RUDE MECHANICALS

By the same author

THE MAN WHO DISOBEYED:
Sir Horace Smith-Dorrien and his Enemies
SIR JOHN MONASH
THE KAFFIR WARS 1779–1877
TOBY
DORNFORD YATES: A Biography
COMBINED FORCES
A NEW EXCALIBUR

RUDE MECHANICALS

*An Account Of Tank Maturity
During The Second World War*

by

A. J. Smithers

With a Foreword by

General Sir John Hackett

GCB, CBE, DSO, MC

'A crew of patches, rude mechanicals'
A Midsummer Night's Dream
Act III, Scene 2

Leo Cooper : London

Hippocrene Books : New York

First published 1987 by Leo Cooper Ltd

Leo Cooper is an independent imprint
of the Heinemann Group of Publishers,
10 Upper Grosvenor Street, London W1X 9PA.

London Melbourne Johannesburg Auckland

ISBN: 0–85052–7228

Hippocrene Books, Inc.,
171 Madison Avenue,
New York, NY 10016

ISBN: 0–87052–499–2

Photoset and printed by Redwood Burn Limited,
Trowbridge, Wiltshire

Contents

Illustrations

All the photographs in this book are reproduced by kind permission of The Tank Museum, Bovington.

Acknowledgments

As always, the writing of this part of a book – the last task to be undertaken – is amongst the pleasantest. Here alone comes the opportunity publicly to thank those people who have, by one means or another, provided information for me to write down. This opportunity I gratefully seize, though a nominal roll of all who have contributed to my stock of knowledge would be altogether too much. By far the most powerful friend was, once again, the Librarian of the Tank Museum, David Fletcher. It was not enough for him to turn up all the archives held by his Museum and for which I asked: time and again he furnished me with Reports and Minutes of whose existence I was ignorant. The information contained in these forms much of the theme of the book. My gratitude to him is much more than formal.

The people upon whom I have drawn for their memories and experiences vary from friends of 40 years and more to chance-met strangers. Amongst the former comes Major J. F. Mayo Perrett, once of 2nd (Cheshire) Field Squadron RE, TA, whose detailed knowledge of the clearing of German mine-fields at Alamein (knowledge acquired along with a Military Cross) probably excels that of any other living man. Mr J. F. Frankish, secretary to Vauxhall Motors, was kind enough to tell me what records survived relating to the Churchill tank and Mr Dean, formerly of the same Company, made me free of his experiences during the beginnings of it. Mr Jock Sutty of Canterbury, a founder-member of REME, was eloquent about the defects of early models. The survivors of 141 Regiment RAC – formerly 7th Buffs – have stuck together all these years and still present a coherent regimental front. To them, and especially to Messrs Allnutt and Bull, I am much indebted for tales of the Crocodile.

For permission to use copyright material I have to thank Colonel A. J. Aylmer for giving me leave to quote from General Spears' *Assignment to Catastrophe*. To the Trustees of The Liddell Hart Centre for Military Archives at King's College, London, for allowing me to use the papers of the late Sir Albert Stern. To Buchan & Enright, Publishers, Ltd, for the quotations from Philip Warner's *Auchinleck: The Lonely Soldier;* to Messrs. Faber & Faber for the extracts from works by General Sir Giffard Martel and to the Estate of Alan Moorehead for the extract from his *Eclipse*.

Lastly to the two friends who were generous enough with their time to read this in typescript and courteously to point out those places where I had fallen into error. It is hardly possible that any book such as this can contain no single mistake between cover and cover. Whatever these may be they are mine alone and I share ownership with nobody. They would have been more had I not had the help of David Fletcher and Major Derek Poulsen. The third and final friend, Philippa Arnott, never fails to astound me with the conjuring trick of turning bags of spoiled paper into immaculate typescript.

Foreword

by General Sir John Hackett, GCB, CBE, DSO, MC

Anyone who has read a history of the tank from 1909 to 1939 entitled *A New Excalibur* will approach this "account of Tank maturity during the Second World War" by the same author with a lively expectation which will not be disappointed. Those who have not read the first book will still find in this one a truly sad, infuriating, pitiful tale of muddle, incompetence and neglect in an area vital to this country's survival in war, a tale which cannot fail to make a deep impression.

"The failure to produce any tank fit to fight the German after more than five years of war," says the author, "and with all the manufacturing capacity of the USA well out of bomber range is a disgrace." This book tells the well-nigh incredible story of how such an extraordinary situation came about.

The writer of the foreword you are reading asks indulgence to introduce here a personal note. He was commissioned as a cavalry officer in the early thirties, in the days when the British Army had long since relapsed into "proper soldiering" after World War I. You joined a cavalry regiment then largely because you liked a life with horses. You would find a little later on that you had, in fact, joined "The Army", as it were by accident. To some, indeed, it became clear that they had joined it by mistake, but they had a little money of their own (the regiment would not have them otherwise) and could always leave. My own regiment was hastily mechanised in Egypt in 1935 for the war with Italy which never broke out, and a few months later I went off to join a real cavalry squadron again in the Transjordan Frontier Force. In the Palestine troubles I took my sword on one occasion into mounted action but remember above all an experience on that same day as unforgettable to me as Saul's upon the Damascus road was to him. We were at that time attacking a guerrilla band holed up in a village, British Infantry, TJFF Cavalry, largely dismounted, and the RAF. I was watching from a hilltop as aircraft came in with bombs and machine guns. As I watched even these little bombs bursting among the houses, with front guns blazing, I suddenly realized that in a real war this would be happening among my led horses. I had never really conjured up this vision before and I doubt whether very many young cavalry officers had. The unhorsing of 18 of the 20 British cavalry regiments of the line in the following year (1939) made me, and a good many others, wonder why it had taken so long. The dismal story told here of the years of frustration, vacillation, muddle and delay which led us into a world war still without a battleworthy tank to replace horsed cavalry is equal cause of wonder.

We could have been far better equipped than with the hopelessly inadequate Vickers light tank which was the main armoured equipment of mechanized cavalry in the BEF. Stalwarts from the First War were, of course, in evidence again, gathered up by the redoubtable Sir Albert Stern into a group known as The Old Gang, which designed a highly promising 76-ton tank to be known as TOG I. Stern looked forward to having thousands of these by 1941. Not one was ever produced. What we did have included 2000 Covenanters. "There were other ill-famed tanks to come but Covenanter was the most comprehensively worthless." Crusader, its successor, "was nearly as bad". One bright spot in the whole sorry story is the success of Matilda II in the infantry support role in North Africa.

The story goes relentlessly on with the emergence of the formidable Russian T34 ("a Christie and the best of them") and the British failure to produce adequate anti-tank guns in good time. The 6pdr and the 17pdr were good weapons but were already, when introduced into service, verging on obsolescence. We saw the appearance of the A22 (the Churchill), the Valentine, the German Tiger, the long and lethal German 50mm gun and the "fearsome 88" dreaded in the Desert. Then we have the appearance of the American Grant (something that with all its faults at last began to look like a real cruiser tank) and Stuarts (my own beloved Honeys) and then the armoured S.P. guns, Priest ("an excellent equipment") and Sexton. It makes a rich and fascinating tale. Through most of it all The Old Gang with some newer members was furiously active. Stern was there, "that unwearying if one-idea'd man", with the enormous support of Martel, with Wilson, Tritton, Elles, Hobart, Kenchington, and now Micklem among the newer members. Mines, unaccountably disregarded for so long, now became fashionable again. We go through the Cavalier tank (with little to commend it), the Cromwell ("even worse than Crusader"), the Centaur ("inadequate"), until the American Sherman appears. The Allies now had, at last, a decent cruiser tank but still not yet the heavy tank we missed in TOG. In 1944, after some five years of war, a 17pdr at last went into Sherman, to create Firefly. The War Office had asked the Ministry of Supply to provide these in July, 1942, and been told it was not possible. A year later it was urgently asked again and this time the request was agreed to and an order placed for 2000, but the order was never carried out. Apart from Firefly no tank existed after four years of war that was fit to go into a tank battle, and only about fifty of these ever saw service, just as the war was ending. But though Valentines and even Matildas were, in the face of the improved anti-tank armoury of the enemy, little better than "coffin-ships" they continued to come off the British factory production lines. The last of 8,275 Valentines emerged in June, 1944, just after D-day. "They should", says Smithers, "have been scrapped long before". He goes on a little later: "It can scarcely be an exaggeration to say that without the products of American factories the war would have been lost".

Not all of the author's judgements will remain unchallenged. Was General Slim "probably the most accomplished professional the War produced" and Alexander "perhaps his only peer"? And what of Montgomery? Monty was surely in many ways the most highly professional of them all, but this author appears to have little time for him. His handling of armour (particularly in trying to force a breakthrough in what should have been an infantry battle) meets with scant approval here. "Montgomery," says the author, "whatever headdress he affected, was not really a tank man". The great and luminous Martel, one of the best tank men ever, back from an exile in Russia, wrote a powerful account of his experiences with Russian armour and sent a copy of it, a few months before "Overlord", to Montgomery. "He told me," Martel records, "he had not time to discuss (it) with me and that he really wanted no advice on how to use armoured forces." As for the much praised TOG tank design (with a transmission weakness which was never wholly cured) was its potential all that the author claims?

Among other aspects of this fascinating book the treatment of special armour deserves particular mention. The Crabs, Flails, Bobbins, Bullhorns, Kangaroos, the heavy armoured cars (Greyhound, Boarhound, Staghound), but above all the DD (Duplex Drive) tanks deserve close attention. The last named played an important part in the invasion of Europe which was the overture to the final act in this tremendous drama.

In spite of all that can be said of the ingenuity, dedication and desperately hard work of a few devoted people, however, the judgement has to be faced that: "The allies prepared to invade Hitler's Fortress Europe with great quantities of obsolescent fighting machines every one of which would be inferior to its opposite number in the same class". The author says elsewhere, with searing directness, "This was the great tank scandal. With the war nearly five years old and with the last two of them largely given over to planning the battles in Normandy it is beyond forgiveness". These are severe judgements. The reader of this notable book will form his own conclusion on how far they are justified.

Introduction

In the Spring of 1914 there appeared in the shops a book that caused quite a stir. *When William Came: A Story of London Under The Hohenzollerns* bore the well-known name of 'Saki' though it was not in the author's customary style. One character is explaining events to a new arrival. '"War between two such civilised and enlightened nations is an impossibility", one of our leaders of public opinion had declared on the Saturday; by the following Friday the war had indeed become an impossibility, because we could no longer carry it on. It burst upon us with calculated suddenness, and we were just not enough, everywhere where the pressure came. Our ships were good against their ships, our seamen were better than their seamen, but our ships were not able to cope with their ships plus their superiority in aircraft. Our trained men were good against their trained men, but they could not be in several places at once, and the enemy could. Our half-trained men and our untrained men could not master the science of war at a moment's notice, and a moment's notice is all they got. The enemy were a nation apprenticed in arms, we were not even the idle apprentice; we had not deemed apprenticeship worth our while. There was courage enough running loose in the land, but it was like unharnessed electricity, it controlled no forces, it struck no blows . . . The war was over almost as soon as it had begun.'

By a high mercy the English narrowly escaped the fate described in the book. Its author did not live to see the end. As L/Sgt Munro, H., Royal Fusiliers, he died by Beaumont-Hamel.

The book went out of print and the islanders went back to their old ways. They had had a nasty experience but it could never happen again.

When William's war did come, the British, after many disagreeable experiences, invented an armoured fighting machine which, for reasons of security, they called a Tank. The word served its purpose well enough but it is a pity that it stuck. As the name of a distinguished Corps it lacks *gravitas*. 'Tank' implies something homely and innocuous, suggestive of suburban villas with Company's water laid on. To the more widely travelled it may conjure up visions of peaceful Indian villages under a setting sun. The Germans, successors to the famous armourers of Augsburg and elsewhere, naturally came up with something fiercer. The very word 'Panzer', possibly because it sounds like 'panther', has a lethal quality. Speed, inexpugnability and killing power are proclaimed even before the machine heaves across the skyline. For the first few years of the second war the contrast between the two spoke for itself.

At the beginning of 1919 Britain had something like a monopoly in tanks. France kept up her fleet of small Renaults but, for a good many years, did little else. America, convinced that wars were relics of barbarism that could never recur, gave up the business altogether. Germany, forbidden to produce any, meditated revenge but for the moment confined it to paper. Only Soviet Russia, in the year 1928, decided that the time had come for examining such things. Perhaps it should not be all that surprising, for Russia under new management had not forgotten its past. Charles XII and Narva, Napoleon and Borodino, the Kaiser and Tannenburg were still remembered as warnings and Russia saw a world of enemies on all sides. More recent was the memory of how on 1 July, 1919, the city of Tsaritsyn, now called Stalingrad, had been captured by Major Bruce and five mechanics in a Mk V tank. There was a Russian equivalent of 'No more Sommes' and Russian engineers were as good as any.

Designing and building tanks is specialized work and is far more than a mere variant on the motor industry. Since it offered no living for a bright young engineer in peacetime, nobody came forward to take it up where the pioneers had set it down. So far as it was anybody's business it was that of the War Office which soon came to be emptied of everybody with the ghost of an idea of how to set about it. The private armament firms, save only for Vickers, had no interest beyond somehow staying in business. BSA, which had made every Lewis gun and many of the rifles for the other war, lived a meagre life on foreign orders for sporting guns and by making air rifles for children. Vickers themselves, now also comprising the ailing Armstrong Company, was still the Vickers of Sir Basil Zaharoff, though the Company did attract on to its Board retired General officers of high standing. The few tanks made for the Army were only a small part of the Company's activities. Worse things happened to the Westland Aircraft Company. At one stage it had to depend for its living upon turning out stainless steel beer barrels. The Schneider Trophy races, largely financed by Lady Houston, brought practitioners like R. J. Mitchell and Sydney Camm into the development of machines that were to lead on to the Spitfire and the great 4-engined bombers but, save only for Sir John Carden, they had no counterpart on the tank side. It is a curious fact that, whereas in the Kaiser's war Britain made tanks and Germany led with the big Gotha and Giant bombers, it was, by Hitler's time, the other way about. The German factories turned out excellent tanks designed by professionals on the State pay-roll. They were not, this time, interested in big bombers. On balance this may have been just as well.

The British tanks of 1916 onwards had been the work of inspired amateurs. Those of Round Two were, for years, also amateur work but without the adjective. During the 18th century when drafts of recruits were regularly sent to the West Indies only to go to the graveyard by way of the hospitals there was a pleasantry to the effect that it would be kinder and much cheaper to knock them on the head before embarkation. Much the same could be said of nearly every British tank made before 1944. In Germany every important matter about the size of tanks, their armour and their guns was settled by Hitler himself. General Guderian has much to say about it, not always as a compliment. Nevertheless Hitler seems to have been right more often than wrong. In this country, Sir Albert Stern wrote bitterly, such things were left to 'a Mr Hopkins'. When manufacturers got into the swing of things they were humbugged by those whom the Managing Director of Vauxhall called 'the Army boys' who could never make up their minds what they wanted. They in turn complained that the factories did not make what the army ought to have.

If there is any amusement to be found in war it lies in comparing the forecasts of the experts with what actually happened. The German victories in France point only one rather obvious thing. If you are determined to rob your neighbour, then go into training, take boxing lessons and you should not find it too hard. Better still, if he has only a stick then buy yourself a pistol. The inexcusable neglect of defence against armour by both France and Britain gave Panzer and Stuka something unpleasantly like a walk-over.

The desert ought to have been the perfect arena for the 'all armoured' school. Indeed it probably would have been but for one marplot device. Tanks had been blown up by mines in 1918 and tankmen had devised ways of circumventing them. The British army retained a few indifferent specimens and gave perfunctory instruction in their use. During the infantry officers' course at the Small Arms School Hythe a single morning was devoted to this low-grade subject. All the skills of our fathers had been forgotten. The Germans, doubtless having brooded over the matter for years, remembered them well. Combined with lethal anti-tank guns, mines prevented the desert campaigns from being Richard and Saladin come again. Then followed some unrewarding campaigns. Sicily and Italy were not designed by nature for tanks. Instead of Arab charges across the sands, usually ending in disaster, came single tanks creeping with difficulty along Kipling's 'dark defile'. The 88 was more than a 10 rupee jezail but it did the business just the same. Burma was rather worse, save for the single round fired by a tank into the tunnels on the Maungdaw–Buthidaung road that exploded an ammunition dump and blew the place sky-high. Better times, for tanks, came later.

The invasion of Normandy certainly taught much about the landing of an army on a hostile shore. Once there, the armies, both British and American, found themselves with one handicap. The new British tanks – the Americans stuck to the Sherman of which 50,000 were made – were excellent. Not, however, for invading Normandy. They had been developed from desert designs and if North-West Europe had been a desert they would have wrought splendidly. As it was they proved, yet again, not good enough for the job. Without the fire from the sky provided by the two air forces it could not have been done. The failure to produce any tank fit to fight the German after more than five years of war and with all the manufacturing capacity of the USA well out of bomber range is a disgrace. This book is an attempt to show how it came about.

CHAPTER ONE
Back to Proper Soldiering

On Armistice Day, 1918, the strength of the British Tank Corps stood at twenty-five battalions. Of these eighteen were in France, the remainder – one being a complete battalion of officers under instruction – were centred around Bovington Camp in various stages of training. Four were ready for embarkation, while the others had some way to go before they could be considered fit for battle. In addition to the fighting units a large maintenance and repair organization, now highly experienced, existed at Teneur, in the rear area of the armies.

This sounds a much more formidable armoured force than it was. The battalions under Sir Douglas Haig's hand were, without exception, worn to rags after their triumph in breaking the Hindenburg Line. Production of machines had fallen off, largely because of a dwindling force of skilled workmen, and the new machines, the Mk VIII heavy tank, the Mk IX troop-carrier, and the relatively swift Mediums B and C, existed only in very small numbers. Had the need for a Spring campaign in 1919 arisen there would certainly have been a strong armoured element but it could not have reached the expectations held in some quarters of a great swarm of modern tanks sweeping everything before them.

The fact remained that the science of war had moved as far from that understood in 1914 as it had done from the Peninsula and the Crimea. Even outside the Tank Corps it was well understood that the horse-soldier and the horse-drawn artillery piece were not merely anachronisms but a positive nuisance. The Division, a miniature army of a dozen or so battalions with its own field batteries and services, had been perfected by the Duke in Spain and had proved serviceable in most of the campaigns of the following century. Only during the second phase of the war in South Africa, with great distances to be covered and speeds greater than walking pace needed, had it broken down. Though all armies counted their strength by divisions the Order of Battle of the BEF had, by 1917, become more sophisticated. Had every numbered division been taken away Sir Douglas Haig would still have commanded an enormously powerful force of medium artillery, heavy artillery, machine-guns, gas-dispensers and aeroplanes. By 1918 there would have been added strong forces of tanks. The division, however, remained, for there was no other way of encadring great numbers of unarmoured infantrymen and their helpers. Nor was the formation yet obsolete, as various monkeyings during the early desert campaigns were to show. What modern armies needed was not a substitute but an addition, a fast-moving component with a concentrated punch that the older arms could not provide.

In the days immediately following the Armistice the mechanized forces demonstrated the extent to which a few men in armoured vehicles could influence events with a power disproportionate to their numbers. The Armoured Car battalion of the Tank Corps led the crossing of the Rhine across the bridge into Cologne, followed by the cavalry. In the Spring of 1919 a complete Tank Group joined the Army of Occupation. A year later, when it had shrunk to little more than a single battalion, the Commander-in-Chief fiercely resisted a call to bring it home, on the ground that tanks inspired great respect among the Germans and were a powerful deterrent to those who might have ideas. Nor was this peculiar to occupied Germany. Half a dozen tanks on the streets of Glasgow in January, 1919, 'in aid of the civil power', had effectively damped down a riot. Far away in Persia General Sir Edmund Ironside, the man later to be assailed on all sides as an old-style bushwhacker who did not understand these things, was observing that given just three half-decent tanks he could have dispensed with three battalions of infantry. For the small wars of the Empire and those regions where the British army kept some sort of peace armoured cars were at least as useful as tracked machines designed for European battlefields and for a number of years they did more than earn their rations. Tanks and armoured cars, however, were clean different things.

The Tank Corps of 1918 was almost entirely a civilian force and on demobilization it practically disappeared. The painfully acquired experience in such matters as bridging rivers, furnishing tanks with buoyancy to make them swim, mining and clearing mines, wireless telegraphy and working closely with aeroplanes was forgotten as the men who had worked these matters out returned to civil life. While twenty cavalry regiments remained horsed and pleased the tax-payers by regular appearances at King's Birthdays and Tattoos the emaciated Tank Corps was banished to Bovington, a place conveniently distant from other centres of military activity. By August, 1920, it numbered about 2,500 all ranks. Around them stood the rusting scrap-yard of machines that had done so much to take order with the Kaiser. With the official announcement that there would be no war for another ten years their occupation seemed gone. The rest of the Army, bowed down under the weight of finding drafts for India, Palestine, Ireland and a seemingly endless catalogue of other places, wanted nothing more to do with them. When the garage man has mended your car you do not ask him to tea. Rude mechanicals must know their place in a horsey army.

It was fortunate that there were still a few men who took another view of the army's raison d'être. Hugh Elles, who had commanded the Corps from its beginnings, was given the command of Bovington and its out-stations. Colonel J. F. C. Fuller – 'Boney' Fuller – remained at the War Office at the head of SD7, the small department in charge of tank business, and Giffard le Q. Martel, reduced to the substantive rank of Major, commanded a Field Company of Sappers in which he interested himself almost entirely in tank affairs.

In terms of matériel the Corps had to content itself with leftovers, for all the makers of tanks during the war had gone back to their ordinary peacetime affairs. No professional armourers had had anything to do with them and nobody was left with the means or inclination to turn his hand to the making of something that might never be wanted. Then, at the end of 1921, the Corps had a stroke of luck. At the top of the War Office tree so far as weapons were concerned stood the Master-General of the Ordnance. Though Fuller's appointment was in another Department, he had for some time been pestering the MGO to persevere with the Medium D tank upon which he had set his heart for the unfought campaign of 1919. The Medium D, the first British tank with a sprung suspension, was a masterpiece of ingenuity designed by Philip Johnson, a professional engineer with a temporary commission in the Tank Corps. For all its originality the Medium D gave nothing but trouble and the

MGO wearied of it. Nevertheless the Army Estimates contained the large sum of half a million pounds for tank development, money that would be lost for ever if it were not spent almost at once. Fuller and Johnson were brushed aside as the War Office opened negotiations with the great Vickers Company.

Vickers were not conspicuously interested in tanks, for they had made none during the war and no big orders were to be expected. Nevertheless, post-war trade being not always good, they agreed to set up a small staff and to see what they could do. The design office moved from London to Sheffield and there it produced plans, starting completely from scratch. The result was not discreditable to them, though it was fortunate that the Vickers Medium (officially the Light Tank Mk 1) never saw battle. It was well engineered, like all Vickers products, which was as well since it would have to last for a long time. It weighed just under 12 tons, was 17 feet long and, with a Vickers-made Armstrong-Siddeley engine of 90 h.p. could travel at a very decent speed. Though designed only for 15 mph it could, says Captain Liddell Hart, go at something nearer 30. This was made possible by a suspension system, something the pioneers had lacked. Each roller-bearing bogey had its own spring after the fashion of railway wagons. Like the Renault FT17, though on a bigger scale, it mounted a turret from which protruded a 3-pdr gun, made by Vickers, and on either side below it were two Vickers machine-guns. Time and again it attacked Bowls Barrows and Tinkers Firs on Salisbury Plain to the satisfaction of the umpires. The facts that its armour would barely keep out small arms fire and that its petrol tank was mounted inside – something that had cost the lives of many good men only a few years before – were not bruited about. The later Mk II was slightly better armoured but neither could have lived for a minute against anything bigger than a rifle. The historian of Vickers says that about a hundred in all of the Mk I and Mk II were made over the next few years. There can have been no fortune in it for the Company. No foreign Government placed orders for either (though half a dozen went to Australia) and so well was it built that few replacements were needed. In 1923 the War Office closed down its Tank Design Department and Vickers were left as the repository of all tank lore. They sold 15 machines to Russia, some of which lived long enough to appear in the war with Finland.

The same year saw the end of the last National Factory that the Ministry of Munitions had set up. All that remained in the way of

State armament institutions were Woolwich Arsenal, the small-arms factory at Enfield Lock and the Waltham Gunpowder Works. Only Woolwich mattered to those concerned with tanks and it had little enough to offer. By 1933 it had a pay-roll of 7,000 as against 65,000 in 1918; most of those on it were working for the Admiralty and there was no spare capacity to waste on unwanted armoured vehicles.

Though the Corps had been given a new tank there was no reason to suppose that the Army was even thinking about bringing itself up to date. Many ideas were bandied about on paper regarding the future shape of war but there was an air of unreality about them. Two schools of thought contended, one of them insisting that wholly armoured formations were the shape of things to come, the other that a judicious mixture of all arms would be more likely to prevail. The oddest circumstance is that nobody seems to have given a thought to the ways in which a tank might be killed. This may have been comprehensible during the few years in which only the Allies of 1918 possessed such a weapon but even when rumours of German reawakening became demonstrably true the matter was still dismissed. The makeshift mines of 1918 had been surprisingly effective, as the fate of the 301st (US) battalion had shown during the storming of the Hindenburg Line. No mine was made in Britain nor were there designs for any. The smallest anti-tank gun could have wrecked the Vickers Medium as it could any foreign machine then known. None existed nor was one contemplated. There had always been a dark suspicion that the hand of the Royal Regiment of Artillery was active. To a gunner the gun is a sacred object, as the altar is to a priest. None but proper Woolwich and Larkhill-trained acolytes could be allowed to place hands on one. Lord Roberts, long ago, had grudgingly allowed the Territorials to exist as spear-carriers but he had strongly disapproved their being allowed to play with artillery. And, of its very nature, the Master-General of the Ordnance and his familiars were for the most part gunners. Even the feeble 3-pdr was grudged to the Tank Corps. Tanks existed to beat up infantry and for that the machine-gun would do perfectly well. Tank-smashing could be safely left to the 18-pdr field gun, even though it was pulled by horses and still ran on iron-rimmed wheels. The Royal Air Force, a separate race of dedicated men, had no interest in the matter.

In 1922 there came a frisson down many spines when the revived Turkish army under Mustapha Kemal drove the Greeks from Asia

5

Minor and squared up to the tiny British force at Chanak. For a moment it seemed that the unthinkable had to be thought about and another war, small but serious, was about to erupt. A Tank battalion would have been invaluable, but none was to be had. It was fortunate that Mr Churchill's signals to Australia and New Zealand brought a reply that if the Turks pushed their luck too hard the Anzacs might have to think about coming back. This served as well as many tanks could have done, but the fact remained that their absence was felt. The civilized world turned over in its sleep.

It was the following year, 1923, that brought the Tank Corps back into the world. Since the end of the war it had continued to exist on sufferance with no guarantee that it would ever have a permanent place in the Army List. On 1 September, after long cogitations, it was announced that the Tank Corps was there to stay, four battalions strong, one for each Division in the Kingdom. The battalions began to move out from the ancestral home at Bovington, to Farnborough, to Tidworth, to Lydd and to Catterick. Major-General Sir John Capper became the first Colonel-Commandant. As a mark of appreciation of the Corps' share in bringing down the Kaiser the King bestowed upon it the coveted Royal prefix. With the new status came the black beret. It all sounded very satisfactory but the Tanks knew perfectly well that it was only one stage better than disbandment. For as long as could be foreseen the 20 mph armoured fighting machine was to be tied to the belt of the 2½ mph infantryman as a kind of optional extra.

Though the founder members of the Tank Corps had, for the most part, returned home the Great Triumvirate of Cambrai remained in the Army. Elles was at Bovington, Fuller at the War Office and Martel went there also in the Fortifications Directorate. For the time being he would be the torchbearer and he deserves scrutiny. Martel had been brought up in engineering. His father had been Chief Superintendent of the Royal Ordnance Factories and his own training, going hand in hand with his inclinations, had been largely in mechanical affairs. Not only was he a trained and experienced Sapper – though this would have been credential enough for most men – but a fully-fledged member of the Institute of Mechanical Engineers. Just after the war he had designed a form of box-girder bridge which became the Army's standard piece of equipment. To complete the picture he was a famous boxer, welterweight champion not only of the Army but of the Combined Services. His reputation for personal courage was outstanding even by

6

Tank Corps standards. Since nobody had given thought to the future of the armoured fighting vehicle once the Vickers Mediums had gone into service Martel decided that he would build a small tank himself. This, quite literally, he did in the garage of his house near Camberley. From the engine of an old Maxwell car, the back-axle of a Ford lorry and a set of tracks made for him by the Roadless Traction Company he fabricated a machine which he showed off in the summer of 1925. Its appearance was comical, as it was only eight feet long by five feet high, the whole crowned by Martel's trilby hat peering over the top. One almost expected to see a key sticking out at the side for it had all the air of a clockwork toy. Nevertheless it worked, and the War Office was induced to order four more to be made by Morris Motors. This marked the beginning of interest in tanks by William Morris, later to be Lord Nuffield. Shortly after it appeared Martel made the acquaintance of the one man in whom, between the wars, glowed the spark of genius in tank design.

Sir John Carden was the sixth holder of an Irish baronetcy. His grandfather had been the famous Colonel Valentine Baker – Baker Pasha – who had been forced out of the Army following a highly suspicious charge of indecent assault upon a young woman in a railway carriage. Carden, after a creditable war, had gone into partnership with another ex-officer named Loyd to run a garage business in London. Encouraged by Martel he produced with great rapidity both a one-man and a two-man machine much like that of his mentor but better. These acquired the disagreeable name of 'tank-ettes'. Their drawbacks soon proclaimed themselves but they taught Carden a lot. His next model, a two-man affair named the Carden-Loyd Mk VI, was a great improvement and sired the Bren carrier and its successors. Eight Carden-Loyds were ordered and they became a familiar sight on manoeuvres during the next few years. All the same they made little or no impact upon an Army that had lost interest.

The cavalry Generals, and they were many, denied all their recent experiences and continued to extol the power of the well-bred horse. Their one aim seemed to be to get the Army back to the lost standard of 1914 with perhaps a few more guns and machine-guns as evidence of their forward thinking. Colonel Philip Neame VC, as a Staff College Instructor between 1921 and 1923, had preached the Gospel of the Tank. Nobody listened. In 1924, at Aldershot, he tried to introduce them into a large-scale exercise and was brusquely told by his divisional General to stop it. At the same time T. E.

Lawrence, always fascinated by machinery, was doing a turn in the ranks at Bovington. When he found that he was spending most of the time on the square he bought himself out.

In 1925 came something that looked like a false dawn. General Sir Noel Birch was both the Army's top gunner and a famous horseman. In spite of these things he was one of the few officers who looked more than a week or so ahead. Neame's cavalry Generals went along with the almost universally held view that nobody who remembered the Somme and Verdun could even contemplate the possibility of another European war. A few, Birch amongst them, were more impressed by Foch's remark upon the Peace Treaties: 'This is not peace. It is an Armistice for twenty years.' In 1925 Birch was Master-General of the Ordnance and in a position of power. He it was who ordered the construction of a self-propelled artillery weapon, made up from the chassis of a Vickers Medium tank and an 18-pdr mounted upon a platform. It was an excellent equipment, better even than the gun-carrying tank of 1916 that had never been used. Its appearance, however, brought to the surface all the slumbering suspicions of his brother gunners. If the thing was half gun and half tank how could they be sure that their hallowed arm would not become the subject of a take-over bid? The unguarded mention in a letter from Colonel Hobart – of whom more hereafter – of something he called The Royal Tank Artillery did not help. The Royal Regiment killed the Birch gun and for ever after looked untrustfully at its designer. Not long afterwards General Birch left the army and became a director of Vickers. The field gunners continued every summer to amuse themselves by firing practices at canvas tanks towed on sleds. These were regarded as great fun and much beer was staked on the results. The gunners retained the effortless superiority of knowing that even their ageing 18-pdrs could smash any tank existing or contemplated.

In the year of the General Strike when the armoured car companies of the Tank Corps stood in the wings, came the last flicker. It came about almost by accident that the best brains amongst the new tank men, Colonels Broad and Lindsay, had an unusual degree of influence in the War Office and at Bovington. They succeeded against the customary opposition in gaining a grudging permission to order from Vickers a genuine tank as opposed to a mere toy. The design team was headed by Sir George Buckham, who had been with the Company since 1895, but most of the ideas came from three relatively junior Tank Corps officers, Major Darwell and Captains Busk and Bloomer. Vickers came up trumps. The Independent – officially the A1E1 – was so named because the word described its function. Groups of these machines could and should operate on their own far ahead of the plodding infantry. With its 350 hp engine, the biggest yet put into a tank, it could carry its 31 tons at a good 20 mph and its four machine-gun turrets plus another mounting a 3-pdr could take on almost anything likely to be encountered during the 1920s. This was the first machine anywhere in the world that deserved to be called a battle tank. The drawback, of course, was that it cost money. Only one was made and it remains in the Museum at Bovington, the mute witness to the spinelessness of the inter-war politicians. It is painful to think what the BEF might have achieved in 1940 given a few squadrons of Independents improved by the experience of the dozen years between. As it was Independent made no mark. The historian of Vickers does not even give it a mention.

All the same the world was slowly becoming tank-minded. In 1928 the Soviet Union produced a new Five Year Plan in which tanks were for the first time given prominence. The French Army, still unaccountably regarded as the best sword of Western Christendom, was working on designs that would become the Somua and the Char B. The United States bought from Mr J. W. Christie his design for a new suspension system and set up an Experimental Armoured Force. Germany was already up to something, though nobody knew quite what. At home the bright little company of Carden-Loyd was bought out by Vickers. Inside the War Office those charged with tank design did nothing in particular. The Majors and Lieut-Colonels doing their two-year tours of duty may have had ideas but they were too sensible to risk their careers by gaining the reputations of heretics or zealots. In any event, the Great Financial Crisis was about to break. It could not have struck at a worse moment. The War Office, headed by the under-appreciated Sir George Milne, had just woken up to the fact that all things had changed. The small book called *Modern Formations 1931 (Provisional)* was a model exegesis of the business of war on land: unlike most official pamphlets it treated not of what the Army was and had but of what it ought to have and how it ought to use it. In his Introduction the CIGS remarked that, although the Army must inevitably lag behind the mechanization of civil life, 'there is no reason why officers should lag behind in thought and study. They must be in a position to make profitable use of the great variety of technical vehicles and other equipment which war will at once produce'. Packed into its 138 pages is a volume of excellent sense: where it deviates into prophecy it is seldom far wrong. There are no pipe-dreams about all-armoured forces. 'Tank brigades depend on speed and fire power to overcome the defence. Open and undulating ground is therefore most favourable to them, since it presents few obstacles to tank movement and offers little cover to anti-tank weapons.' On the other hand 'Enclosed country is favourable to infantry action. In this type of country the machine-guns of the defence are hampered, and opportunities thus occur for infiltration by infantry in co-operation with armoured machine-gun carriers and armoured mortar carriers.' Desert and bocage, in fact. Anti-tank defence should be the work of a 6-pdr gun and contact mines – ('one 3-ton lorry carries 550 mines') – and 'anti-tank defence may be given to 3-inch anti-aircraft guns which are quite efficient for the purpose'. A proportion of Medium tanks should carry a 15-lb mortar; infantry battalions needed the 3-inch variety. A specification is given for this invaluable weapon that was to be issued to them six years later. Light tanks should not be used in a serious attack. With a few obvious exceptions such as unavoidable remarks about cavalry – plainly regarded as an embarrassment – and a lack of clairvoyance about the extent to which air power would dominate everything, the book was ahead of its time. It might usefully have been issued to any training unit during the first years of the war that was to come. Needless to say it would be many years before a 6-pdr anti-tank gun would appear. Far more blameworthy was the fact that no effort was made to use the existing 3″ 20 cwt AA gun for its proposed secondary purpose. This was delicate ground. The author of the book was Colonel Charles Broad, a faithful son of Woolwich and Larkhill for a score of years before he took to the tanks. In the section on medium tanks they are allowed only rifle-calibre machine-guns and, almost apologetically, 'a gun capable of destroying similar machines'. Intercourse between gunners and tank people hardly existed. The CIGS was a Gunner. By encouraging Broad to say even this much he was risking the heavy displeasure of his peers. Any suggestion that a tank should carry a weapon which might even seem to compete with those of the Royal Regiment would have been blasphemy.

Whether all the issued copies of the pamphlet were the same I do not know, but bound in with mine is an extract from the *Daily Telegraph*. It is dated simply November, 1931, and is more flattering than any publisher's blurb. The first line reads 'Authority Endorses

Voice Of The Prophet' and the writer was 'Our Military Correspondent'. The then occupant of that office was Captain Liddell Hart.

The reputation of prophets is best served by their utterances being reserved to the Delphic, Sibylline or at least ambiguous. Captain Liddell Hart disdained circumlocution. Having headed his last paragraph 'Doom of the Large Army', he went on, 'The nation will no longer be used to swell the encumbered ranks of a large conscript army but to furnish the material for its mechanized spearhead'. Where the rest of the spear would come from he did not explain. As a dip into the future it did not earn him high marks.

Three years before General von Seeckt had even begun to encadre the first of Germany's panzer divisions the British Army had a sound doctrine of armoured warfare, complete with Establishments for everything and instructions for the handling not only of tank formations but even of Bus Columns for infantry. Broad's little book had wisdom for everybody, ending with the words: 'It behoves all officers to study the methods of mobile war in the past and to apply those lessons which are applicable to modern mobile forces, in war games and Staff exercises. In this way only will they fit themselves to use the weapons which on the first hint of serious war will at once be placed in their hands.' This last suggests a rare triumph of hope over experience. Prophecy is not the business of serving soldiers.

Having approved the pamphlet, and with advance copies in the hands of cavalry officers, the War Office became worried about its venture into the occult. The red and brown manuals from Gale & Polden had always been available to anyone who cared to disburse a shilling or two. An exception was made for *Modern Formations*. It did not go on sale nor was it issued, as all other Army publications were, to the Territorials. There was no point in giving them ideas above their station. By these means the leaven was kept well away from the dough. Kipling's *The Army of a Dream* had come again. Rich in academic interest, but barren of practical importance. Aldershot went on as in King Edward's day.

CHAPTER TWO

Warriors at Ease

So matters plodded on for the next few years. The Tank Corps, under officers of the quality of Broad, Pile, Lindsay and later Hobart, became highly efficient; its gunnery and its wireless communications were kept constantly exercised and improved. That said, it could not be reckoned to be fit for battle until it had been completely re-equipped with better machines. Many variants of the tankette were made and played with; they were all of them unworthy of Carden's skill in design and Vickers' production capacity. Nor was their function clear. Very small tanks moving at speed might have some mosquito value in another encounter battle such as Mons, moving ahead of an army and annoying another one walking towards it. Nobody can have seriously expected that Mons would come again. With the beginning of work on the Maginot Line it became clear that the French did not think so. The only use for tiny tanks could be in the duties known compendiously as 'imperial policing'. This was the long-standing curse of the British Army. The Continentals kept their armies at home and could train them to a programme. The British Army, once it had found the drafts for India, Palestine, Egypt and half a dozen other places, could only number at home the Colts and the Veterans. These would have to spearhead any future Expeditionary Force as they had done in 1914. There was always talk by politicians about the need for a small army to be up-to-date and highly efficient in order to compensate for its lack of numbers. By about 1930 this meant the tankette and the hickory-wheeled 1905 model 18-pdr. Wry amusement was sometimes felt by those opening the little red manual called Field Service

Regulations Vol. 2 for the first time. Among the pink pages of advertisements there stood one for the Danish Pedersen self-loading rifle. Three decades later a similar weapon was issued to the British infantry.

With the absorption of Carden Vickers began to design and make machines weighing about 6 tons, based on the tankettes but far more refined. Sir Charles Craven, the Chairman, cast about for markets abroad and found them. To begin with he moved the design office south to Chertsey where Carden was given a free hand to design whatever he reckoned the most saleable. Something about £20,000 a year was set aside for experimental work. This soon justified itself with orders coming in from Poland, India and, rather surprisingly, from the War Office. The surprise comes from the conditions of 1931, the year of the Economy Act and of the naval mutiny – if that be the right word – at Invergordon brought about by a sudden and brutal cut in pay. Craven was well pleased, writing that 'The tank side of the military business is certainly a profitable one, and I really do not know what we should have been able to do with the machine shops at Elswick without the large orders for tanks secured during the last twelve months'. Though they seemed large orders by the standards of the day they amounted in all to no more than a few dozen.

The army's share was the very small Vickers Light Tank, the cheapest of Carden's new designs. It turned the scale at just over 3 tons, had a road speed of 35 mph and carried a crew of 2. The armament was a single .303 Vickers machine gun of the excellent 1915 model. A better machine, the Vickers 6-tonner armed with a 3-pdr gun, was available but was reckoned to be beyond the financial ability of the Treasury. A number of the Mk II version of the light tank was sent to India for trials on the North-West Frontier and it served that purpose fairly well. The pace of production was pretty leisurely for none of the new machines actually reached their units until 1934. In 1932 and 1933 half a dozen amphibians went to Russia and the same number of experimental artillery tractors to Poland. The War Office was content with about 120 'dragons', gun-towing machines made from the chassis of the old Vickers Medium.

There had been a spasm a few years earlier when, in 1929, the War Office had demanded a successor to this machine. The Vickers 16-tonner, properly called the A6, was a very good tank indeed, a better climber of obstacles than the Independent, though smaller and less well armed. It was one of the few British tanks that could boast of having an engine tailor-made for itself and this was its un-doing. The cost of £16,000 was undoubtedly very high and only three were made. Major-General Peck, whose responsibility it had been, left his appointment as Director of Mechanization soon after A6 appeared and his successor, Major-General Brough, was told firmly that, however good the new tank might be, he must find something cheaper. Much cheaper. And smaller, and with an ordi-nary commercial lorry engine that would cost only a fraction of that with which Peck had indulged himself. It took eight years for the first pilot model to put in an appearance. During these there were two misfires, an A7 and an A8 designed, at any rate in part, by no less than Sir William Morris.

The A8 never got beyond a very early stage of development but A7 seemed a little more promising. It had been started years before on paper as a medium tank and the brain behind it was that of Sir John Carden. Once the drawings had been laid out, however, the business was turned over to Woolwich Arsenal where work pro-ceeded at the customary snail's pace. It was not accelerated by the Disarmament Conference of 1932 which arrived at the interesting conclusion that tanks of less than 6 tons weight were legitimate because they could not be expected to breach a trench line whereas anything bigger was reckoned aggressive. In spite of this the work ground slowly on. A7 seemed to hold out promise of being a more advanced machine, for it was powered by twin diesel engines – the first to be used in any tank – made by AEC and it had a fair turn of speed at 25 mph. It displaced 18 tons but still wore only about half an inch of armour. Woolwich produced three trial models and played around with it for several years during which it became stead-ily more out of date. It was not until 1937 that A7 finally received its quietus and during that time much had happened.

The most sinister occurrence, in 1933, was the arrival of Adolf Hitler as Chancellor of Germany. Already an armoured force was coming into existence under the subterranean guidance of General von Seeckt but the first German tanks, copies of the Carden-Loyd tankettes, were not formidable. When better ones were demanded the pace was a lot faster than that of Woolwich. The first models of the Panzer I, begun soon after Hitler's arrival in the Wilhelmstrasse, looked suspiciously like the good but neglected Vickers 6-tonner.

Quite fortuitously 1934 also witnessed the arrival in the MGO's chair of the man whom everybody expected to take the whole tank business firmly by the scruff. Sir Hugh Elles, who had led the tank assault at Cambrai, had been off the stage for a long time. After re-linquishing the command at Bovington in 1923 he had been given an infantry brigade until 1926, had been chief General Staff Officer at Eastern Command until 1930 and Director of Military Training until 1933. His last appointment had been as GOC of a Territorial Division, the 42nd (East Lancashire). All these non-armoured func-tions had kept him away from the tactical developments of the cur-rent generation of Tank Corps leaders, Colonels Broad, Pile, Lindsay and Hobart. Fuller had vanished from the scene in 1927 never to return to the Army List.

If the Royal Tank Corps expected its old Chief to bring about a revolution which would make the army into a modern force fit to take the field in an European war it was in for disappointment. Elles had, over the years, become doubtful about the value of the arm he had pioneered. It may be that the tiny tanks about him – the worn-out Vickers Mediums hardly counted – did not inspire the confi-dence of the massive affairs of 1918. He thought nothing at all of the Vickers Light tanks and the events of a few years later proved him right. Elles, who after the 1927 exercises had favoured the creation of an armoured division, had changed his mind. The only tank worth having was something heavy and powerful, fit to slug it out with modern anti-tank weapons and once again to clear the way for the infantry. This was not the business of armoured divisions. After talking it over with the CIGS's Research Committee Elles instruc-ted Vickers to go ahead and make such a machine.

Before this had got very far Fate took a hand. Vickers had agreed to produce two new tanks, substantially the same but with a light model to do the old cavalry work and a heavier one for the infantry co-operation role. They were known as A9 and A10. One condition was imposed. The work should be left entirely in the hands of Sir John Carden and nobody from the War Office would be permitted to show his nose about the factory until officially notified that the new machines were running. This demonstrates as nothing else could the respect in which Carden was held. On 10 December, 1935, when returning from Brussels to Croydon in a small Belgian airliner, he was killed along with all the other occupants in a crash near Biggin Hill. Vickers mourned him because, since he had teamed up with them in 1928, his tanks and tractors had brought them orders worth more than three million pounds. Liddell Hart, who was in a position to know, called him a man of genius. Those left to carry on his work were no more than good journeymen.

Carden's *spécialité de la maison* had been suspension systems and within months of his death something spectacular happened in that context. Colonel Martel, having done a stint as Instructor at Quetta Staff College, came home for a year's course at the Imperial Defence one. At the end of this, in June, 1936, he was appointed to the War Office as Assistant Director of Mechanization with special responsibility for tank development. In that capacity he accompanied General Wavell to Russia. There he saw things of which nobody in the West had had the faintest idea. During the Red Army Manoeuvres of September, 1936, it seemed that all the dreams he and Fuller had once cherished had actually come true.

It was not merely the number of Russian tanks that kept Martel at gaze, though the 1200 that defiled before him represented something like a dozen times the number of serviceable machines with the British army. In quality also they were streets ahead of anything that Salisbury Plain had ever seen. Apart from light machines of the Carden-Loyd kind that were plainly on their way out, they fell into two groups, the new cavalry and the armoured infantry. Most impressive, apart from the march past of a thousand tanks with no faults worse than an occasional engine missing fire for a moment, was the medium machine, the BT2 made in the great Kharkov factory. This owed nothing either to Carden or to any other European designer for its suspension was built to serve Russian purposes. It was common knowledge that what wore out tracks was not cross-country work but the ''ammer 'ammer 'ammer on the 'ard 'igh road'. Because of this all tanks during the Kaiser's War had been carefully moved by rail to the nearest possible place from which they could debouch for battle. Onė of the still existing crosses that British makers had to bear, and would bear for a long time to come, was that they must make nothing too big to be thus transported. The Russians, not having railway lines everywhere, had struck out a path of their own. The BT series ran on five pairs of wheels with a track carried round the circumference of the whole. Each wheel was shod with a solid rubber tyre and the machine was perfectly capable of travelling long road distances without using the track at all. It mounted a 45 mm gun, more powerful by far than the Vickers 3-pdr, and the engine was a 12 cylinder affair that could serve equally well for aircraft. The design was German, a variant on the BMW. BT 5 – the initials stood for Bystrochodniya Tankov, Fast Tank – was demonstrably faster on tracks than anything known in Britain as well as being well armoured, well armed and utterly reliable. In a few years time its later model became better known as the famous T34. Martel wrote of it at once to Elles, saying that he had watched it going along roads at at least 30 mph and across country at only a few miles per hour less. 'We saw several machines pass at 30 mph over a prepared bank which had a vertical drop of 5 feet on the far side. The whole machine leapt through the air and cleared a 30 ft gap. There was no apparent damage to the suspension or the crew. The engine is an aircraft engine of some 300 hp output.' It was, he added, 'at least twice as good as the A9'. The heavy tank, the T28, was not so good but still 'far superior to the A7 which is being built at Woolwich Arsenal'.

These were sobering thoughts. Wavell, a fluent Russian speaker who had spent some time in the country in 1911, introduced Martel to a number of the Russian Generals, including Voroshilov and Budyenny, with whom he seems to have got on well. In a way this was a pity for when, in 1942, it was necessary for Churchill to send a senior officer to Russia Martel was the only possible choice. This deprived the Royal Armoured Corps of his services when they were sorely needed. He came home this time brimming with ideas.

The designer of the BT suspension system, it turned out, was an American named J. Walter Christie who owned a firm called Front Drive Motor Company which he had formed for the French Grand Prix of 1907. His design had first appeared on a gun-carrier made at the end of 1916 and his first tank had been produced for the US army three years later. As Uncle Sam had set his face against tanks, and as other components were less good than the suspension, the Front Drive Company had fallen upon hard times until 1931 when the US army bought five of its T3 tanks and the Russians two. How Martel managed to buy a stray one in America and have it worked on by Nuffields is a story that has been told elsewhere.

He got little enough help from his old Chief. The idea of using an aircraft engine in a tank was not new, for the 300 hp Liberty engine had been designed and made in the States at the end of the war with exactly that purpose in mind. It had, like so many other things, been forgotten. Martel cast around and found out that the RAF had a stock of 600 Napier Lion engines of 500 hp for which it had no use. In October, 1936, he sought leave to acquire these since the Air Ministry was prepared to let them go for a nominal price. Elles turned the idea down flat. £500 was far too great a price to pay. Work continued on the A9. Colonel Justice Tilly, a founder member of the Tank Corps, was permitted to inspect it, in his capacity as Chief Instructor at Bovington. He described it succinctly in a letter to Lindsay, now banished to India in accordance with the usual practice. 'It's a dud. Too small for cross country work, the crew are too cramped to work their weapons or wireless; it bounces like a rubber ball; the tracks come off.' Interestingly Tilly mentions a conversation with 'Roseway, a WO Financier'. The Treasury, it seemed, was quite willing to find whatever money the tank people needed if only the General Staff could make up their minds what they wanted. For the new light tank, the Mk VI, Tilly had little good to say. He was not alone in this.

The War Office, however, had not been in complete hibernation. Captain Boys, Assistant Superintendent of Design at Enfield Lock, had designed a tank-killer which he demonstrated during a chance visit by Mr Leek of the BSA Company. It was a rifle of .55 inch calibre with a magazine containing 5 rounds and worked by the usual bolt action. There was a monopod mounting to take the weight and a recoil reducer on the end of the barrel to prevent it dislocating the user's shoulder. Mr Leek went away with an order to make 2,000 of the things; the first appeared in January, 1936, and by 1943 nearly 69,000 had come off the production line. A good cross-bow would have been just as useful and far cheaper.

Even the man who might fairly have claimed to be its inventor seemed to have concluded that the tank was no longer a serious weapon of war. The American correspondent Virginia Cowles, who had seen something of the war in Spain, tells of a meeting with the son of Lord Birkenhead, a member of an anti-tank unit, who had recently lunched with the Churchills. Over the meal he had spoken of a recent lecturer who had assured his audience that the life of anti-tank gunners would be short. His host had become indignant. 'What a monstrous thing to say. On the contrary, you'll be sitting there picking off tanks one by one.' It may not have been a considered judgment but, coupled with other remarks of a similar kind made years later and to be set out in their proper place, it does seem that the Churchill of Hitler's war had modified the views of an earlier day.

When the Spanish Civil War broke out in 1936 most people expected to learn something about the advances in tank warfare since 1918. General Martel saw nothing new. 'The nearest approach to a blitz was in Catalonia where a distance of 180 miles was covered at a rate of 4 miles a day.' There was, however, an eye-witness, Major-General (ret'd) J. F. C. Fuller. 'Boney' was under a cloud. Not only had he become a Fascist of high degree but he was known to have been in regular correspondence with Aleister Crowley. Crowley had been regarded as a harmless crank specializing in the absurder forms of black magic until he was unwise enough, in 1934, to begin a libel action against Constable & Co, the publishers. In the course of this the vileness of the man was plainly disclosed, as drug-fiend, sex-maniac and possible murderer. Plainly not a fit associate for a General officer. All the same 'Boney' could do one last service to the army. As he was going to Spain in any event and as there was no British representative with Franco, he was asked by the CIGS, Sir Cyril Deverell, to send back reports of anything that the War Office might like to know. Fuller obliged, with many words of fascist propaganda and some useful observations. One was quite firm. Light tanks were wretched little machines of no military value. The Royal Tank Corps had little else.

It was in 1937, with the threat of Hitler fortified by knowledge that he already had an air force and four armoured divisions at his service, that the Government screwed up its courage and decided to re-arm. For the army this meant high priority for anti-aircraft guns and little for armoured fighting vehicles. A wooden model of a proposed medium tank was produced. Martel and Hobart approved it; Sir Hugh Elles did not. It would take too long to build. Instructions were given to press on with the three types already existing in one form or another. A9 suffered from suspension troubles, troubles that could probably have been overcome by Carden but were apparently beyond his successors. A10 was almost identical though heavier armour justified the description of 'interim heavy cruiser'. Nuffields were working on their Christie which would become known as the cruiser A13. Elles himself had tried his hand at designing an infantry tank. The first model came out in September, 1936, when Martel was in Russia. It was a two-seater, weighing 11 tons and carrying 2½ inches of armour with a Ford V8 engine to push it along at 8 mph. In appearance it looked small and grotesque with what seemed to be an inverted saucepan on top. This was a .5 inch machine gun, the only weapon bigger than something of rifle calibre that would fit its diminutive turret. As it waddled slowly before him Elles christened it Matilda after a duck in some forgotten comic strip. The ugliness of his duckling must have impressed him, for Elles promptly ordered a better and quite different model to be made. Plans for the A7 were dusted off at Woolwich and contracts were placed with the Vulcan Foundry at Warrington to manufacture a modified version. Officially it was the A12: it goes down in history as the famous Matilda II. As a gesture towards something battle-worthy two pilot models of heavier machines, designated A14 and A15, were to be put in hand, the former being entrusted to the London Midland & Scottish Railway Company. Neither ever saw daylight. Nor did the proposed A16 of 21 tons.

There can have been little pleasure for Martel during his tour of duty at the War Office, even when in March, 1937, he was joined by Hobart in a new appointment within the Staff Duties Directorate. Both men had a sound grasp of the business and Martel in particular had seen in Russia what the skills of 1937 could produce. The obstacle was Sir Hugh Elles, who seemed incapable of making up his mind what the army needed or of pressing hard enough for any serviceable tank at all. Martel, with all the loyalty of a good officer, never by written or spoken word criticized his Chief and his private feelings must be left to the imagination. It can only have come as a relief, however, when the new Secretary of State, Hore-Belisha, got rid of Elles at the end of the year. With much good sense he seriously considered promoting Martel, still only of Colonel rank, to fill the vacancy. It seemed fair to assume that he consulted with his resident oracle, Liddell Hart, before arriving at the decision merely to raise Martel to Brigadier, whilst abolishing the ancient office of MGO and transferring its functions to the new Director-General of Munitions Production, Admiral Brown.

By early 1938, Munich year, it had become accepted that the cavalry must at last be sent to the knacker's yard. Even then the opposition was intense. Only quite recently had the Secretary for War, Duff Cooper, announced ex cathedra that: 'I think it is too early, if the time ever comes, to assume that the function of the cavalry is finished'. There was another argument against progress, this time rather better. In peacetime a regiment does its duties using those men actually with the Colours. On completing his service, normally after seven years, the soldier transferred to a reserve of two categories of readiness. On mobilization the reservist, of course, rejoins. Mechanize a cavalry regiment and for a number of years to come you will find it, on mobilization, to be swamped with ex-horsemen who do not know one end of a tank from the other. This was undeniably true, but the decision had to be taken if the army was to be fit for anything other than a museum. The decision to mechanize all but two regiments of the cavalry of the line, along with eight Yeomanries, was taken at the worst possible moment, in the Spring of 1939. The Royal Tank Corps, now increased to eight battalions, one of them in Egypt, suffered along with the rest of the army from a desperate shortage of both men and officers, but at least its reservists were tank-trained. The Royal Armoured Corps, successors to the cavalry, for the moment had no great accretion of strength from its old members.

Nor was that the worst of it. Hampden Gordon, who had entered the War Office in 1908 and had been assistant to Sir Reginald Brade during the Kitchener days, wrote a book on the subject in 1934. A passage on the Staff Duties Directorate asserts that 'The British Army, small in size, must at least be highly scientific, and a clear duty which falls to the War Office is to keep abreast or ahead of modern developments in every department of war material.' In this it had utterly failed. Martel had told of what the Russians were doing; it was common knowledge that Hitler's Germany had six armoured divisions in being; the French had excellent tanks in the Hotchkiss, the Somua and the heavy Char B. The British Army had nothing but a collection of machines that compared with these as the London to Brighton race compares with the Motor Show. No officer at the War Office in a rank below Major-General could wield any influence. The Sappers had three, the Gunners several and the Tank Corps not one. None of its officers had even reached that rank. Of the Brigadiers experienced in tank business – Broad, Pile, Lindsay, Hobart and Martel – all save the last had been, in the words of Tilly's letter of 2 December to Lindsay in India, 'buried'. He had, he explained, tackled Elles about this. 'He didn't like it, but was fairly cornered and said it was the system.' This was probably true. The army has always tried to make of its future leaders well-rounded men, not keeping them long in any one job, no matter how great their aptitude for it. It was rather like taking Lord Nuffield away from building cars in order to learn the grocery trade. All that came out of the War Office was a constant tinkering with designs, nearly all from men with no engineering experience, which made the builders' lives a burden.

They were burdensome enough without assistance. J. D. Scott, in his history of Vickers, tells how, early in 1938, the Company had completed its order for light Mk VIB machines for India and were still turning out twenty of the useless little machines every month. They had orders for sixty A 11s (Elles' Matilda) and fifty A9s, but all Sir Noel Birch's pleadings could not get an order for a new medium tank from the War Office. 'The company was too hard-pressed on design and development (for foreign orders) to go on even with the various research projects which were particularly close to Birch's heart; the self-propelled mounting for field guns, the tank destroyer, and the wireless controlled tank were all pigeon-holed.' Delivery of the 'dud' A9 began in 1939; the A10, officially dead, was resurrected and an order for 100 of them arrived. Vickers, however, did manage to strike one blow. In 1937 the Company had put up a plan for a 17-ton tank to be called the Infantry Tank Mk III; it was to be fairly well armoured and present a low silhouette. The main innovation was to be a manganese track, 'which had a revolutionary effect on track life'. It was turned down. 'Like a child abandoned in the snow, and rescued in improbable circumstances, this redesigned A10 was destined to make some mark in the world. Submitted to the War Office on or about St Valentine's day it adopted the Saint's name and, when the war broke out, the Company was told to give it priority over everything else!' Whatever its faults, the Valentine had one unique and compensating virtue. It was the only British tank of the day that could be trusted not to break down in moments of crisis. When the final report on AFVs (Armoured Fighting Vehicles) in the Mediterranean Theatre was published in 1945 Valentine's 130 hp GMC diesel engine was the only one to be rated 'Very Good'. Bedford and Liberty were both reckoned 'Poor'. Its one weak point lay in the absence of any skirting armour to protect the vulnerable suspension. This was a controversial subject. The Tank Board records for June, 1942, contain a report from one expert saying: 'I am convinced that this tank (Matilda II) would be much better without a skirt'. At almost exactly the same time Dr Dadswell, Chairman of the Tank Mission to the US, was writing: 'The British stressed the need for skirting plates to protect the suspension from HE'. It is beyond argument that many Valentines were put out of action from this cause.

Nevertheless the tank certainly did make its mark in the world. It was uncomplicated and robust, with an electrically driven turret traverse and no power assistance for either brakes or steering. Fair space existed for the crew of four and there was room enough for 62 rounds of 2-pdr shot and more than 3,000 rounds for the co-axially mounted Besa machine gun. When the 2-pdr became outdated, the turret was just able to accommodate a 6-pdr at the cost of dropping one crew member. The gunner had to be his own loader, a circumstance that put too much of a burden upon an individual. As such, the Valentine could only be a makeshift, but eleven Marks were made before it finally bowed out.

Thus the jig-saw pieces were fitted loosely together. Matilda 1, the original Infantry tank, was practically condemned before it went out to the RTR. *Infantry Training 1937*, the official training manual for the foot, contained several paragraphs explaining how sub-units should work with tanks. It might have been written twenty years before. Matilda could waddle in front at the speed of a not very good cross-country runner and had armour so thick that any projectile less than an artillery shell would bounce off it. In the cramped turret one gunner could just operate a heavy machine-gun. There was no more to it and only 139 of them were ever built. The A12, Matilda II, was superior in every way. There were 24 tons of it, with the first diesel engines (two of them of the kind used by London buses) to be mounted in a British tank and a 2-pdr gun which could kill any German tank known to be in service. Of cruisers there were some A9s and 10s, with the Nuffield-Christie A13s beginning to appear, plagued by what were tiresomely called 'teething troubles'. Numerically the greatest, though quite ineffective, were the under-powered, under-armoured, top-heavy light machines, mainly of the Mk VIB type.

Whatever might be said in Whitehall or Westminster, the army, at any rate on the regimental officer level, had no doubt at all that it was only a matter of time before we should have to take on Hitler and the politicians' touching faith in the French was not widely shared. Sooner or later a new BEF would have to embark for France, though everybody with even a little knowledge of the state of things would have agreed with Lord Gort's observation to Hore-Belisha of 17 March, 1939: 'It would be murder to send our Field Force overseas to fight against a first-class Power.'

There was no popular demand for the re-equipment of the army. The great fear, naturally enough, was of the German air weapon. Such modernization as took place was concentrated on the Royal Air Force and the suddenly modish Air Defence of Great Britain. Anti-aircraft gunnery was, to judge from the newspapers, the main business of the land forces. Vickers went ahead fulfilling small and belated orders for the new 3.7″ and 4.5″ guns. Tanks and other armoured vehicles trailed along at the end of the queue. The experience lacked novelty.

If the armoured forces did not have much for which to thank the tank producers they had even less cause for gratitude towards the Military Secretary's Branch. Of the RTR Brigadiers most likely to become the successors to a younger Elles two names stood out.

Hobart was sent to Egypt and on his return placed on half-pay. Pile was sent to organize Anti-Aircraft Command. There was no obvious successor to either of them for command of the Mobile, or Armoured, Division when it should finally move from paper to Tidworth. In February, 1939, as the functions of the MGO were being taken over by a new civilian Ministry of Supply in an unhurried confusion, the best brain in the business was removed from it. Martel, promoted to Major-General's rank, left the War Office to take command of a Territorial division, the 50th (Northumbrian). The system had made a completely clean sweep. Martel had been in turn Sapper and tank man; the one thing he had never been was an infantryman. The rounding-off process was, no doubt, felt to be to his advantage. The RTR took a different view.

Elsewhere there was a complete indifference to tanks and anything to do with them. In 1939 Ian Hay, of *The First Hundred Thousand* fame, was brought back to the army with Major-General's rank in order to drum up recruits, especially for the Territorials. His new book, *The Citizen Soldier*, was widely read. In 282 pages he treats of all the established arms of the services. Something like half a page, in the chapter on the artillery, speaks rather vaguely of anti-tank gunnery. On tanks themselves, apart from a photograph of a Vickers Medium going over a bank, there is a great silence, save for a few banalities.

Outside the islands there were strange stories going about. Raymond Gram Swing was the predecessor of Alistair Cooke as the voice of America in England and of England in America. His experience of men and affairs equalled that of any American foreign correspondent, for he had been in Berlin at the outbreak of the other war, had watched the progress of the Dardanelles campaign from Constantinople and had gone on to become a man of power in the world of US newspapers. When Swing made a broadcast men and women on both sides of the Atlantic listened with respect. His voice over the wireless on 9 March, 1939, said surprising things. He spoke of the announcement in the papers that morning by the British Government that, 'It is preparing an army of three hundred thousand men to send to France in event of a European war. Three hundred thousand men, nineteen mechanized divisions, that is a huge array. It is four times larger than the British Expeditionary Force, the "contemptibles", sent to France at the outbreak of the Great War, and, being mechanized, it will be far stronger than just four times as strong.' The General Staff doubted its ability to scratch up any force at all; the most optimistic figure, that of Colonel Hawes, of the Plans Department, was three battalions and a few guns. Where Swing, resident in New York, got his information is unclear but he had a nation-wide audience in America and was universally believed. It can hardly be reckoned odd if they raised their eyebrows a few months later.

CHAPTER THREE

Supply and Demand

The Ministry of Supply, created in the Spring of 1939, inherited the entire business of tank production. The War Office, in theory, laid down what was needed; the manufacture was entirely in the hands of Vickers and Woolwich Arsenal. No shadow factories of the kind built to expand the RAF were available to help them out nor, save for a few orders called 'educational', had civilian industry been put upon anything resembling a war footing.

When armies mobilize the first thing they do is summon back their reservists. In September, 1939, this produced something of a family party atmosphere, except perhaps with the newly mechanized cavalry. Old friends who had not met for years put on their harness, sometimes letting out a notch or two, and reported to their regimental depots. The younger men now in the saddle sometimes looked a little sideways at the new arrivals, mostly men with ribbons of an earlier war on their chests but, owing to the slowness of between-wars promotion, only two or, at the most, three stars on their shoulders. In some quarters there was unease, for it occasionally came hard to a man to have to touch his hat to the contemporaries of his sons. The new generation felt, reasonably enough, that the older men had had their chance and that this war was the business of others. They need not have worried. The veterans soon settled down, the habit of addressing them as 'Uncle' grew and few of them felt like supplanting their juniors.

It was not only the fighting side that called back the victors of 1918. When the Ministry of Supply was formed its first head was Dr Leslie Burgin, who would have strenuously denied that military

26

affairs had ever bulked large in his blameless academic life. Being a sensible man and by no means blind to what was happening on the continent he felt deeply uneasy about the prospect of pitting a few score Vickers light tanks against the six German armoured divisions that already existed. If this was the best the War Office could do he must needs look elsewhere. Lieutenant-Colonel Sir Albert Stern, demobilized these twenty years, had been one of the quadrumvirate who had invented mechanical warfare and made a reality of it. He was now 62, several years below retirement age for a full General, and a public figure. In the exotic world of money he occupied a great position, being a director of three Banks – Midland, Clydesdale and Bank of Romania – as well as being head of Stern Brothers and a member of the London Committee of the Ottoman Bank. At the moment Dr Burgin called him to mind he was heavily engaged in a hopeless attempt to prevent German interests taking over the Romanian oil industry. Under the mantle of the great banker, however, still dwelt the old Bertie Stern who had demonstrated between 1915 and 1918 that he had a dynamic power of getting things done and feared no man, however exalted. His fierce quarrel with Mr Churchill in 1917, when he had been sacked from organizing British tank production, had long been composed as a number of 'Dear Winston', 'Dear Bertie' letters among his papers proclaim. Stern had had a better grasp of the design and production side of armoured fighting vehicles than any other man and, although he had long been out of touch with military affairs, such talents were not to be neglected.

In June, 1939, Stern took his wife to Paris to watch the French Grand Prix, observing glumly that it might be her last opportunity. While he was there a letter was forwarded from Burgin, whom he did not know, asking whether he would meet the Minister to talk about tanks. Stern jumped at it. He knew enough about the present state of affairs to have serious misgivings about the kind of tank the army was getting and of the languid pace of production even of these. Burgin and Admiral Brown, the ex-Chief Engineer to the Fleet who was in charge of production, told him that they were 'very disturbed at the condition of mechanical warfare' and asked for his views. Stern replied: 'I should be a something fool to give views without study,' and asked the Admiral to arrange for him to talk to somebody at the War Office. An interview was fixed with General Sir Maurice Taylor, the Minister's Senior Military Adviser, and his Deputy General Davidson. There he received the treatment proper to an impertinent reservist. 'Sir Morris [sic] Taylor expressed surprise at the visit and said he was perfectly satisfied with the development of mechanical warfare, that he knew nothing at all about it and relied upon General Davidson.' Davidson was more forthcoming. He took Stern aside and said that 'I should be very disappointed at the position of affairs as nothing had been done in the development of mechanical warfare during the last twenty years. Very little money had been provided and Vickers had really been the only firm to develop a tank, that he and his deputy had great difficulty in making any developments as he was unable to get skilled draughtsmen.'

Stern reported back and sought out his old associates who had begun the entire armoured warfare concept. First he looked up Sir Ernest Swinton, ten years his senior, a director of the Citroën car company, ending his time as Chichele Professor of Military History at Oxford and himself chairman of a similar ad hoc committee. On 26 September, 1939, they formed up together to see the new CIGS, Sir Edmund Ironside. The CIGS, who could see further through a brick wall than most people believed, or affected to believe, was cordiality itself. Nobody knew better than he the nakedness of the army and the wretchedness of its tanks in comparison with those of other countries. Ironside and Burgin resolved them into the Special Vehicle Development Committee (SVDC) of the Ministry of Supply and gave them an office and secretary in the Adelphi. As the CIGS explained, the tank that the Army needed would weigh something in the order of 60 tons.

The Ministry, in accordance with age-old habit, had sprouted Boards and Committees charged with advising its Minister on almost every imaginable subject. Some of these, no doubt, were manned by practitioners skilled and experienced in their various arts. The Tank Board was not such a one. For the most part its civilian members were as obscure as the reasons that had suggested their part-time appointments. Stern's SVDC was no more than a small offshoot of the Board proper, though it did confer upon him full membership. Meetings showed little that he could admire.

The more Sir Albert learnt about the state of tank affairs the more indignant he became. It had been no great surprise to be told by Admiral Brown, in a letter dated 6 July, 1939, that 'the strategy and therefore the type of tank is a bit outside my province' or that 'we have had a devil of a time getting started!' Admirals were not expected to understand tanks. There had been Admiral Moore during the previous war with whom Stern had had much the same experience. Admiral Brown did at least understand what mattered when he wrote of a 'super-heavy tank, a land battleship'. General Davidson was less forthcoming. A note went to his Chief enquiring, 'Shall I help Sir Albert Stern or shall I damn him?' To begin with he blew hot and cold. Stern wanted information about the French tanks. Brigadier Hollebone was packed off to see them without Stern being told; when he returned he announced that he had given his word as an officer and a gentleman not to tell anyone in England, including the Minister, what he had seen. By the following April Stern's indignation boiled over. 'I make a definite statement now about the hopelessness of your Department now running tanks,' he wrote to Burgin. 'General Taylor knows nothing about tanks and General Davidson has no right to be where he is, in charge of design of tanks.'

Not only Generals incurred Stern's scorn. In June, 1940, he was to write in one of his numerous Minutes that 'I believe Liddell Hart, a friend of Hore-Belisha's, wrote a book which became Hore-Belisha's *Mein Kampf*, in which he said that in the next war England would fight on sea and in the air but there would be no expeditionary force in France ... [which] led to a very serious crisis with the French government.' By then he was laying about him, writing of 'the appalling incompetency of General Davidson and his Department'. Stern may not always have been right; indeed the fact that he was behind the times eventually became demonstrable, but it seems a pity that his driving energy could not have been put to better use. In the Kaiser's War, to which he constantly refers, his great contribution had not been to the development of the technical side of things but in goading others into action. As in 1916, he invariably went straight to the top. There are in his papers copies of many 'Dear Winston' letters pointing out all these things. When his friend became Prime Minister Stern took to so addressing him in letters but as time went on the replies became shorter and shorter; eventually they were no more than curt acknowledgements over the signature of an under-strapper. All the same his work was not valueless. He alone, as he told Burgin as early as December, 1939, had badgered the Admiralty into making cemented armour of 2½ to 4 inches thickness. Before that he was asserting that we had had a 6-pdr gun in 1916 and badly needed another. By April, 1940, the Admiralty had tested one and 'it went through 3″ carburised plate like butter'. Years were to pass, and many good men to die, before the army had such a weapon.

There was, of course, another prophet from an earlier age who might seem to have been overlooked. 'Boney' Fuller had visions, some of them apocalyptic, but he was banished from power. Late in 1940, when things looked at their blackest, Martel wanted him dug out from retirement and appointed all-purpose sage of the Royal Armoured Corps to advise on the shape of things that ought to come. 'He might come to the conclusion that in this future war the campaigns might be won by using half a dozen immense tanks like small battleships that could traverse land or sea as well. . . . There was nothing impossible in this from a mechanical point of view. It all wanted sorting out; it might be that the time required to evolve such machines would be prohibitive, but no one could say this without investigation. Perhaps a less ambitious design might be the right answer.' Fuller was not asked to do it. In his capacity as a Fascist he had been in Berlin just before the war and had written a letter to Unity Mitford, Hitler's admirer, prophesying that the war would be over in a few weeks and Germany would win. This soon leaked out and put paid to any chance of bringing 'Boney' back into the fold. It was a pity that this piece of typical eccentricity settled the hash of a man whose patriotism could never have been in question, but fatal it was.

Stern and Swinton went to France for a week at the end of November, taking with them Brigadier Pratt who commanded the 1st Army Tank Brigade – the two RTR battalions that were the army's entire battle tank force – along with General Hotblack, Gort's adviser on armour, and Lieutenant-Colonel Kenchington, RTR. Stern's thinking was clear, though it is impossible to say how far it was shared by Pratt and Kenchington. To understand how his mind was working it is necessary to forget all that we now know about the shape of the campaigns between 1940 and 1945. In November, 1939, the main facts were the existence of two lines, the Maginot covering the belly, if not the heart, of France and the newer Siegfried performing a similar office for Germany. The BEF would, presumably, build itself up as quickly as possible to something like the BEF of 1918 and, one day, it would have to set about the Siegfried works as its fathers had set about the Hindenburg Line. This would demand tanks of the largest possible size carrying the biggest guns they could mount. All else, light tanks, cruisers and the futile little Matilda 1, was an irrelevance.

Stern went home convinced that the work must once again fall to

30

him and his old collaborators. His 1918 contempt for the War Office and its ways were unabated. 'I believe this is all due to the efficiency of the Tank Board being destroyed by the elimination of the civilian element. . . . A soldier is not trained to be a designer or producer of mechanical weapons.' Of the civilians so eliminated he named the man he had long ago described as 'the father of the tank', Sir Eustace Tennyson d'Eyncourt. His first task was to seek him out, along with Walter Gordon Wilson, whose gear-boxes had made tanks workable, and Sir William Tritton. All were willing to come in with Stern and the tank they designed was to be called TOG – The Old Gang.

Tritton's Company, Fosters of Lincoln, had built 'Mother' and many of the tanks that had helped to break the Kaiser's army. For the past couple of decades it had been back to its old business of making agricultural machinery, but the memories had not gone. The company's headed writing paper had a drawing of a Mk 1 Tank at each top corner and, within the last years, they had built some tanks for Italy which, to Tritton's disgust, had been used against the Abyssinians. Fosters could still build tanks if anybody wanted them. To furnish them with engines the Gang recruited another old member, Harry Ricardo, whose engines had powered the Mk V and much else. With his professional colleagues at Davey Paxman & Co he designed and produced, with a speed that seems hardly credible, a 600 hp diesel motor to be called the Paxman-Ricardo.

One of the causes of Stern's downfall in 1917 had been an ill-judged liking for a form of electrical transmission which had failed dismally during the Oldbury Trials of that year and had led to the great quarrel between him and Wilson. He was, however, still convinced that he had been on the right lines and brought back to the Gang the electrical engineer who had then advised him, Charles Mertz. He was put to work in designing an arrangement of generators driven by Ricardo's engine that would make steering and gear-changing no more difficult than in a London bus. TOG, the name the Gang gave to their creation, was to turn the scales at 70 tons, the weight of six Matilda 1s.

Wilson, the only member who had remained in touch with tank affairs over the years, does not seem to have been as fiercely dedicated as the others. His epicyclic gear-box, designed in 1917 and a masterpiece of its kind, was still in service and would long remain so. Since the end of the First War he had devoted most of his time and skill to the subject and had invented the first self-changing system. The firm he had founded, Self-Changing Gears Ltd of Coventry, understood this mystery better than any other in the world and he had never been a man to suffer fools. The attitude of the War Office, so he claimed, was more than he could stomach and very soon he resigned. This was a calamity for TOG. Its design was sound, its engine excellent and its gun-carrying ability far in advance of any British tank of the time. The weak spot was its transmission, for machines of this weight demand more than adaptations of commercial systems. Wilson, of all living men, could have given the tank what it needed. He chose not to. One may fairly surmise that Stern had not forgotten their furious quarrels of two decades earlier and that he could not bring himself to exercise the necessary smoothing down. Very probably he came to regret this, though he would never have admitted it. Instead he decided to manage without him. It was not absolutely clear whether Mertz was brought in after Wilson had marched out or whether the quarrel arose over his system being considered. Had that been so, it would have been an exact replay of the events of 1917 when Wilson and Stern had raged at each other in terms hard to forgive over exactly the same matter. Electric transmission had failed then; it was hardly reasonable to expect it to do better now.

Tritton remained both faithful and enthusiastic, putting Fosters to work on tanks again in February, 1940. Before they had got very far, and at the time that Stern was planning to have a thousand TOGs built for the campaigns of 1941, a Memorandum was delivered to them. It bore the date 16 February, was over the signatures of Hotblack, Pratt and Kenchington and it cut the ground from under Stern's feet. Because of 'the appalling conditions of mud encountered by the BEF in Flanders' the entire specification would need to be changed. The new one, containing all-round tracks, unditching beams and sponsons, sounded exactly like a re-make of the 1918 Mk V. The reasons behind the Memorandum can only be guessed at. The BEF was not in Flanders, not at least as Flanders is generally understood. Nor was it troubled by mud. In February, 1940, it was deep snow and intense cold that were the enemies. The BEF was, in fact, dangerously near freezing to death, with little protection offered by the flimsy battle-dress blouse. Knowing men had chamois leathers sewn inside the back to protect the kidneys and the issue of some 1918 leather jerkins was a Godsend. Hotblack, of course, knew all there was to be known about tanks and mud from his experiences in the other war and it may be that he was anticipating events. A possible explanation is that other counsels had prevailed and TOG was regarded as no more than an irrelevant nuisance.

Stern took no notice. All through the Spring and the Dunkirk summer The Old Gang worked away and the great tank grew under their hands. The German armoured divisions now numbered ten, with the conversion of four light divisions used in Poland to full tank status. Hotblack, who had recently been Military Attaché in Berlin, knew all about this. One cannot avoid considering the possibility that he saw further ahead than the elderly gentlemen and took the view that their efforts, being misdirected, ought to be brought to an end without hurting their feelings. If this was his intention it did not succeed. Bertie Stern was a tenacious man.

He was also a man gifted with an uncommon degree of foresight, a foresight that was not merely visionary but mitigated by much commercial experience. His immediate pre-war concern, jointly with the French, to scotch German attempts to take over Romanian oil had taught him a lot about that commodity. In 1939 the biggest tanker afloat displaced some 17,000 tons. Stern came up with a plan for an oil-carrier of 100,000 tons to be built in a French yard. Doubts were inevitably raised about its feasibility but the thing was done after a lapse of a good many years. Technically it ought to have been possible in 1940 but in that interesting year there were more important considerations than imaginative naval architecture. His fancy had always been for the biggest machines possible, from the absurd Big Wheel of 1915 to Martel's unformed idea of a monstrous tank with a pair of 14-inch guns that would blow the Siegfried Line to Kingdom Come. For the moment, however, TOG 1 held the field. By the end of February, 1940, Tritton's people had produced a wooden mock-up and were making ready to turn it into a serious weapon.

33

CHAPTER FOUR

'We have had no End of a Licking'

RUDYARD KIPLING

It is time to return to the main stream. In 1938 a new kind of formation then called the Mobile Division had been formed under Major-General Alan Brooke; it comprised, in theory, two mechanized cavalry brigades, an Army Tank Brigade and Divisional troops, thus carrying out the 'all-armoured' idea. Brooke did not like it, preferring the alternative plan of having a balanced force of all arms working together. Before he could influence events he was translated to the world of anti-aircraft gunnery. The function of the Division remained – strategic reconnaissance and limited offensive operations in suitable conditions. Being made up mostly of light tanks, it was not considered fit for the task of taking on any sort of strongly defended position. In the summer of 1939, when Brooke was replaced by Major-General Evans, the name was changed to the Armoured Division. It may have sounded more menacing but did not increase its effectivenes.

The bullet was, however, bitten in April of that year and all but two regiments of the cavalry of the line were unhorsed, along with eighteen Yeomanries. The only survivors, picked on grounds of seniority, were the Royals and the Greys, the latter being already in Palestine. The Royal Tank Corps became the Royal Tank Regiment and the whole mechanical force became amalgamated under the style of the Royal Armoured Corps. Plans were made for its expansion into three Armoured Divisions, five Army Tank Brigades (to be the heavyweights) and a single armoured car regiment which already existed as the 12th Lancers. Included would be eight TA battalions, converted to armour and numbered 40th to 46th RAC.

The idea was that the divisional cavalry regiments – each division had had one since Wellington's day – should coalesce and form armoured reconnaissance brigades. As the establishment of each consisted of Vickers Mk VI light tanks and Bren carriers they could be fit for nothing more, if, indeed, even this limited task would not be too much for them. It was painfully obvious that a few proper tanks with proper guns, of which every other European army of consequence possessed plenty, could make mincemeat of them. The French Army included fifty-three tank battalions, many of them armed with the Somua or Char B which could take on any known enemy with more than a sporting chance of success. Their High Command, held out for so long to credulous foreigners as the repository of all military wisdom, had made from these only three Light Mechanized Divisions; the remainder were scattered about in packets, four of them encadred into under-sized armoured formations to support attacks that would never come. The Germans, under Guderian, would soon have ten divisions, well equipped and battle-hardened.

It is curious, and it seemed so at the time to many people, how little effect the knowledge of this had upon the men in power. German air strength was considered awesome, but few bothered much about their land strength. Though the matter is unprovable, there is strong suspicion that Hitler went out of his way to help this along. Reports of massive traffic jams during his picnic-march to Vienna were blamed on mechanical defects in the tanks; the jams were real enough but the cause was more probably simple lack of experience in policing large scale movements. It was all of a piece with the cardboard tank stories current at the time. No harm could come from making those who were soon to be Germany's enemies believe that they had little to worry about on that score. There was certainly no sense of urgency in England over making anti-tank weapons that were worth having.

Vickers had produced the 2-pdr gun in the Spring of 1938 with a great flourish of trumpets. Though small, it was explained to students at the Small Arms School at Netheravon, it was of an unbelievable power and could kill any tank with its solid slug. Originally it was intended as a weapon to be used by both the Royal Artillery and the infantry, but it was soon made plain that the infantry did not want it. Already it had been given, or promised, the Bren, the Boys rifle, the 2″ and 3″ mortars and a platoon of small tracked carriers. These were quite enough to be getting on with and battalion guns had been dropped two centuries before. In any event General Wavell was urging infantrymen to cultivate the arts of the game-keeper, the poacher and cat-burglar, arts that did not depend upon possession of this clumsy and unfamiliar tool. Later on the cause was altered and infantry clamoured for guns. Martel, like some others, needed no warning that the 2-pdr might be just good enough to cope with the tanks of 1938 but that thicker armour against which it would be impotent could not be far off. He received no encouragement. A bigger tank gun meant carrying fewer rounds and an increase in the size of its turret. It would be better to wait until change was unavoidable.

Then there was the matter of mines. These had proved their effectiveness in 1918 and were both cheap and easy to make. *Infantry Training 1937* spoke airily of them, proclaiming mines to be Sapper business. In the summer of 1939 few, if any, British-made ones existed. During the first post-mobilization course at Hythe a few hours were taken up with digging holes in Sandling Park and laying the three which made up the Small Arms School's stock. Two, shaped like slab cakes, were the British Mks I and II; the third, about the size and shape of a Stilton cheese, was called the French mine. The Instructors admitted handsomely that nobody knew very much about any of them. The *Official History* mentions the existence of mines in the arsenal of the BEF but nobody remembers encountering any.

In July, 1939, there appeared Captain Liddell Hart's new book *The Defence of Britain*. It implied that the 'teething troubles' of the Christie cruiser were over and praised the light tanks for being much better protected than their predecessors, and for having gone far towards beating the anti-tank gun. Mr Hore-Belisha's guru must have known that this was stretching the truth. The Mk VIb light tank had actually added a vice of its own to those of the earlier models. Unlike them, it was top-heavy. All the same, July, 1939, was not the time for outstanding candour about the state of British armour. The Germans were known to be regular readers.

When the order for General Mobilization went out at the end of August the horse-trained cavalry reservists were replaced by men who had done their Colour service with the Royal Tank Corps. This put a severe strain upon the new RTR, but it managed. The 1st Armoured Division was formed and, Martel says, 'carried out some training but was dreadfully short of equipment'. As the first four Regular Divisions went to France each carried with it a mechanized cavalry regiment that had hardly got used to the sight and smell of its new weapons. The undertaking to France that we would put two complete Corps into the field within thirty-three days was honoured, but their condition was, to put it mildly, less than perfect. To make good the pledge whole divisions of the Territorial Army followed them, each with its Yeomanry in slightly worse case, for lack of training time, than the regular cavalry regiments.

The striking force of armoured fighting vehicles provided by the country in which the tank had originated consisted of one battalion, the 4th RTR. Its weapon was a half-hundred of the unprepossessing 'I' tank, the Matilda I. After wintering at Domart it moved in the Spring of 1940 to a training area sixty miles west of Paris, at Pacy-sur-Eure. One armoured car battalion, the free-range 12th Lancers, completed the Order of Battle.

The BEF set to work building a firm defensible position along the Belgian frontier, work being most done by every form of Sapper and Pioneer who could be clapped into battle-dress. There was only one bright spot. Horses were gone and mechanized transport, mostly 3-ton lorries, had turned all infantry into mounted infantry. By the end of November the first snows had begun to fall and the beginnings of the great freeze were being felt. The main task of the BEF was to remain alive and in good heart. This it did extremely well.

The constitution of the army in France is an awful example of how military affairs become the victim of politicians. It was not so long ago that they had been talking bravely of a small but highly sophisticated force, technologically superior to all competitors, that would emerge from the pavilion when the time came. Because of this practically all spending on the third eleven, the lightly regarded Saturday night men of the Territorial Army, had stopped, except so far as it affected the anti-aircraft forces; these were very largely Territorial business to which two infantry divisions had already been converted. The remainder, still armed with the identical weapons once used by their fathers, had no particular role beyond that of home defence. In the other war several divisions had been sent early on to India; the troops relieved by them had made up five new Regular divisions, given some Territorial gunners and Sappers. Mr Churchill made the point strongly in a letter of 1 October addressed to the Prime Minister. 'Do not imagine,' he said, 'that Territorial divisions will be able after 6 months' training or so to take their part without needless losses and bad results against German regular troops with at least two years' service and better equipment . . . The only way in which our forces in France can be rapidly expanded is by bringing the professional troops from India and using them as the cadre upon which the Territorials and conscripts will form.' Brooke said much the same thing, pointing out that there were enough infantry battalions in Palestine to complete a division. Mr Chamberlain's Cabinet took another view and the BSA Company was put to work. Its Lewis gun production line had stood idle since 1918. It was now given all the old weapons from the Ordnance stores to recondition. They would do for the 'terrier' divisions.

Though the Mediterranean was still open and a re-play of 1914 would have been perfectly possible, it did not happen. Brooke blamed Ironside's obsession with the Middle East. After the 5th Division had been formed in December (the 6th of 1914 had come from Ireland and was only a memory) there were no regulars left at home. For political reasons it was needful to brag about the number of divisions in France. On paper a division was a division, no more and no less. Five of the first-line Territorials went out in the course of the winter and spring to be followed soon afterwards by three second-line ones. The small but very high-class army soon became, in cricket terms, half county class (most of the Test material was in India or Palestine) and half village. More advanced training for the better formations was not possible. Instead a number of good senior TA officers with war experience, one of them a VC, were unceremoniously sacked and replaced by regular officers, some of them dug out from minor staff appointments and of no obvious superiority. The only other formed Territorial division, the 49th, fared even worse. It was sent to Norway.

Even the best informed of the men shivering on the Belgian frontier had not entirely grasped what they were in for. Martel, still GOC 50th (Northumbrian) Division, visited his Corps Commander (Brooke) on 30 January by order for a talk about the campaign to come. Brooke noted in his diary that '[He] seemed quite oblivious of the fact that, instead of attacking this spring, we are far more likely to be hanging on by our eyelids in trying to check the German attacks'.

The 4th RTR were, at least, complete professionals. They could do some sort of training and make their preparations for when the day came. The remainder of the 1st Armoured Division was less well placed. During the winter it had been broken up and used for anti-invasion and internal security. Suggestions that Marlborough Downs would serve nicely as a training area were turned down; it would interfere with the gallops of nearby racing stables. Ingenious artificers passed their time in making plywood mock-ups of what should have been armoured command vehicles. In due time these were to accompany them to France.

The Support Group of two RHA Regiments, two battalions of Greenjackets and some Sappers was commanded by Lieutenant Colonel – in due time General Sir Frederick – Morgan, who described his Division as 'more of a basis for argument than an instrument of war'. Nearly all its transport was hired from civilian sources and loudly proclaimed the fact. Morgan himself did well enough with 'a pompous old dowager of a saloon', lately the property of HBM Ambassador to Athens, but others fared less sumptuously, especially one company of Rifles who went off to war 'in the vehicles of a travelling circus, including barred lions' cages, all still bearing their striking, not to say blinding, decor of scarlet and gold'. Nobody seems to have remarked upon these being the colours of the 11th Hussars.

During the winter the cavalry were formally encadred as two Light Armoured Reconnaissance Brigades coming directly under GHQ. The 1st was all Yeomanry, the Fife and Forfar and the East Riding; the 2nd was Regular, the 5th Royal Inniskilling Dragoon Guards and the 15th/19th Hussars. As both had started from scratch there was little to choose between them in efficiency. The rest, the 4th/7th Dragoon Guards, 13th/18th Hussars and the Lothian and Border Horse, remained unbrigaded.

Nobody had much enthusiasm for the posture which the BEF had been constrained to adopt. When Major-General Sir Edward Spears went back to France as the eyes and ears of Winston Churchill he naturally sought out the French Generals he knew. General Georges, Gort's immediate Chief, deplored 'our backwardness in tank construction'. The consensus of opinion was that we needed the heaviest type that bridges could carry. This conversation took place pretty nearly on the same day that the CIGS, Ironside, was demanding from the Ministry of Supply a battle tank of 60 tons and a cruiser of half that weight. He was told that two committees were considering it, one under Stern and the other headed by Swinton. Of Stern's thoughts we know; the other committee, being desperate, was pressing for adoption of a French machine, a Hotchkiss described by Ironside's biographer as 'already obsolete, under-armoured and under-gunned'. It is small wonder that Swinton made common cause again with Stern, but there was no message for the CIGS from the professionals whose business it was to see that the army had what it needed. A few Matilda IIs crawled out of the works of Vulcan Foundry, Fowlers and Ruston & Hornsby and that was all. Nor were tanks the only missing essentials. Ironside's diary entry for 3 December records that 'Even Fortington, our statistician, says that we are running a great risk in sending the troops over with so few anti-tank guns and anti-aircraft guns'.

Those whose responsibility it was to find out about these things knew perfectly well what the Germans were up to. Captain Joseph Summers, commonly called 'Mutt', was Vickers' chief test pilot and had been the first man to fly a Spitfire. In October, 1937, he had paid a routine visit to Germany where he had met Ernst Udet, the ace pilot of the earlier war and now a General and considerable grandee in aircraft manufacture. At the Heinkel factory Udet had headed Summers off from the most secret things but he had allowed him to fly a Ju 87 dive-bomber. Summers told the Air Ministry that he would not care to be on the receiving end of it. The Air Ministry was as uninterested as was the War Office when told of the six panzer divisions and their constitution. The capacity of mankind for deluding itself when it wants to is infinite. Stukas, as the Ju 87s were commonly called, were the essential complements to the armoured fighting vehicle, providing them with what amounted to their own private heavy artillery that could be switched on at a moment's notice. With machines like these having the freedom of the skies the power of the tank became almost irresistible. Steady infantry could, up to a point, take care of themselves by digging and by shooting back. Men imprisoned in their vehicles could not.

On paper the German Order of Battle did not disclose any great superiority in numbers or matériel. By the spring of 1940 they mustered on the western front 136 divisions, ten of them being armoured. The French opposed them with 101 divisions along with fifty-six tank battalions of varying degrees of effectiveness. The British divisions had reached the ominous figure of thirteen, the bulk of the infantry now coming from the Territorial Army. It has to be repeated that all this was on paper. The German Army was organized as an army. The Allies were not. The BEF was no more than a miscellany of divisions varying greatly in quality.

A German armoured division counted 300 tanks in the original six divisions and 220 in the former light divisions. In all they put into the field 2,574 tanks of which 627 were mediums, the Panzers III or IV, and 334 Czech-manufactured light mediums from the Skoda works, the booty of Munich. The figures are Guderian's. The remainder were almost all Panzer IIs, 10-ton machines with a speed of 30 mph and a 20 mm cannon. In reserve, and readily available at a pinch, were another 800 Panzers I and II. Their strengths were mainly in two matters – first an excellent system of wireless control (the French had only ordered theirs in November) and second a high degree of reliability. Whereas any British designer had to hawk around for a lorry engine that might serve to push his tank along the Germans (prominent amongst them Dr Porsche) had only one address to which they need go. The Maybach AG had been in the business of making big engines since the day they had powered the first Zeppelin. Practically every engine used in any German AFV throughout the war was designed and more often than not made by them. British tank crews for a long time went in constant fear of mechanical breakdown. For their German opposite numbers the thing was a rarity.

The French, had their High Command known its business, could have put against them an equally formidable array, for they had fifty-six tank battalions to the German thirty-five; these varied greatly in establishments from eighty machines to a former cavalry regiment down to thirty-four in those equipped with the Char B, a tank better than anything opposed to it. Though the Rue Ste Dominique still dreamt wistfully of Napoleon, the grandees of the army had forgotten one of his sovereign maxims: 'Scatter to forage; concentrate to fight'. It is easy to be highly critical of the French, but having regard to our own miserable contribution it is hardly becoming.

With the advent of sunshine and the long days the sword of Damocles fell, beginning with an air attack on Arras on 10 May. This was regarded in some quarters as little short of cheating. Spears tells of how, some months earlier, he had suggested to the Air Ministry that it might be advantageous to bomb the Black Forest which was known to harbour great dumps of ammunition and was ripe for burning. He was told by a shocked Kingsley Wood that this was out of the question. The place was private property.

Spears expressed his feeling about the move into Belgium so beautifully that it is a positive duty to quote him. 'I felt slightly uncomfortable. Were our forces by any chance doing what the Germans had expected them to do? Quite apart from the fact that the Germans had probably a very fair idea of the French plan, the simplest reasoning would have told them what its main lines must be.

Would the Allies allow the small nations, neutrality-intoxicated though they were, to be destroyed on their doorstep? Certainly not. The Nazis were perfectly aware that they had but to start beating up these babies for the nanny democracies to rush out in cackling protest.' It had already happened in Norway. It would happen again in Greece.

As the BEF abandoned the positions upon which so much work had been lavished for so many months the German air force made no attempt to prevent them. There was indeed a feeling that if any unit were to lose its way the Germans might very well send out guides to lead them to their destination. Nothing could have suited Plan Yellow better. The Belgians had refused to allow any inspection of the positions they were offering. When the BEF, headed by the armoured cars of the 12th Lancers and the Vickers Mk VIb tanks of the cavalry, arrived they found themselves in a position ill-prepared and hardly defensible. Hitler's original plan for November, 1939, had been to hit them as soon as they arrived but the crash of a German aeroplane containing all the details and the inclemency of the weather had compelled him to think again. The second thoughts were, from a German viewpoint, better. His main thrust would be through the Ardennes as soon as the Dutch and Belgian armies had been bombed out of the war. Accordingly, this prerequisite having been attended to, the Stukas set to work upon the French First Army and, for some days, the BEF was left in peace. In his book *The Defence of Britain* Captain Liddell Hart had spoken admiringly of the formidable barrier to invasion posed by the pill-boxes, the forts and the deep belt of demolitions guarding this approach through the Ardennes. They proved practically useless. Guderian's Panzers made tracks for the Meuse and, in particular, for Sedan. Before long his columns were roaming unhindered well to the rear and the BEF was outflanked.

It was a demonstration of how, whatever mathematicians may say, two parts can be greater than a whole. Most German tanks of 1940 were not particularly formidable; by the standards of four years later they were puny affairs. Minefields a fraction of the size of those to be used at Alamein would have halted them. Any piece of artillery could knock them out. That is, of course, on the assumption that both guns and gunners were in their proper places. It was the business of the other partner to see that they were not. The Ju 87 dive-bomber was easy meat to the fighters; even musketry and light automatic fire from the ground could keep it at arm's length. When either the troops did not stand or the fighters were absent, however, the combination of Panzer and Stuka was irresistible. The sheer speed and surprise of numbers of aircraft, apparently with the eyesight of vultures and carrying punches almost equal to medium artillery, gave the tanks an easier run than anybody had bargained for – including General von Kleist, Guderian's Chief. *Gott* indeed appeared to be *Mit Uns*, for the skies remained peacock blue throughout as the Stukas required them. A week of low cloud and rain might have altered things considerably.

The British Armoured Reconnaissance Brigade was, in the words of Brigadier Vyvyan Pope's famous letter to the War Office of 26 May, 'a wash-out. It might be able to carry out recce alone but cannot fight a delaying action'. It was by infantry tanks of the Army Tank Brigade, the 4th RTR now joined by the 7th, that the armoured battle was to be fought. The 4th still manned its fifty Matilda Is; the 7th, arrived only at the beginning of May, mustered twenty-seven of these along with twenty-four Matilda IIs and seven light machines. The Brigade had been moved by rail from Pacy to the Forest of Soignies where they harboured during the night of 15 May. By then the first panzers were over the Meuse and were cutting loose in the rear areas with only the three Territorial labour divisions – divisions merely in name for they were nothing but lightly-armed infantry battalions – to stand in their path. The four French armoured divisions had been swept ignominiously aside. At noon on the 16th Brigadier Pratt, commanding the Army Tank Brigade, received his orders. He was to move his command back to Tournai at once. The train drivers at Enghien had disappeared, the place was being bombed heavily and there was no possibility of entraining the Matildas. Pratt, having no choice, decided to move everything by road, though he needed nobody to tell him that the tracks of his tanks could not stand such punishment for long. His only towing vehicles were three Scammell lorries from Brigade Workshops which at one time had to pull thirty tanks that needed repair. At Ath a message arrived from the Corps commander. Lieutenant-General M. G. H. Barker. He was not one of the finds of the war and was removed shortly afterwards. Barker's order, sent direct to each of Pratt's battalions, was for the Brigade to retrace its steps and deal with some German tanks around Hal. Most fortunately, before the order could be fully carried out, Pratt had a visitor. Brigadier Pope, head of the AFV Branch at GHQ in succession to Hotblack, had come to see what was happening. In a great rage,

he told Pratt to take no notice of Barker and to move through Tournai to Orchies, some 16 miles south-east of Lille. It was a journey
usual at the time, very slow through roads crammed with refugees,
and the pavé was hard on the Matilda's iron tracks. The Brigade
arrived at about midday on the 20th. Of the hundred or so tanks that
had left Soignies there remained fifty-eight Matilda Is and sixteen
Mk IIs fit for service. They would all be needed, for Lord Gort had
decided to fight his way south to join up with the French. The *drôle
de guerre* was over.

There came a pause in Rommel's headlong progress. For one
thing he was led to believe that a French armoured division had cut
across his tail. Then he was delayed by the labour divisions. There
were three of these, the 12th, 23rd and 46th, all second-line Territorial formations made up from the less-trained element left behind
when Hore-Belisha had doubled the strength of the TA overnight in
the summer of 1939. Their function had been to build a railhead
near Rouen for a BEF of 1916 proportions and, when opportunity
offered, to carry out a little training. This had been denied them so
far since all had passed the bitter winter of 1939/40 in guarding what
had been called Vulnerable Points, an activity which had demanded
their splitting up into posts of platoon or even section size. For the
most part they were very young. They were not, however, the half-
armed mobs that they are popularly held to have been. The TA officers and NCOs had been leavened by a fair number of Regulars
from overseas battalions and every man had at least carried out his
individual training and fired one course. They could use their
weapons well enough but they were weapons of the wrong kind.
There were no artillery, engineer or signals units. The battalions
lacked everything prescribed for them save only for a short Lee
Enfield apiece with a cotton bandolier of fifty rounds, a few Brens
and some Boys rifles with half-charge practice ammunition. Officers, save for the few who had privately acquired pistols, carried
stout walking-sticks. None the less, they were in good heart, well
disciplined, physically fit from their labours, and entirely determined not to let down the regiments whose badges they wore. They
had been rushed up by lorries during the night and had observed
with mild amusement the French units in the area, every one of
which seemed to have a previous appointment. Worst of all, when
they had been snatched from their pioneering tasks, they had been
ordered to leave behind all their tools. In most battalions there was
not a single pick or shovel, nor had entrenching tools been issued.

1. Lord Gort, Matilda I and visiting foreigners

2. The Vickers Light Tank Mk VIA

3. The Vickers Light Tank Mk IVB

4. The 'duds'. Prototype of A9

5. The 'duds'. A10

6. Matilda I. Named, aptly, for a comic-strip duck

7. Matilda 2. The best tank of 1940

8. Panzer II. The scythe of Guderian in the same year

9. Valentine in London

10. Valentine in the Caucasus

11. Canadian-built Valentines for the Red Army

12. Valentine Victrix. Tripoli 24 January, 1943

13. Up-gunned. The 6-pdr Valentine

14. A voice crying in the wilderness. The Old Gang with TOG 1

15. The bruiser denied its fight: TOG 2

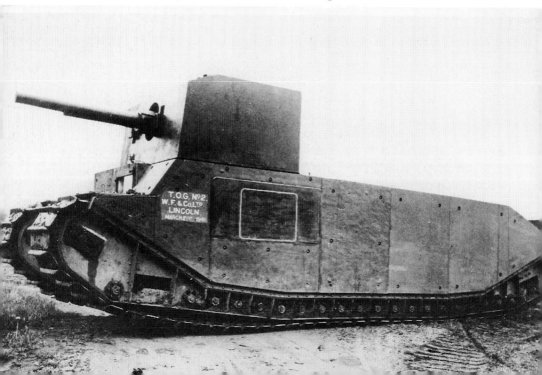

Nobody in his right mind could have expected them to achieve anything, but General Brownrigg, Adjutant-General to the BEF, would not allow it to be said that they had run away and abandoned the French. Strung out across roads crammed with refugees moving at a slug's pace, they made such positions as they could out of the open fields and farm buildings, grubbing with their bare hands and the rims of their helmets. Then they waited, having little idea of what had happened beyond the fact that the sky had fallen in. They did not have to wait more than a few hours. The War Diary of the German 8th Armoured Division tells of how they met for the first time 'English troops who fought tenaciously (a battalion of The Buffs) ... The battle for Doullens claimed the whole attention of the troops. In spite of the use of numerous tanks it was only possible to break down their resistance after two and a half hours.' It seemed longer.

During that time the Army Tank Brigade reorganized itself after moving on to Vimy, within sight of the Canadian War Memorial. Seven of the sixteen Mk IIs were transferred to 7th RTR to support the powerless Matilda Is with their 2-pdrs. Then came one of those odd coincidences that happen in war. The Brigade came under one of the improvised organizations that had sprung up, this one being called 'Macforce', from its commander General Mason-MacFarlane. In theory it comprised two divisions, the 5th – the last Regular division – and the 50th, Territorials from Northumberland. The commander of this last was back on his old battlefields of Arras and Cambrai, the only survivor of the great Bermicourt days. Major-General G. le Q. Martel took over direction of the first tank battle of his second war. The chain of command having broken under the strain of events, his orders came direct from Lord Gort, beginning with a warning that an attack was to be delivered by the 50th Division, or such part of it as could arrive in time, with the 1st Army Tank Brigade under command. This was on the evening of 19 May. Later the same day it was decided that any elements of Major-General Franklyn's 5th Division which could reach the scene would also take a hand. Arras, Martel was told, was securely held by a garrison based upon the Welsh Guards, and the French 1st DLM (light mechanized division) of some seventy Somua tanks was to the east of the town on the River Scarpe. All the information available, both of the enemy and our own troops, had been gathered by the armoured cars of the 12th Lancers, who were doing splendid work. No intervention by the RAF against the swarms of dive-bombers could be expected. The airmen were putting up a tremendous fight but their machines, save only for the Hurricane, were hopelessly out-classed and their losses formidable. In particular the Fairey Battle light bomber was to the RAF what the Vickers light tank was to the army. Whenever it appeared it was slaughtered. The French pilots stayed resolutely on the ground.

Martel's battle was designed as an Anglo-French affair with the French Vth Corps advancing from Douai. Spears tells of how it was organized. No French commander turned up at the planning conference fixed for the 20th. At 12.30 on the 21st Gort received a letter from General Blanchard saying that his troops could move on the 22nd or the following night. With the German armour cutting round the rear from Abbeville and still moving fast, this was far too late. Martel's men must do the business alone. The huge 'Tiny' Ironside, who was at Lens, 'lost my temper and shook Billotte (GOC 1st Army Group) by the button of his tunic'.

Martel sent two infantry brigades to relieve the 1st DLM and thus make their 20-ton Somuas available to pitch in with his Matildas. The 150th Brigade of the 50th Division arrived at Vimy just as dawn was breaking on the 20th. As Arras seemed to need it more, Martel handed over their only 2-pdr battery to the garrison. His second brigade, the 151st, along with the two RTR battalions, fetched up early on the following day, all hands being very tired indeed after some long marches. Martel sensibly ordered a compulsory rest and forbade any discussion of what was going to happen. After an early morning conference with Franklyn, he issued orders to his commanders at 7.30. The attack would begin from a start line along the Arras–St Pol road, rounding Arras to the south and clearing the enemy out as far as the River Sensée, an area 10 miles deep by 4 wide. It would be carried out by two columns. The Right Column would be the 8th Durham Light Infantry, 7th RTR, an 18-pdr battery and a 2-pdr anti-tank battery with one company of motor-cyclists. The Left would be 6th DLI and 4th RTR, supported in the same way. Each column would be under command of the infantry CO. The routes were to be, for the Right Column, Maroeuil-Duisans–Warlus–Wailly–Mercatel–Henin; for the Left Column it was Dainville–Achicourt–Beauraines–Wancourt – all of them names familiar to the men of 1917. Martel's HQ would be at Vimy. The start line was to be crossed at 1400 hrs.

In fact the crossing was late, for German outposts, hitherto undiscovered, were found before the line was reached. They were duly mopped up. Then the battle began. On the left 4th RTR were engaged almost at once as they and the 6th DLI, following in artillery formation, met the enemy headlong. The Matildas shot up his transport and killed a lot of Germans. Then they pressed on towards Achicourt, knocking out or running over many anti-tank guns. The DLI took at least 100 prisoners. So far only artillery fire had met them and the thick armour of the Matildas was unworried by it. Pratt asserted in a letter written soon afterwards that many of the German anti-tank gunners left their weapons and fled and that even field artillery shells bounced off. One Matilda I was hit fourteen times by 37 mm shells and only lost a bit of armour. Some tracks, however, were broken and a few machines were put out of action by tracer bullets in the engine compartments. The dive-bombing went on incessantly, mostly on the DLI, but one Matilda was turned over, killing its commander. The RTR battalion commander was shot dead; there was no room in a Matilda for a CO and he was obliged to use a light tank. It went the way of most light tanks. The CO of the 7th battalion was killed in the same way. Progress, inevitably, was slow and by 1830 it was obvious that the Sensée was not going to be reached. The exhausted infantry, bombed and shelled almost beyond endurance, could go no further. The column halted at Beauraines, on the personal order of Martel, who had come to find out how things were going.

The Right Column found the going even harder and got no further than Warlus. It was not helped by the French Somuas, which took it into their heads that the anti-tank battery with the 8th DLI was hostile; they opened fire, knocking out a gun and killing two of its crew. Apologies followed. German tanks were certainly in and around Warlus and, accordingly, Martel decided to halt the Right Column at Duisans until things became clearer.

Once the columns had halted the Germans set about them. The idea was plainly to hammer them remorselessly from the air until they had to move out and then the panzers would attack them in the open. Martel says: 'Their plan met with a good deal of success'. Over a hundred planes pounded the tired garrison of Beauraines. It would have been madness to leave the infantry as a sitting target with no weapons beyond small arms with which to retaliate. As they moved they were attacked, Martel says, 'by great numbers of tanks'. 'The 4th Tank Battalion, although very outnumbered, helped to stem the tide and the anti-tank guns did their best, but the column was forced to withdraw to Achicourt.' Six Somuas appeared from nowhere to lend a hand and make amends. When a heavy German tank attack was put in the 2-pdrs knocked out twenty 'and left them burning on the ground'. Four of them fell to the gun of Major King's Matilda II.

Rommel's own account of the matter adds quite a lot. He says that the thin-skinned vehicles shot up by 4th RTR were part of the SS Totenkopf Division which seems to have been unaccustomed to such rough play. Part of it undoubtedly took to its heels. More sinister is the first mention of British tanks being knocked out by the 88mm anti-aircraft gun used as an anti-tank weapon.

That night the entire force, what was left of it, was pulled back to Vimy where in the morning of 23 May it was attacked by strong German forces debouching from the old 1915 positions on Notre Dame de Lorette. 7th RTR, from a hull-down position, bagged seven panzers and left their mark on the infantry. It was the end of the affair, for soon afterwards the remnant marched north to Carvin and the main body of the BEF. The tanks had done splendidly, but the infantry deserve a word. There is Martel's authority for saying that the Northumbrian Territorials had vowed that no man would be taken prisoner unwounded. When they reached Dunkirk and were ordered to embark with rifles only they made it a point of honour that every unit would take all their machine-guns and not a single one was left behind. Not every formation could make such a claim. On 3 June Brooke told Ironside that no further TA divisions should be sent as they 'would never stand up to the bombing'.

There was still much fighting for Martel and his Northumbrians to do, mostly around Ypres, before the final evacuation. None of it, however, relates to this story. When the dust had settled he came in for criticism, not all of it deserved. In his *DNB* entry it is said that 'his conduct of the operation and its faulty co-ordination led to much sharp criticism from the tank officers taking part, who felt that his powers as a commander and tactician did not match his gifts as a technician'. This is harsh measure. Time was pressing hard on him, the fog of war was even thicker than usual and scrambling fights of this kind cannot be planned like 18th century sieges. With no staff, no communications and a force far too small to carry out the given task he deserves our commendation. Somebody, at any rate, thought so. When, in February, 1944, he returned from an unrewarding mission to Moscow, and lost an eye when the 'Rag' was bombed, his existence was not forgotten. A minute went out from the Prime Minister to the Secretary for War dated 19 April. 'I think we ought to do something for Martel. You cannot blame him for his ill success in Russia. They treat all our people like dogs. Martel fought a good fight with his tanks about Armentières [sic] in France ... I do not agree with him in some ways about tanks, but I am sure he is an officer of exceptional quality.' That is a compliment worth having.

When the war was over Liddell Hart dug deeply in order to find out why the German armour had not pressed home its attack on the Dunkirk perimeter when the going was good. He came to the conclusion, upon the testimony of von Rundstedt (though unshared by Guderian) that Martel's battle had been the sole cause. The action of a few tanks had given the Germans, for a change, wild ideas that a substantial armoured force was in being ready to cut them off. But for the neglect of decades it might have been true. As it was the 'strong force' that was encadred at Carvin on the 23rd, as a composite 4/7th battalion, comprised eighteen Matilda Is and two Matilda IIs, all of them with their tracks on the point of collapse and almost out of ammunition. It was still able to mount a small operation as it travelled north, helping to extricate the Cameronians from an ugly situation at Givenchy. This cost eight of the remaining runners. The battalion reached Dunkirk with the last two survivors on 27 May. Thus ended the blooding of the First Army Tank Brigade. It gave no cause for discouragement about the future. Matilda I was useless but Matilda II was a winner. And the regulars of the RTR were a match for any German.

The second stage of the piecemeal destruction of the Armoured Division took place at Calais and it came about in this fashion. On 21 May 3rd RTR, at Fordingbridge in Hampshire, was under orders to move to Southampton with the object of joining the two battalions at Pacy. Because this was not an operational move equipment was carefully packed away, every gun being heavily greased with mineral jelly. The vehicles had all been embarked when a sudden order arrived at 8 pm which altered everything. All personnel were to entrain at once for Dover. They reached the port during the small hours and were rushed across the Channel, arriving at Calais by tea time on the 22nd. With them went two motor battalions, also part of the Armoured Division, the 2nd 60th Rifles and 1st Rifle Brigade along with a Territorial battalion from the London Division, the 1st Queen Victoria's Rifles. These last were, on paper, a motor cycle battalion but, unsurprisingly, embarked as simple infantry. Paper is seldom to be trusted implicitly. The *Official History* gives the strength of a RTR battalion as fifty-two cruiser tanks. 3rd RTR had on charge the usual mixture of light Vickers Mk VIbs and Nuffield A13 cruisers of the Christie kind, with more Mk VIs than cruisers. They arrived during the afternoon of 22 May and the men were set to work at the irksome business of de-greasing. As soon as a few light machines were fit to travel they were sent to St Omer to find out what was going on. They came back reporting the town empty. A second patrol was never seen again. The rest of the battalion set off by the same road and bumped into a column of German tanks when just short of Guines. The fight that followed cost 3rd RTR a dozen of its cruisers. On orders, the battalion retraced its steps into Calais. Three panzer divisions followed it. That night an attempt was made to break out eastwards towards Gravelines. Major Reeves' squadron – the name was just beginning to replace 'company' – reached the canal there after passing through German troops through mutual misunderstandings. There they waited. First came the dive bombers, then the panzers. In the football crowd conditions of refugee-crammed roads B Squadron took them on as they tried to force a crossing. The 2-pdr of Reeves' A13 accounted for five tanks and two troop carriers before the fighting died away as the light thickened. A second squadron, with some infantry, attempted to follow B but was roughly handled. Only nine cruisers and twelve light tanks were left when the order came to evacuate the place. 3rd RTR had ceased to exist. The defence of Calais and Boulogne doubtless satisfied national honour. It also threw away large numbers of troops, some of them of the highest quality and very hard to replace. How anybody could seriously have believed that a single tank battalion, particularly one equipped as was 3rd RTR, could have made the slightest impression on three armoured divisions with complete mastery of the air passes understanding. And the end was not yet.

There remained of the Armoured Division its HQ, a brigade of light tanks at Pacy, a few Lewis guns and 2-pdrs called a Support Group and two RTR battalions, the 2nd and 5th, which reached Cherbourg on 23 May. In all they numbered 284 tanks, 134 light Vickers, the remainder cruisers. The Divisional Commander, Major-General Roger Evans, was a heavy dragoon who had won a Military Cross in Mesopotamia and would not have claimed to be England's Rommel. It would have made no difference if he had been. The task laid upon him was impossible from the start.

The name of Armoured Division still stuck but Evans' force was nothing of the kind. Not one of his tanks was strong enough to withstand even the fire of the small 37 mm gun with which the Germans were lavishly equipped. Nor were they mechanically reliable. In Brigadier Pope's letter, parts of which have been quoted before, he makes the point very firmly: 'All of our tanks must be mechanically simple and reliable. 75% of our casualties have been due to mechanical failures and slow repairs.' He goes on to say: 'Moves by rail cannot be relied upon. The Boche can always cut the lines by air attack. All our tanks must, therefore, he capable of moving long distances at reasonable speeds by road.' The German tanks had already given convincing proof that the thing could be done. Pope also mentions that 'the 2-pdr is good enough now, but only just. We *must* mount something better and put it behind 40 to 80 mm of armour'. None of this sounded revolutionary.

It is hardly necessary to follow the two brigades, faced by two first-class panzer divisions, through their depressing retreat across the Vexin. General Sir James Marshall-Cornwall treats fully of it from the commander's point of view in his *Wars and Rumour of Wars*. From the most advanced point to the East of Rouen, order was followed by counter-order from the French commanders; it was a discouraging business. On one day the 3rd Brigade – the two RTR battalions – lost eleven cruisers and seven lights. On 29 May the losses in the two brigades amounted to sixty-five, 'though some were recovered'. At one stage they found themselves defending the Andelle, a pretty little trout stream but no sort of obstacle to anything. Eventually they crossed the Seine at Les Andelys and made their way to Cherbourg, narrowly beating Rommel in the race. Fourteen of the A 13s and a dozen lights reached the port and were safely embarked. The 2nd brigade, the three cavalry light tank regiments, had been withdrawn beforehand as unfit for further service. Its tanks entrained for Cherbourg and were not seen again. Pope summed it up in his last paragraph. 'I do hope the powers that be realize that the Boche has succeeded solely because of his mass of tanks supported by air attacks. Man for man we can beat him any day and twice a day, but dive-bombing followed by tank attack is too much on our very extended fronts. If only 1st Armoured Division had been out here in time, it might have made all the difference.'

The anonymous author of *The Diary of a Staff Officer*, an army officer with the RAF in France, is quoted approvingly by Fuller * in saying that '500 fighters could have saved Sedan'. He also gives an interesting glimpse of Evans' men and what they had to endure.

* In *The Second World War*, p 81.

Under the date 10 June he wrote: '1500 hrs. A quartermaster of a tank battalion forming a part of our armoured division turned up here today with two cars and twenty men. They represent a few of the survivors of the gallant but abortive action of this division when counter-attacking with the French. The French infantry arrived on the scene five hours late. The tanks had done their work, the ground being cleared, but the French infantry were not there to consolidate the gains. The tanks pottered about trying to hold the ground they had won and were then shot to pieces in detail by the heavier-armoured German tanks. Our armoured division did not attack the strong points but drove into the line between them. They cruised up and down between these strong points over the shallow trenches and crushed the Germans in them under their tracks. They could not depress their guns enough to deal with the enemy close round them and the crews opened up their tanks and fired their revolvers down the sides of the turrets.' The code name given by the French to the division was, he tells us, 'Roger's dogs'. One can imagine the tone in which they used it.

Though the BEF had been annihilated, it had left some impression behind. In August the German formations making ready for invasion were told of what they might expect. 'The English soldier,' said von Bock's report, 'was in excellent physical condition. He bore his own wounds with stoical calm. The losses of his own troops he discussed with complete equanimity. He did not complain of hardships. In battle he was tough and dogged. His conviction that England would conquer in the end was unshakeable ... The English soldier has always shown himself to be a fighter of high value. Certainly the Territorial divisions are inferior to the Regular troops in training, but where morale is concerned they are their equal. In defence the Englishman took any punishment that came his way. During the fighting IV Corps took relatively fewer English prisoners than in engagements with the French or the Belgians. On the other hand, casualties on both sides were high.' It was matériel rather than men that had ruined them. Next time it would have to be better, much better.

For the two Brigadiers there would certainly be a next and better time. John Crocker, of the 3rd Armoured Brigade, would in due season travel back along what the French now call 'La Route Fleurie' as Commander of I Corps, British Liberation Army. Richard McCreery, of the cavalry light tanks, finished the war in Italy as the last commander of Eighth Army.

CHAPTER FIVE

'There Was Not English Armour Left'

Ballad Of The White Horse

G. K. CHESTERTON

Between the wars Anthony Armstrong had written a series of small books describing life in an infantry battalion which the initiates found very funny. In *Warriors at Ease*, first published in 1926, there appears a spoof operation order. The paragraph on tanks is succinct: 'Tanks are very rough things and ought never to be used in any war.' His view was widely shared for the next dozen years or so. In his famous novel *Royal Regiment*, which came out ten years later, Gilbert Frankau has a conversation between a CRA and a battery commander, both of them men who had done course and distance against the Kaiser. The CRA speaks: 'You're well over forty with twenty-five years service, four and a half of 'em active, behind you. If war were to break out tomorrow what would be your command? Six eighteen-pounder bundooks, four of 'em 1918 vintage, and about a hundred flannel-footed soldiers.' He was quite right.

In the blink of an eye all that had changed. Tanks and other kinds of armoured vehicle had suddenly become *à la mode*. Some may even have remembered Sir Douglas Haig's dictum of late 1916 that a division of them was worth more than ten divisions of infantry. Unfortunately there were few tanks about during the summer of 1940 when the main business of everybody seemed to be the walling in and roofing over of the island. Brooke says that over 700 had been sent to France and only the twenty-five from Cherbourg had returned. Those apart, there was little enough available and most of the runners were unfit for combat.

The spirit of the islanders, still people of the same ancient stock, reflected their traditional perversity. How the war could now be won seemed an impossible question but the relief at being shot of the French was almost tangible. Though tanks had suddenly become chic they were still not the first priority. Mr Churchill minuted to Lord Beaverbrook on 9 August that 'If it came to a choice between hampering air production or tank production I would sacrifice the tank'. Since the future of the world depended for the moment upon a few hundred fighters and a couple of score destroyers this could hardly be called into question.

It was at about this desperate time that a small tragedy happened, though nobody now admits to knowing exactly when it occurred or who was answerable for it. A little while before the war the Tank Corps had suffered an attack of conscience about all the veteran machines still lying around Bovington and had begun to refurbish them for the Corps Museum. Some zealot, probably at about the time when strange demands were being made for aluminium saucepans to be turned into Spitfires, decided to scrap the lot. 'Mother', the first real tank, Wilson's gun-carrier, the Mediums B, C and D, along with the Mk V Star, the last of the 16-tonners and various other irreplaceable machines went under the torch. One can only hope that their ingredients saw service once more under other names. The ancestor of them all, however, managed somehow to escape. 'Little Willie' was made to run again and is reputed, though uncertainly, to have been packed off to defend an airfield. At least one Mk IV did duty guarding the coast in Dorset. They were not the oddest of defenders. At the fighter station of Acklington in Northumberland the Station Adjutant, Robertson-Campbell, produced his own AFVs. Some heavy lorries were kitted out with wooden boxes, a large one containing a smaller one, the gap being filled with shingle and holes bored through the lot for rifles. They were capable of movement, just. To such straits was one of the world's leading industrial nations reduced.

Whilst on the subject of Heath Robinsonry there is a fine example that deserves its place in any book. A little before the war a firm named County Cars submitted to the War Office plans for a machine which its designers reckoned a valuable addition to the armoury. On the chassis of a Bren carrier was mounted a pair of arms protruding forward and ending in a kind of gimballed bucket. In this would crouch two men with a light machine-gun. At the touch of a lever the arms would raise the bucket high in the air and its occupants would be able to bring down fire on targets otherwise concealed by such obstacles as houses or haystacks. The General

Staff were enchanted, though but slowly. In 1942 a prototype was ordered; General Richardson inspected it a year later and recommended that it be produced in quantity. At the end of 1943 the only specimen in existence passed its trials and was exhibited to the AFV Directorate. These humourless men ordered immediate cancellation. 'Praying Mantis' now sits apologetically in the Tank Museum alongside other monuments to misplaced ingenuity.

The Order of Battle during the summer of 1940 comprehended five armoured divisions and three army tank brigades. In sober truth there existed a single Regular battalion, 8th RTR, with fifty Matilda Is. The 150 or so cruisers that remained, including what were left of the pre-war Vickers Mediums, were on charge to the six ex-Yeomanry regiments whose numbers began with 40. Crocker's brigade had, of course, the assorted twenty-five that had been brought home from Cherbourg. An AFV Directorate was at last set up under the experienced Brigadier Vyvyan Pope. There was still no overall commander of the armoured forces, big though they would soon be as new machines came out of the factories.

Throughout the summer and autumn it was upon Pope that the burden fell of deciding what kind of armoured force was needed, what sort of machines it should have and how it was to be manned. The large training establishments that came into existence were his work and his memorial. Fortunately he and Brooke, now C-in-C Home Forces, were of one mind about the ultimate objective. The two kinds of armoured forces used in France, the armoured division for mobile operations and the army tank brigades for the slogging match, were retained. An establishment for the former, rather on the lines of Guderian's panzer divisions, was set up and lasted for the next couple of years virtually unchanged. It consisted of three armoured brigades, each of three regiments and a support group. This comprised a regiment of RHA, two motorized infantry battalions and a mixed AA/AT regiment of artillery.

On 10 August a brave decision was taken, originally by Sir John Dill and Anthony Eden, that a cruiser tank battalion of fifty-two machines, a light tank regiment of the same number and 7th RTR with its fifty Matilda IIs should be shipped at once to Egypt to thicken up 7th Armoured Division. With the entry of Italy into the war the state of affairs in the Middle East had become menacing and Wavell needed tanks more immediately than did Brooke. Undoubtedly this was the right course to have taken but it creamed off the top of the small armoured elements left at home.

Tanks, however, were beginning to arrive in appreciable numbers. The biggest single contribution came from Vickers who between September, 1939, and June, 1940 handed over 269 out of a national total of 739. The Company's main concern now was the Valentine, for orders had been received to turn out as many of them as was possible. This work was carried out in a corner of the Elswick shop in cottage industry style. No such thing as a production line existed. In the beginning plates were put together and secured by a few bolts in order to make a skeleton. Then the whole thing was riveted before being moved down the shop for 'suspension and wheeling'. That done, the hull went back again to take aboard its engine, transmission, fuel tanks and the rest. Much ingenuity and improvisation followed and by mid-summer Valentines were coming out at about forty a month. The Valentine had many shortcomings but Vickers boasted, with justice, that it was the most reliable tank of its day. The Nuffield cruiser – variously called A 13 and Mk IV – was not reliable. The design, based on the Christie suspension, was by no means a bad one, the road speed was quite good and it carried a 2-pdr gun. Martel, who should have known, reckoned it superior to the German Mk III 'as a design'. Unfortunately the quality of engineering was less good, for which Martel placed the blame squarely on the Ministry of Supply. On the heavier side, Matildas were now coming out of Woolwich in increasing numbers and would have to carry the weight of the fighting for some time to come. Again a good design was flawed by bad manufacturing work. Weak mechanical features, particularly in the fan drive and water pump on the cruisers, and clutches on the Matildas were never properly investigated and put right. Martel says grimly that 'This cost us dearly on the battlefield'.

There remained the heaviest tank of them all. Stern's Gang – he would not have objected to the word even though it came later to mean something else – had worked for months with their usual energy. On 23 April a letter had gone to Ironside beginning: 'I ask the General Staff to give an immediate order for 100 so-called "Stern" tanks.' It pointed out that a pilot model was due in August; if it proved no good little harm had been done, but if it was a success 'large numbers of these Tanks could be ready for a 1941 offensive'. Stern had managed, as only he could have done, to prise out of the Admiralty a quantity of heavy armour plate and now he needed 'test benches, jigs and tools etc'. Not for the first time he reminded the CIGS that d'Eyncourt, Tritton, Swinton, Symes, Ricardo, Rigby and Mertz were assisting him and that 'We were responsible for the design and production of all the Tanks in the last war'. 'I cannot believe that our advice can be disregarded even at the instance of the present authorities in charge of design and production, who have never designed a heavy Tank nor have been in charge of production of Tanks on a large scale.' Stern and 'the present authorities' were not on terms of cordiality. The reason for his letter to the CIGS can be found in a meeting with the Minister four days earlier. 'I told the Minister that I have seen General Kenchington who said that the Army wanted heavy Tanks.' Kenchington was an important figure in the tank world. After three years in France with The Buffs he had transferred to the new Tank Corps and was by 1940 the second man in armoured fighting vehicles at the War Office. 'I told him that my present engine had been taken over by the Naval Land Equipment Department, which confirmed my previous forecasts regarding this engine.' Presumably the excellent Paxman-Ricardo had been the Admiralty's price for the thick armour plate. 'He [Kenchington] said that they had not yet had time for another meeting of the Co-ordinating Committee and no further meeting had been called. I told him that I could not keep my manufacturers any longer. I showed him the letter dated 18 April from Windeler saying that Mirrlees Bickerton & Day had resigned from the TOG Group. I said that it would not be fair to keep them. I said I was appalled to think what would happen in a year's time. I had hoped, for the country's sake, that a Tank Board would be constituted. It takes nine months to design and nine months to produce a tank. A Tank Board need not interfere at all with present production. I asked him whether he could give an order for the jigs and tools for the engines and transmissions. He said "No, I cannot. Kenchington tells you one thing and us another. After all, General Carr* made his statement and did not ask for your tanks. It is the Co-Ordinating Committee which decides on the programme. It is nothing to do with me or the Secretary of State for War. If you get an order from the Army then it will go through".' Dr Burgin sounds much like Alice's White Rabbit. The note explains much. Nobody, in solid fact, was in charge of tank production save for a Committee which seldom met. General Pownall, Vice-CIGS, says that it was usually called 'The Crazy Gang'. Nevertheless, work on TOG 1 continued thanks to the faith of Sir William Tritton.

* In his last days as Assistant CIGS. Soon afterwards he was given command of 1 Corps. A Gordon Highlander and not experienced in tanks.

Whatever Dr Burgin may have thought of him, Kenchington was fully aware of what was happening and was taking an important share of it himself. TOG was not the only candidate for adoption as the Army's heavy tank. You may remember the pre-war A 20. This had been withdrawn from its pigeon-hole, dusted off and handed to Harland and Wolff, the Belfast shipbuilders, for working over. Even before the *drôle de guerre* had ended it had been agreed in the War Office that something bigger than Matilda would be needed before very long. The usual limitations, however, must apply. Any tank built inside the island would, one day, have to be shipped out of it. Before reaching a ship it would have to travel by rail. There-fore, it was argued, the machine must not be so heavy that ordinary rolling-stock could not carry it nor so wide that it could not go through the tunnels. It must, for obvious reasons, have a low sil-houette. Though heavily armoured, it must not weigh more than forty tons. Mr Churchill, not without tank experience of his own, interested himself in the business and allowed Kenchington free access to him to talk about it.

The task of building a heavy tank was something outside the ex-perience of any organization, save only for Vickers and Woolwich Arsenal, both of whom were more than fully employed on other things. Fosters were not even considered. In the end it was entrus-ted to Vauxhalls, the British end of the great US company, General Motors. Vauxhall, with much work on hand in building cars and lorries, had not sought the job. No Minutes of the Board survive to show that the Company ever had anything to do with tanks at all. There was no tank tradition nor had the oldest hand any experience of the right kind. In spite of that the Company put up a remarkable performance. With the help of Major Raikes, lent by the War Office, they worked throughout the summer and autumn at a speed not known before.

It was by no means a painless business, as Stern found out when he visited Luton on 23 June, 1940. He held a long meeting with the Managing Director, Mr Bartlett, the Chief Engineer, Mr King, and the American Alex Taub who had designed the Bedford engine which was to power the new machine. The efficiency of the factory and the obvious quality of the workmen made a very favourable im-pression but Mr Bartlett had a tale of woe to tell. The only specimen of the A 22 – ex A 20 – in existence had been sent over from Belfast and had been taken from Luton station by Mr Dean of Vauxhalls to their borrowed testing ground at Luton Hoo. There he and Harold

Drew, the Company's expert on suspension systems, had put it through its paces. Much had been found wrong. To begin with, the bogey wheels had an unaccountable habit of coming adrift. Cinematograph films had been made and played back in slow motion until the cause was found. This promised well but it was only one of the difficulties. Was there no data, Bartlett asked, nor any useful guidance that the Mechanization Board could give them? Stern answered that there were none. All the mistakes of twenty years before were being repeated and there was no point in seeking help from the Tank Board. The only member of it with a glimmering of knowledge of the subject was Mr Durrant of the London Passenger Transport Board.

It is greatly to Vauxhall's credit that they produced any tank at all. A good share of this must go to David Raikes, a serving soldier who, for all his lowly rank of Major, feared no man. He it was who acted as go-between, much as Stern had done in the earlier war, prodding laggards in Government Departments until the Company got what it needed. Not even Mr Churchill awed him. When, on one of his visits, the Prime Minister demanded to know why so big a tank carried so small a gun Raikes told him. Vauxhall had produced a complete tank in less time than the Ministry had needed to furnish any gun at all.

It certainly had refinements that seem unexpected for 1940. At the driver's feet were the usual pedals for accelerator, clutch and brake. The last two were power-assisted by means of a Clayton-Dewandre air compressor mounted on top of the gear-box. There were two sets of brakes, each designed for a distinct purpose. The 'stopping brake' was a powerful hydraulic affair of the conventional kind. The 'steering brake', which worked more lightly on the tracks, was operated by a bicycle-style handlebar. Four forward and one reverse speeds were engaged by means of an old-fashioned crash box of a kind not seen in other kinds of vehicle for several years. The Instruction Book remarks, fairly, that 'Driving and steering are made as easy as possible'. The system also provided much that could just as easily go wrong. Much the same could be said of the electrical arrangements. Behind the front gunner's seat was a petrol-driven charging plant for the batteries upon which depended the rotation of the turret and the three wireless sets, one for internal communication. With the engine switched off the turret could be cranked round by hand but it was a slow business. Under ideal conditions all these things worked well but Churchill was not the simple and robust tank that the soldiers demanded. To keep it in action called for considerable exertions by all five crew members.

Even its makers would not have called the Churchill a handsome tank. Its top part proclaimed solidity but the tiny bogie wheels, eleven on each side, gave it an odd look. The big wheels of the Christies suggested speed, whereas Churchill's small ones certainly did not. Nor was this deceptive, for it was never able to manage anything better than about 15 mph, half of the cruiser's pace. The first model was armed with a 2-pdr and co-axial Besa in the turret with an additional 3″ howitzer protruding from alongside the driver. Roomy though the interior was, it had insufficient space for both and the howitzer soon had to give place to a second machine-gun. The tank's weakest point lay in its engine. Mr Taub's flat 12-cylinder Bedford, with an output of 350 bhp, was well suited to the heavy lorries for which it had been intended. It was not nearly powerful enough to push 40 tons of metal on tracks at any respectable speed and the strain on it naturally led to over-heating. Though Churchill was to go through eight Marks and the last models differed in detail from the first, no better power unit ever came its way.

Hardly any Vauxhall records of that period have survived but the present Company Secretary, Mr Frankish, recalls that when he first joined there was a cartoon in the office 'depicting the desires of the differing disciplines in tank design; thus the engine man desired nothing but a simple platform for his engines, the armourer wanted nothing but guns etc'. It is hardly surprising that the Churchill was not quite the machine the Army needed.

Stern, never an outstandingly patient man, had no high opinion of the Churchill and he was becoming more and more exasperated with officialdom. There is, among his papers, a note saying that the continuance of the Tank Board in its present form would end disastrously. 'The Board only meets once a month for two hours when England is fighting for its life.' The members were indeed stridently undistinguished, save only in their usual business affairs. To set out their names would be quite pointless for none was widely known for any reason. Among the Tank Museum archives is a photograph, undated but probably taken some time in 1942, of them at a celebratory luncheon at the Savoy. What they were celebrating is unclear but the speaker on his feet is unmistakeably Lord Beaverbrook. The rest of them, save only for Lord Nuffield (who looks miserable), resemble a David Low cartoon of capitalists holding high revel. Sir Albert Stern is not present.

The Secretary to the Ministry of Supply was Sir George Gater whose background was entirely in education. Stern sent him a letter on 16 August pointing out that the one military member of the Tank Board (Pratt) was in America and the Chairman, Sir Alexander Roger, was heading a Ministry mission to India, South Africa and half a dozen other countries. Like the other members, Sir Alexander did not devote all his time to tanks. He came from Callenders Cables, was a great authority on telephones and had been Director-General of Trench Warfare Supplies during the earlier conflict. Other matters were mentioned, inspired by the apparent levity with which the Ministry was behaving. 'Perhaps tanks are not wanted. Why then waste public money on them? If they are wanted, why not constitute a proper Tank Board?' Sir Albert's bitterness was justified. 'It is our firm conviction that in eighteen months England will wake up and find itself with out-of-date tanks equipped with out-of-date armaments.' He was entirely accurate in his forecast. Eighteen months after August, 1940, came the spring of 1942 when no British tank existed that was fit to be used in battle. Such prophets are seldom popular. When Stern was told that the War Office considered Ricardo to be 'not much good and too old to be of any further use', he called it 'scandalous'. As it was. Henry Ricardo was one of the country's most talented engineers. At 55, he was seven years younger than Sir Alexander Roger and the same age as General Hobart. When Lord Beaverbrook, during his short tour as Minister of Supply, proposed that Sir Albert Stern become Chairman of a new Board the War Office threw up its hands and cried 'Veto'. This was understandable, for Stern would have been a hair shirt to everybody in the tank business. It was not, however, a sufficient reason for turning down a man with his credentials. The cry went up that he was not a qualified engineer. This drew a dignified letter suggesting that a few years' apprenticeship long ago would not have added much to his present knowledge of tanks. The first Chairman had been in no better position. The War Office won, as it could hardly have failed to do. What frightened the General Staff was not the gaps in Stern's knowledge but the whip in his boot. Any laggard behaviour, or even suspicion of it, and Bertie would be off to see Winston. It is a pity that the opportunity was denied him, for it is plain that much was kept from the Prime Minister on the subject of armour and its development. Nor should Stern have been regarded as an enemy. He picked up the business where he had put it down in 1919, but he was not a man to be so consumed with vanity that he would refuse to learn new things. Instead the appointment went to a Mr G. W. Thomson who left scant evidence of his tenure when, in June, 1941, he gave way to Sir James Lithgow, the Clyde shipping magnate. He in turn was succeeded in the following year by another Glaswegian, Lord Weir. He was 63 and in 1918 had been Director-General of Aircraft Production. Tanks were not his subject.

Another member of the Gang, Sir Ernest Swinton, was every bit as worried as Stern about the way things were shaping in tank design. He wrote down his misgivings in a letter to the Minister, Herbert Morrison, on 24 June. Morrison sent a soothing reply: 'The Prime Minister has decided that the Board shall study future plans for a heavy tank.' It did nothing of the kind; not, at any rate, for a long time to come.

Instead of that the Ministry furnished the Army with a tank that may fairly claim to be the worst of them all. Covenanter was intended to be the next successor to the indifferent A 13; the design came from the LMS Railway Company, with some Ministry assistance, and the railwaymen built it. The engine was a 12-cylinder one made by the firm of Meadows. Covenanter was an elegant tank with a low silhouette but that is the only compliment it deserves. Before it was even issued the fact became plain that it was quite useless. The power unit was not up to the job, the cooling system did not work and the armour was proof against nothing much more than bird shot. Nearly 2,000 Covenanters were made before being withdrawn from service soon after they had been issued. There were other ill-famed tanks to come but Covenanter was the most comprehensively worthless.

To replace it there came a tank that was nearly as bad. This was not the fault of designers, for Crusader, in Martel's words, 'had the makings of a most excellent cruiser tank'. The engine was a survival of the Kaiser's War, the 1917-designed Liberty, which, worked over by Nuffields, had been exhumed to power most of the tanks which fought Hitler. In 1940 it had no competitor. The trouble with Crusader was that it was shockingly badly made. Before long it acquired a wretched reputation with the Army because it broke down with unfailing regularity even in peacetime conditions. Nuffield, perhaps justly, blamed this on the shortage of skilled examiners, most of whom had been press-ganged by the Navy. Many of the Crusaders handed over to the Army had never been tested at all, though every component demanded careful scrutiny.

First came the motive power. The Liberty Low-compression Flying Engine, to give it its original and proper name, was not so much chosen as inescapable: there existed no other capable of even attempting to do the work demanded. General Ironside blamed this on the horsepower tax which had discouraged manufacturers from turning their hands to more powerful ones, and he may well have been right. General Guderian grumbled that captured British lorries were, for the same reason, of little use to him. Back in 1917, before most of the new soldiers had been born, much work had gone into the Liberty, mostly on the American side of the Atlantic. As it combined the best features of the Rolls-Royce and Sunbeam designs it was, by 1917 standards, a very good engine indeed for either tank or aeroplane. One weakness demonstrated itself: the engine of an aeroplane had the advantage of streams of cold air working on it. Tanks must make other arrangements as best they can. The Ricardo engine of 1918, almost identical with the Liberty, had given much trouble through over-heating. It seemed probable that the resurrected Liberties would present similar difficulties.

The Crusader tank was cooled, intermittently, by two fans which, along with the two water pumps, were driven from the crank-shaft by a long Coventry chain. This served reasonably well on Salisbury Plain but the desert found it out. A little sand in the works and the chain jumped free from its sprocket; it was a three-day workshop job to change this. Only moderate amounts of sand and heat were needed to disable the pumps. After a little running they began to leak. There were no facilities in the desert for attending to this. Then came the suspension arms. Because of faulty castings these snapped off 'like carrots'.* There were ten of them to each tank and they weighed about 2 cwt apiece. It was possible to fit reinforcing plates but it was a long business for workshops already overburdened. Other weak points existed but there would be little object in cataloguing them. To find any matter for congratulation to the makers is a task of some difficulty.

One thing cannot be denied to the War Office. Some, at least, of its members were already looking ahead to the day when there might be a return to Europe. In conjunction with the Admiralty they asked Tritton to interest himself in both amphibious and flying tanks. The latter could hardly be taken seriously in the summer of 1940 but Fosters went to work on the first. During the month of August Sir William Tritton had designed a self-propelled lighter powered by,

* Report by the Chief Mechanical Engineer, XIII Corps.

of all things, a jet engine which would avoid all the snags of an under-water propeller. Like so many other promising ideas it was quietly dropped.

Stern never flagged in his pursuit of a proper heavy tank. On 17 December, 1940, he met General de Gaulle who, whatever his faults, knew as much as most men about the subject. Stern mentioned the common objection, that they would never cross the bridges of Europe without breaking them. De Gaulle was of his mind. 'He considers that heavy tanks were needed – about 60 tons – to average 20 mph.' On weight etc 'he never found one bridge give way'. On 24 February, 1941, he lunched at the Savoy with Martel, who was of opinion that there was little to be learned from the African campaign but reckoned that infantry tanks and cruisers 'would tend to come together'. Stern, naturally enough, turned the conversation to the TOG tank. On the principle that when gentlemen meet compliments pass Martel observed that he liked the roominess of its inside. Beyond that he did not seem prepared to go. On 26 October the guest was Lord Beaverbrook. This was the occasion when the Beaver told Stern that the War Office had refused to have him as Chairman of the Tank Board. One matter, however, united them. 'The army needed two basic tanks in enormous quantities, a lightly-armoured fast and a heavily-armoured slower one.' Several new models of the former kind were to appear before the war was over but no heavy tank followed the Churchill.

Quite apart from the tanks themselves, Stern was worried about armament. His note for 13 May, 1941, reads: 'At the present time there are no tanks in sight that can carry the 6-pdr gun. I have begged for a 12-pdr for the heavy tanks.' Although this was a standard naval weapon and readily available, he begged in vain. Nor was he the only one. At the September meeting of the Tank Board in 1941 the ACIGS, General Macready, laid it down that the War Office would like an Infantry tank with 100 mm of armour and carrying a 17-pdr gun. The Chairman, Mr Burton, soon dealt with that. Such a machine, he said, would probably weigh over 50 tons and it would, therefore, be difficult to ensure reasonable reliability and arrangements for transport. This, incidentally, was the only Tank Board meeting to which Martel was bidden. In reply to questions he told them flatly that light tanks were useless, even for aerodrome defence. The Board accordingly put in an order for 2,400 of them. It was all of a pattern with an earlier decision, made on 6 July, 1940: 'The 6-pdr is quite unsuitable for tanks because of the increased weight and space.' Not for the only time the Board's order for light tanks does not seem to have been carried out.

The only cannon still readily available was the 2-pdr, good enough against the Panzer II but incapable of penetrating the new models now known to be coming into service. There was, however, a better secondary weapon on the way. When, in 1937, the Army adopted the Czech ZB light automatic in place of the Lewis it demanded certain changes. The rimless cartridge, though far less a cause of stoppages, was replaced by the Victorian rimmed .303 and nitro-cellulose by cordite. There was also a belt-fed version of the gun which the RTC agreed to accept provided that it remained in its original form with the 7.92 round. Contracts were placed with the BSA Company from which came the name Besa. Just after Munich the Company surreptitiously intruded one of its engineers into the Zbrodovka Works; upon his return a team of five was set up at Small Heath and production began. The first gun appeared in June, 1939, but much work was needed and the run did not begin until the following Spring. In May, 1940, 200 guns came out of the factory; by the time of Alamein the figure was 2,600 a month. By the end of the war BSA had turned out 59,322 Besas of the 7.92 calibre and 3,318 of the bigger 15mm model. This was in addition to 468,098 Brownings for the RAF. So great is the country's debt to BSA that an irrelevance to the tank story may be permitted. Perhaps the oddest weapon to emerge from a British factory was their Welrod Silent Pistol, designed for the French Resistance and making 'only the faintest noise which would pass unnoticed in the normal chatter and clatter of a cafe'. 'With them,' records the Company's archivist happily, 'a new reign of terror was instituted against the men who were shooting hostages by the score and wiping out whole villages.'

Such irregular activities lead naturally to an obscure Department of the War Office charged with, among other things, producing some sort of weapon that an infantryman might use against a tank with the hope of knocking it out. One of Mr Churchill's known characteristics was that of, from time to time, taking a fancy to some slightly eccentric character to whom he would give unusual rope. Not all of them justified his faith but in Major (later Major-General) Millis Jefferis he found a useful ancillary. Under Jefferis there came into existence MIRc (Military Intelligence Research – c). His second in command, Stuart Macrae, had until recently been editor of *Armchair Science*. Of their many freakish weapons one is of interest here. The idea was for a form of grenade that could adhere to the side of a tank for a few seconds during which an explosive charge would be detonated. All manner of people, from the Professor of Colloids at Cambridge to the only maker of bird-lime in the country, were brought in to help. The upshot of it all, after a year of trial and error, was the 'Sticky Bomb', brought into service in 1941 as the 74 Grenade. From the same stable came the Home Guard's Blacker Bombard and, later, the PIAT.

On the more regular side a command structure was beginning to emerge. In October, at Mr Churchill's personal insistence, Hobart was brought back, translated from Home Guard lance-corporal to Major-General and given an armoured division. And on 8 December came the appointment of a Commander, Royal Armoured Corps. The lot fell on Giffard le Quesne Martel. On the same day, far off on the Libyan border, General Wavell was beginning a classic operation with his 7th Armoured Division.

CHAPTER SIX

'Destruction of an Army'

Title of 1941 War Office Booklet

Mr Churchill, in his war memoirs, makes the point that his prime concern was to accumulate all the regular troops he could find 'as wars are not won by heroic militias'. Wavell's first campaign demonstrates the wisdom of this. Although he was outnumbered by something in the order of 10 to 1 he had an army far better trained than ever had been at the disposal of Lord Gort. In particular he had an armoured division which, though poorly equipped, was a great deal more formidable than Morgan's 'basis for argument'. Only experienced professionals could have done what he demanded of them.

During his time in Egypt General Marshall-Cornwall had the strategic roads and railways to the frontier greatly improved and Wavell made good use of them. He had no intention of waiting to be attacked by the Italians but planned to knock them about in a kind of Cambrai as originally devised by Fuller – a five-day raid designed to hammer his enemy hard and send him reeling backwards. In the event his battles went on for two months and ended only with the destruction of an army.

The *mise en scène* and the troops involved were very different from those of the earlier battles. No roads crammed with refugees – indeed very few roads at all – no incessant dive-bombing and no need for haphazard operations to be carried out with a minimum of reconnaissance and planning. General O'Connor, commanding the Western Desert Force, had at his disposal a very good division of the old style, the 4th Indian, under a very good divisional General, Beresford-Peirse. 'B-P', as he was inevitably known, was a gunner and a distinguished one. The armour was Hobart's legacy. The 7th Armoured Division, re-inforced by one of the Arras regiments, 7th RTR, was poorly equipped by the standards of later on but for 1940 it was not too bad. Its two armoured brigades were reorganized before the battle into similar formations each of a light and a heavy regiment with fifty-two tanks of some sort apiece. Whatever name they bore, however, each mustered only about a half of its strength in anything bigger than Vickers Light machines. Although these were nowhere near good enough for a regular battle they still retained one virtue. They did not break down with anything like the regularity of some later and bigger affairs. The armoured-car part of the business was carried out by the 11th Hussars, whose ubiquity was equal to that of the 12th Lancers in France. They retained some traditional Cherry Picker panache for a while as several of the Rolls Royces that had been in their care since 1927 were still present on parade, but they were soon replaced by lowlier Humbers and Daimlers. The tanks despatched by Mr Churchill while the island was under siege had by then arrived: two RTR battalions, the 2nd and 7th, and the 4th Hussars, whose presence brought the regular cavalry regiments up to four. The RTR units were now equipped with cruisers, mostly the new A 13, but still with a number of the outmoded A 9s and 10s. All of them had fetched up at Port Said during September and they had had plenty of time to learn the tricks of the desert. In late November Wavell had put them through a big exercise during which 7th RTR and 4th Indian Division – despite its name mainly composed of British Regulars – had carried out a 40-mile approach march followed by an attack on an entrenched and fortified camp.

That is exactly what his formations were required to do when the order went out for battle to commence. The Italian positions consisted of a string of seven forts running from Sidi Barrani on the coast to Nibeiwa in the south, with large unpatrolled gaps between them. General O'Connor was charged to rip them up, using the 7th Armoured Division. At dusk on 7 December the light tanks of the 7th Hussars led the cruisers of 2nd and 6th RTR across the desert at a steady 8 mph. By courtesy of the RAF no enemy airman molested them. The heavyweights, 7th RTR, had gone on ahead, taking a couple of days over the journey and allowing comfortable time for maintenance and adjustment. A desert moon helped the last stage of the approach march to Nibeiwa. Behind 7th RTR came the 4th Indian Division, the power of its artillery greatly increased by 7

Medium Regt RA with eight 6" howitzers and eight 60-pdrs. Beresford-Peirse grouped his guns in the fashion of Napoleon's Grand Battery and the result was entirely successful. At 0715 on the morning of 9 December the Italian garrison of Nibeiwa awoke to salvoes of shells falling around their beds, to be followed five minutes later by the crashings and creakings of 7th RTR's Matildas. A few minutes after that the Cameron Highlanders, fresh from their lorries, were on them. In an hour the business was over.

It is part of British folk-lore, largely civilian, that the Italian soldier had only one ambition, to head for the nearest prisoner-of-war camp and bang on the door. Certainly Mussolini's army was not Caesar's Tenth Legion but folk-lore is seldom noted for accuracy. General Slim, who had measured swords with them in Abyssinia, was tolerant of most things but he would never allow Italian jokes in his presence. At Nibeiwa the garrison, especially the Italian gunners, fought manfully. It was not their fault that they had no chance.

With Nibeiwa gone, Beresford-Peirse turned his guns on the next objective, the forts of Tummar East and West. The Matildas were in high feather, having knocked out a score or so Italian M 11 tanks with their 2-pdrs. Tummar West went the same way during the afternoon, though a sand-storm proved unhelpful. Brigadier Mirrlees, CRA to 4th Indian Division (whose Staff included a future CIGS, then plain Major Baker), moved his guns as one and the performance was repeated. Everybody concerned agreed that the garrison, which had at least had some warning, fought hard and skilfully. Tummar West did not go under until 1600 hrs. As a result only nine Matildas were available to set about Tummar East, partly because of mechanical troubles but also because it was reckoned expedient to leave some for protection of the infantry against any possible counter-attack. This, in fact, happened – a brave but futile effort to recapture Tummar West.

While the Matildas had been engaged in their proper work of infantry support the two brigades of 7th Armoured Division had been giving a demonstration of cruiser business. Moving parallel to but south of 7th RTR, they passed under the guns of Nibeiwa and swung north-west to cut the Italian line of retreat, the road from Sidi Barrani to Buq Buq. Contrary to expectation, they met with little resistance. Some generalship of a high order followed. Scenting an Italian collapse, Beresford-Peirse lorried an infantry brigade to straddle the road to the west of Sidi Barrani. Another was already on the eastern side. B-P's brigade was soon in trouble, the Italian gunners firing fast and accurately into them soon after they had debussed. A composite squadron of ten Matildas, hurriedly put together, drove the gunners from their places. Sidi Barrani fell shortly afterwards.

This was the factor that decided Wavell to turn his raid into a full-dress offensive. Two matters weighed heavily with him. First, his troops were already 140 miles ahead of the railway terminus at Matruh and they had no third-line transport. Second, his crack infantry, the 4th Indian Division, was wanted in the Sudan. To replace them he had the 6th Australian Division, sardonic and indestructible men looking forward to their first fight, well aware that the AIF of the other war had given them a lot to live up to. The armoured element remained the same, though much reduced in numbers of effective tanks. It was the light Vickers that had come through best and the cruisers worst. 7th RTR managed to field about twenty-six Matildas for the next phase. The assault on Bardia, the next stop on the journey west, followed the well-tried plan. 166 guns, expertly served, put down a traditional barrage. An Australian battalion moved in the dark to the western side, attacked at once and made a bridgehead over which the Matildas could pass. By afternoon Bardia had gone the way of the others. 7th Armoured Division, which had moved at the same time even further westward, drove on beyond Tobruk with the now customary task of cutting off retreat. For the first time they came under air attack but there was no serious resistance from the Italian army. The assault on Tobruk on 21 January, 1941, was made by the last sixteen Matildas of 7th RTR in company with the Australians, who thoroughly enjoyed it. Matilda may have been named after a duck but she waltzed satisfactorily and the Australians swore by her. Had there only been a few more runners it might have been possible to prevent the Italians from destroying many of the harbour installations.

Such was the shortage of tanks by the time Tobruk had fallen that a complete RTR battalion, the 6th, had to be sent back to Egypt after handing over its few serviceable machines to the 1st and 2nd Battalions.

Though operations still had some way to go it may be convenient to look back for a little and examine what was happening at home. At about the same time as the Tobruk garrison was learning that the Australians were off to see the Wizard, the wonderful Wizard of Oz, General Wavell was receiving orders to move into Greece. The experiences of Norway, Belgium and a near-miss over Finland did not seem to have left any indelible impression. Not for the first time in history all was to be lost save honour.

CHAPTER SEVEN

'Embattled Armies Clad in Iron'

MILTON – *Samson Agonistes*

Martel, newly promoted to Lieutenant-General, formed up to the
War Office on 8 December, 1940, to assume his duties as Director,
Royal Armoured Corps. He can hardly have been unaware that he
was not the first choice of the CIGS. Sir John Dill would have preferred Hobart, Churchill's discovery, as the tank expert. In the
lower reaches of the army, however, Martel's name was known after
his Arras fight and there his appointment was welcome.

All War Office Directorates have Charters, setting out with fair
precision what their duties are and how they tie in with other departments. Martel asked for his. The reply was: 'Do you mind if you do
not have one because we have tried to write it but found it very difficult to do so?' Martel, who hated rows, accepted this. In the most
general terms his job seemed to be to raise and train a new kind of
army, additional to the old-fashioned one already existing, but the
design and production of the next generation of tanks would be in
other hands. Above all, he was not to have a seat on the Army Council, he was to serve two masters (Dill, CIGS, and Brooke, C-in-C
Home Forces) and he must not get ideas above his station. Tanks
were not everything.

One thing worried him greatly and the subordinate status of his
Directorate barred him from doing much about it. Long before the
war it had been fairly obvious that the 2-pdr gun could only dominate tank battles for a very short time. Arras had shown the Germans that they needed thicker armour; the Matildas captured
during the summer scramble gave them all the information they
needed for making their own bigger gun. The 6-pdr sketched out by

Martel and his cronies would serve for some time but it was already on the way to obsolescence. Or would have been had it existed. As long ago as June, 1939, the General Staff had put forward a specification of sorts for such a gun and the Director of Artillery had reduced it to working drawings. A complete 6-pdr was in existence during June, 1940, and the Ministry of Supply formally requested that an order for 400 of them be placed at once. In August the General Staff laid it down that the number of 6-pdrs be 'governed by the effect on 2-pdr production, which was poor'. The most it would do was to order fifty more pilot models. In December the Ministry, off its own bat, though with War Office approval, increased the order tenfold merely to get production under way.

A depressing choice was put to the War Office. In February, 1941, it was given the alternative of either 100 of the 6-pdrs during the year or 600 of the 2-pdrs. It elected to have the larger number of the weaker weapon. Not until November, 1941, did any worthwhile number of the more powerful guns put in an appearance. Thirty-two arrived during that month, 146 in December, 341 in January, 1942, and by May the number had risen to 1517. By then the gun was very near to obsolescence. With the full knowledge of what Martel called 'the Powers that be' British soldiers would be sent into battle in unreliable tanks with impotent weapons. It would have been bad enough if they were to be no worse off than the Matilda Is at Arras, unable to strike hard but well protected. What happened was that the superior German weapons could riddle their tanks from distances at which they were unable to make any reply. Murder, the term used by Gort, is a strong word, but a case can be made for charging Martel's powers with it. The plea that they knew not what they did would have been less than honest.

Captain Liddell Hart had come to share the view of General Fuller that the war was lost and its continuance would loose on the world the Four Horsemen of the Apocalypse. In a paper circulated at the beginning of December he called for a peace upon any terms we could get. The Admiralty smelt in it a flavour of German propaganda and the First Lord, A. V. Alexander, had scathing things to say about the author. This, though unsurprising, was less than just. Indeed, on a cool professional appreciation of the situation he was perfectly right. By equally professional and scientific means it has been proved that a bumble-bee cannot fly.

On a wider view of matters it was necessary to consider what the new armoured force was for. At the end of 1940, and for as far as most men could foresee, it would be part of an anti-invasion army with some elements being sent to Egypt. Wavell's short campaigns in the desert and Eritrea had been in truth defensive, for the burglar had been crouched outside when the door had opened and the householder had knocked him down. It might be possible to clear a part of the North African littoral, but what would that achieve? It was the outermost skin of the onion and the armies of the Empire could never, on their own, break into Europe and bring down the German. There was much brave talk, but it was whistling in a grave-yard at midnight. All that could be done was to build up Bomber Command, give the Royal Navy all it needed to blockade a Germany with no eastern front, and hope that some ally, possibly America, would some day take a hand. The army must make itself as effective as possible and hope some day to find a role. Martel, who had seen the power of Russian armour, needed no lectures about this. And Russia, her Red Army apparently purged pink, was still actively helping Hitler.

All that said, the Royal Armoured Corps would some day, some-where, have to fight the German armour. It was tantamount to asking a businessman of sedentary habits to take on the Olympic gold medallist. Nevertheless it had to be done. The groundwork had been completed. At home there was now five armoured divisions in various stages of imperfection and three army tank brigades. The 2nd Armoured Division was soon on its way to Egypt. Those left behind were numbered 1, 6, 8, 9 and 11. Nos 1 and 9 had, or were getting, cruiser tanks; 6, 8 and 11 were equipping with Valentines. This was neither one thing nor the other. Originally it had been des-ignated the Infantry Tank Mk III but it had not the robustness of Matilda; nor had it the speed of A 13 or the new Crusader. It was, however, reliable and the cruisers were not. The Crusader was reckoned to run well enough for a few hundred miles but after that it developed all manner of small but fatal defects. The Ministry of Supply insisted on rushing out as many of them as possible and no proper time was given to testing. Half the number of decently engineered machines would have been of far greater service.

After machines came men. Martel was determined that he must somehow get the pick of the new intakes and he did all that a man could to achieve this. The Germans sent their choicest men to the tanks in the same way that the best of the British went to the Brigade of Guards, and if armour was to perform as it must the same would have to apply at home. The draft that came in during the second half of 1940, men in their late twenties, was very good indeed. Not overgrown schoolboys but men who had already begun to pursue civilian careers of one kind or another for a noticeable period. It was permissible for a man awaiting call-up to volunteer for anything he might choose. As the army had little to boast about most put their names down for the Navy or the RAF. Martel, like an 18th century sergeant drumming up recruits for an unfashionable line regiment, made many broadcasts inviting aspirants of the right quality to go into tanks. This produced quite a fair number but less than it would have done a generation earlier. Every war seems to throw up new things, the kind that appeal to the young and adventurous. In the American War it had been the Rangers of Tarleton and Simcoe, in Napoleon's day the Rifle Brigade, in South Africa the Mounted Infantry and in Martel's own youth the Tank Corps. The novelty of this last, however, had now worn off and the ardent spirits looked more towards the Commandos and the Parachute Regiment. Martel, from his HQ at High House near St Paul's School, proselytised all he could but on one point he was scrupulous. He refused flatly to call for volunteers from existing units, thereby depriving them of badly needed men of quality.

Even more than raw but promising recruits he needed good officers and good technicians. Among those already on the strength, especially among the officers, there was 'a good deal of indifferent material' that had to be weeded out. Along with weeding went planting. A Young Soldiers Battalion was set up at Bovington and it throve from the start. There was no nonsense about an 'officer caste'. By the time the business was properly under way it was reckoned that about a third of the new subalterns were public school boys, a third from secondary schools and the remainder older men who had seen something of life. Martel (Wellington and 'The Shop') reckoned that the public school boys came off worst. The pick of the young soldiers went to their own OCTUs and turned out a fine generation of leaders, fully as good as the German once experience had come.

Technicians were a serious problem. This kind of war was not going to demand the great Central Workshops that had been such a feature of the Tank Corps in the last one. Minor repairs were unit responsibilities, helped by Light Aid Detachments RAOC; behind that came the 2nd and 3rd line workshops manned by the same Corps. Today the RAOC, as the army's bomb disposal experts, has

75

a reputation second to none, but it was not always so. On those infrequent occasions when the Corps parades as a body it marches to that fine tune 'The Village Blacksmith', appropriate for a tradition of rude smithery. Its original business had been guns, making them and servicing them. Of late years it had become a body of storekeepers. *The Vocabulary of Army Ordnance Stores** makes the Army & Navy Stores catalogue look like a pamphlet. The Ordnance officers, masters of their work though they were, were not engineers and did not even speak the language. Martel asked that a separate corps of RAC engineers be raised, for without something of this kind a tank disabled by a minor fault would remain as a corpse on the battlefield. His stature was insufficient to compel the Army Council to agree at once. It was not until 1942 that the Royal Electrical and Mechanical Engineers were added to the Army List against strong opposition from the Ordnance officers. This opposition had dangerous consequences. Spare parts, their amassing and their issue, remained an Ordnance responsibility. As they were not trained to this specialized work they constantly produced either the wrong article or a compelling excuse for not having it. The CQMS philosophy never quite died.

There were minds other than those of Martel and his associates at grips with the difficulties of making an effective tank force and learning how to use it. Cruiser tanks were a necessary concomitant of armies fighting the great sand-table exercises with real blood that were going on in the desert and looked like continuing for a long time. All the same, no decision was going to be won there. If the army was ever going to strike home it would have to be in Europe and there it would be a matter for big-gunned heavyweights. Two streams were running parallel. At Christmas, 1940, Martel had been shown the pilot model of the Churchill. It had armour of 80 to 90 mm, turned the scale at just under 40 tons and was made to carry the not yet existing 6-pdr. Martel thought fairly well of it but the prototype was far from perfect. 'It seemed a pity that the firm used steel bogie rollers on a steel track. Rubber and steel run so much more smoothly together.... The front prow was somewhat unnecessarily high. This was a relic from the last war. A long tank like the Churchill can nose its way out of holes and obstacles without a very high prow, which adds considerably to the weight of the machine.... There were clearly some weak mechanical features. It

---

* Including, so one was told, the mystical 'Bowls, porridge, india-rubber, handles without, officers, lunatic, for the use of'.

was, of course, essential to clear these up before production was ordered. Unfortunately this was not done and the tank was released for production too soon.'

At exactly the same time Sir Albert Stern and others of the Gang were at Fosters' Lincoln works examining the wooden mock-up prepared by Sir William Tritton. The main discussion was on one topic only. For an engine of 600 hp 'much heavy gearing would be required', as Stern wrote in his report for posterity drawn up after the war. They settled on something 'of great promise ... a system of electrical transmission which would eliminate mechanical gear changing'. This was the idea of Charles Mertz, who had much experience of the use of such things in London trams. The first specimen machine, known as TOG 1, was built around it. A second machine, variously called TOG 1A and TOG 2, incorporated an hydraulic system. Neither of them proved satisfactory. The electrical system failed completely because the length of the tracks demanded a power that it could not provide. The hydraulic version worked through fluid couplings 'which could be filled and emptied at will'. This was fatal. 'It was estimated that the couplings would take one-third of a second to fill or empty, but in practice it took much longer and resulted in considerable damage to buildings, bridges and walls at the side of roads.' In Germany the renowned Dr Porsche was having much the same difficulties with an electrical system of his own which was intended for the Tiger.

It was for want of more than a nail that TOG was lost and after covering something over 500 miles on its tracks it was condemned. The great tank, however graceless, looked and was formidable. With a weight of just under 80 tons it was the only genuinely heavy fighting vehicle made in Britain before the war ended. Its engine, the Paxman-Ricardo diesel of 600 hp, was entirely suitable, its tracks were well designed and honestly made and its armour, which covered every part exposed to enemy gunners, was the thickest yet known. The inside was capacious and the turret mounted a wooden mock-up of a very big gun. To replace it with a real one, such as the 3″ AA gun, would have been simple. Though its top speed was not much over 8 mph there were battlefields upon which speed was of no importance. TOG's weak point was in the transmission. Even in the absence of Wilson, this could have been put right, for the existing Merritt-Brown system proved entirely equal to the strain of the 76-ton Tortoise, of which more in due time. Wilson's defection had compelled Stern to try out rather freakish expedients but that need not have been the end of the matter. A conventional Merritt-Brown should have worked perfectly well.

The premature death sentence came about through several causes. First was the deep-rooted belief held by the Board that anything of more than 40 tons must necessarily be uncontrollable; second was the fact that TOG could be of no possible use in the desert, beyond which few people were looking. Lastly, there was undoubtedly strong personal animus against Stern in some high quarters and his work was seen as a monstrous nuisance. All of which was a great misfortune. When the time came to fight in the Normandy bocage the slow, heavy unsinkable TOG with a mighty gun would have been of more value for Tiger-shooting than a troop of cruisers.

The obituary was not read out to Mr Churchill. As late as 23 April, 1943, when the demand for heavy tanks was beginning to be taken seriously, he wrote a Minute on Tank Supply Policy. 'Pray let me have a report on the Stern tank or any alternative that can be devised.' It was too late. TOG 2 had been certified dead and was on the way to the Museum, where you may still see it. And there was no alternative. TOG 1 had been broken up. Stern had made one last effort to save the Gang's creation by showing it to the Canadians. General Macnaghten was known to be of a mechanical turn of mind and he was suitably impressed. For all that he had to give the same answer. It was too late.

If TOG's stream had dried up, others were still running. You will remember that Martel had desired the return of 'Boney' Fuller as his armoured oracle but that his Fascist posturings had made him unemployable. For all that, he had not quite vanished from the scene. Back in the days of the Kaiser's war, when the tank was beginning to show its virtuosity, both he and Martel had dreamed dreams. One of Fuller's was to do with Lord Kitchener's tactics at Omdurman where he had had the desert lit up overnight by the searchlights of his gunboats, thus avoiding being surprised by the Dervishes and causing them much what soldiers call 'wind up'. The idea did not seem to have outlived its usefulness after twenty years, for Commander Oscar de Thoren RN had come up with a suggestion. Let searchlights be mounted on tanks and they will not merely dazzle the enemy but will sweep a path under which an attack can go in. A test had been made in 1917 but no business resulted. Fuller's strange friends included a Mr Mitzakis, who, apparently, made projectors and had in 1933 formed a syndicate with de

Thoren. Fuller had talked the War Office of 1937 into trying the thing, with the result that the taxpayer bought out the syndicate and one armoured searchlight turret was built. In September, 1939, Mitzakis produced a new and more powerful version. Six were ordered and in April, 1940, they were handed over. No amount of fire directed at the Matilda-mounted light seemed able to extinguish it and three more were ordered. On, of all days, 18 June, 1940 – just as the last of Crocker's tanks was leaving Cherbourg – the War Office put in an order for 300 more. That amounted to roughly twice the number of tanks of all kinds then in the country. As it had nothing to do with either canals or defence it was given the jargon name of Canal Defence Light and a school of instruction was set up at Barnard Castle. Others sprang up later on in the Middle East and the USA. Mr Mitzakis' light was modified so that it could give not merely a fixed beam of great power but could also flicker. This could, at the least, disconcert any defender. Mr Mitzakis was appointed Technical Adviser; 6,000 all ranks passed through the British schools and 8,000 through the American. Whether this was a nonsense or a battle-winner remained to be seen. Over a long period some 1850 tanks were converted to CDL, engrossing the entire 1st Tank Brigade of three battalions and two more in the 35th. In due time the US Army was to raise six further battalions. Nothing could be expected during 1941 but Fuller's last brain-child was taken very seriously.

CHAPTER EIGHT
Diversions and Defeats

To the men in the Middle East all this might been happening on another planet. After Tobruk Wavell, with a dash uncharacteristic of British generals, knew the scent to be breast high and sent his troops off westwards at the best speed they could manage. The 4th Armoured Brigade bounded 100 miles to Mechili, starting off on the same night that Tobruk had fallen and arriving within 48 hours. The 7th Hussars galloped at the fort in their light tanks but were equally swiftly chased back by the Italian mediums. Then arrived a Matilda squadron of 2nd RTR which knocked out six of the enemy and sent the rest scurrying for shelter. Before the 7th Armoured Brigade, with its supporting foot and guns, could be brought up the Italians were away.

The 4th Armoured Brigade and the armoured cars of the 11th Hussars pounded in pursuit over some pretty rough going. On 4 February the leading troops reached Msus and on the day following the road running south from Benghazi had been blocked by the Support Group of riflemen and guns some twenty-five miles west of Antelat. Next day the Italians headed towards the road block with 100 new medium tanks and 25,000 men. General Creagh moved the twenty-four cruisers which were all that was left of 4th Armoured Brigade to Beda Fomm, eight miles from the road and on the Italian flank. Then came the moment of hubris. Desperate efforts by desperate men failed to break through the trap. At dawn on 7 February General Bergonzoli launched his last tank charge. When the guns of the Support Group and the 2-pdrs of the cruisers weighed in he surrendered without further ado. The bag on this occasion was 120 tanks in varying condition, 190 guns and 26,000 men. The grand total for the whole campaign was, in round figures, 400 tanks, 1300 guns and an army of 130,000. British and Australian losses totalled 500 killed and just under 1400 wounded. There had been some remarkable journeys by tank. 7th RTR, for example, had covered more than 300 miles of desert in two months. This does not disguise the fact that far more tanks fell out with mechanical trouble than arrived. Hubris did not last for long. Nemesis was at hand.

Mr Churchill had a mediaeval sense of honour. To him it was better, as old Sir Colin Campbell had said, that every man of the Queen's Guards should lie dead on his face than that the enemy should see the colour of their knapsacks. One King had given promises of help to another and they must be kept. It was useless to suggest that when a friend is attacked by an armed gang you do him better service by going away to buy a gun rather than by pitching in with bare fists. American public opinion would not see it in that fashion. Wavell's orders were to send the strongest possible force to Greece and he obeyed. Honour, no doubt, was satisfied but the satisfaction was to cost many stout ships and good men. The pity of it was that so many of these came from Australia and New Zealand; they were the choicest of their small populations and could never be replaced.

Cyrenaica was stripped to the bone, reducing all signal services to the civil telephone lines manned by Italians and Arabs. The tried New Zealand and 6th Australian Divisions embarked. Martel, when told by Mr Churchill what was in the wind, said that we should rue the day that we sent forces to fight the great German armies in Greece. It was far worse than the rush into Belgium. Nor was it a matter of land forces only. Such scratch formations as the RAF could find would have no chance at all. On the tank side there was the 2nd Armoured Division, good material (it included Mr Churchill's own 4th Hussars) but still green. One brigade and part of the support group would go to Benghazi; the other, the 1st, to the Piraeus. It was made up of about fifty old cruisers A 9s and A 10s, and the same number of the inevitable Vickers lights. The Germans were now well equipped with the Panzers III and IV. Half a dozen of either could have slain the entire brigade. It began to assemble at Aliakmon on 21 March, the anniversary of the beginning of the great retreat of 1918. History soon repeated itself. A few Matildas were sent to Crete where they performed famously in the defence of airfields. No tank returned from Greece, however, and the entire

Brigade was lost. The absence from the desert of Force W, as the expedition was called, gave Cyrenaica to Rommel for the taking. One man, the proprietor of the Hotel Britannique in Nauplia, probably spoke for his nation. 'Goddam you. You son-of-bitch English no come here this no happen. Beat it. Go. Go now. You hear me? Go.' Then, in tears, he turned back to the heap of rubble that had been his livelihood. The obligations of honour had been met.

Rommel arrived at Tripoli on 12 February, six days after Beda Fomm. He came by air and was accompanied in the Ju 52s by a reconnaissance battalion and an anti-tank battery. A tank regiment, advance guard to the 5th Light Division, disembarked a few days later. At about the same time, far across the desert, General Sir Philip Neame, VC, had taken over from O'Connor and received a visit from the CIGS, along with General Wavell. Neame told them of the wretched state of his army, of the deficiencies in training, the shortage of armour, anti-tank and anti-aircraft weapons, air support, MT, signals and everything else. His aerial photographs and agents' reports made it plain beyond a peradventure that the German convoys were coming in regularly. GHQ could do nothing to help him. Greece was the top priority. Dill took his leave with the encouraging remark: 'You are going to get a bloody nose here, Philip, and it is not the only place where we shall get bloody noses'. Once again the army, neglected in peacetime and sacrificed by politics, would have to put up with it.

In place of the experienced 6th Australian Division he had the 9th which was 'quite unready for a campaign; it had not completed its preliminary training and had done no higher training whatever'. It had little transport and few weapons except rifles. Not that this greatly bothered the Australians. As Neame said later, 'I could have had no better fighting troops under me'. Armour was even worse. The 2nd Armoured Division was only half a division, the other half being in Greece. Its commander, Justice Tilly, was one of the most experienced tank officers in the army, having begun his career at Cambrai. His death soon after arrival in Egypt was a grievous blow. His successor, Gambier-Parry, had come from a different stable. If matters had not been so serious the condition of the 3rd Armoured Brigade – which for all practical purposes was the whole division – would have been comical. 5th RTR began with fifty-eight or so worn-out cruisers; by the time they had been driven across the desert the number had dropped to twenty-three. The 6th RTR had arrived ahead of their tanks and were given in their place a number of captured Italian M13s rigged out in makeshift fashion with No 11 wireless sets. As there was no third battalion Neame lent the brigade the 3rd Hussars. They had travelled all the way to Beda Fomm and back and their light tanks were fit only for scrap. They too were put into M13s and told to get on with it. The M13 was not a bad tank by the standards of the day but it had one great drawback. Like Matilda, but unlike all others, it ran on diesel fuel. This meant that it required supply arrangements of its own, again cobbled hastily together.

With all that said, the 3rd Armoured Brigade ought to have been a match for Rommel at that time. His own 5th Light Division was also a scratch formation and mustered only about 130 tanks of which no more than a third carried any gun bigger than a 20 mm. When he tumbled to the fact that the British had no intention of advancing further and decided to put in his own attack he had no more than about fifty. The difference was that between an experienced pack of hounds and the inmates of Battersea Dogs' Home. They bumped into each other on the road from Agheila to Mersa Brega early on 31 March. After a sharp little fight 5th RTR began, in accordance with Neame's orders, to withdraw. Rommel smelt blood and decided to take a gamble. Without waiting for 15th Panzer Division, which had not yet disembarked, he set to work harrying the 3rd Armoured Brigade eastwards. 5th RTR lost five tanks the following day to Rommel's three and immediately afterwards the whole Brigade was in headlong retreat. Thus heartened, the Italian Ariete (Armoured) Division dogged Rommel's steps. The No 11 sets in the commandeered M13s did not work and all cohesion was lost. In forty-eight hours the tank strength of the 3rd Brigade was down to a dozen A13s, twenty-six M13s and a few lights. 5th RTR came near to having a pitched battle with 6th RTR. The artillery of that part of the Support Group that had not gone to Greece vanished into the desert. When air reconnaissance reported a patrol of the Long Range Desert Group and the Brigade's Recovery Section as being a hundred enemy tanks approaching Msus some pessimist put a match to the petrol and supply dump there. It was the only one of any size and the only one containing diesel oil. Most of the M13s were destroyed in order to keep at least some fuel for the survivors. The next couple of days were taken up with hunting around the desert in search of a filling station. This was to become standard practice, with each side filling its tanks from the other's cans. It does credit to both armies that neither possessed a mind sufficiently depraved to leave out for capture a dump of petrol spiked with iron-filings or something else that would wreck an engine within the hour. It smacked too much of poisoning wells. The Special Operations Executive was supplying its saboteurs with quantities of abrasive grease, guaranteed to ruin any machinery. Real soldiers did not stoop to such activities.

The ultimate humiliation came at Mechili. A few German tanks, led by dust-raising lorries, closed menacingly in on Divisional HQ. Generals Gambier-Parry surrendered. Later on he was joined in captivity by General Neame and O'Connor who, travelling in the same car, had blundered into a German reconnaissance unit. In their prison camp in Italy Gambier-Parry led the choir and proved adept at forging papers. Such talents were not wasted.

Tobruk, however, held firm. Morshead's 9th Australian Division, plus a brigade rushed in from Egypt – eighteen Matildas and a score or so of cruisers, crewed by men from the 3rd Hussars and three different RTR battalions, along with a sufficiency of guns defied all comers. Rommel, having no appetite for a large and dangerous garrison on his flank, tried on 14 April to take the place at a run. He underestimated his opponents. When his infantry moved forward to clear the mines and make a gap for the tanks they met the 2nd/17th Australian battalion. Untrained they might have been but they set about the pick of the Wehrmacht in a way of which their fathers would have approved. This obliged the German tanks to try their luck unaided and they fared no better. Thirty-eight panzers, mostly the big Mk III and Mk IV, collided head on with the 25-pdrs of the 1st and 3rd RHA as well as the 9th Australian A/T Battery and the few remaining cruisers. After about three hours 5th Panzer gave it up as a bad job, leaving seventeen of their thirty-eight tanks knocked out. The RHA had not expected too much, as only a few armour-piercing shells were still with them; it was interesting to learn that the ordinary HE variety was quite effective for the purpose that became known as 'brewing up'. On 30 April Rommel tried again, this time from the west and with better preparation. The 15th Panzer Division, just arrived, lent its infantry for the purpose. By then eighteen Matildas of 1st RTR had been shipped in to thicken up the defences. For the first time mines, hastily made in Egypt, played a significant part. Forty panzers drove into the newly laid field and the tracks of seventeen were blown off, though all but five managed repairs and got away. The next wave of thirty-four encountered the cruisers of 1st RTR in hull-down positions waiting

84

for them. Three Germans were set ablaze for the loss of an A 13. It was not, however, all like that. When the Matildas tried a counter-attack against fourteen Germans they came off decidedly the worse. Matilda had been a useful tank in her day but that day was already over. Experiments on captured sisters had given the Germans an antidote. It was a long-barrelled 50 mm gun of very high velocity which would henceforth be the Matilda's executioner.

Rommel had lost half his armour at Tobruk but he still held Sollum and Wavell badly wanted it back. He could muster twenty-nine reconditioned cruisers, mostly old A 9s and A 10s, along with a motorized Guards Brigade and the much-tried 11th Hussars in their armoured cars. New arrivals were the 4th RTR with twenty-six Matildas, though one squadron had been packed off to Eritrea.

The Matildas made a 100-mile journey across the desert through ferocious sand storms and fetched up under the guns of Sollum early on 15 May. The Italian garrison was surprised at breakfast and Sollum fell quickly. Once again the Italian gunners put up stout resistance, picking off seven Matildas from underneath as they reared up over the low stone walls. Encouraged by this success, a stab was made at Fort Capuzzo, though the surprise element was gone. Nor was the garrison all Italian. German artillery, fortunately lacking the long 50 mm gun, knocked the tanks about and a counter-attack seemed to be coming. The Matildas sensibly withdrew. They had started twenty-four strong; six remained serviceable. The cruisers, down on the left wing, had no better fortune. Though twenty-two remained after some messy and inconclusive wheeling and shooting they were too ramshackle to be risked again. General Gott, in charge of the operation, decided to content himself with the gain of Halfaya Pass. His content was short lived. Rommel recaptured the place on the 26th. Six Matildas were lost in a brave attempt to cover the retreat. The Germans dug in, laid mines and brought up some of their 88s which 4th and 7th RTR had come across long ago at Arras.

Mr Churchill, one may fairly suspect, was becoming disenchanted with Wavell. In the past he had produced famous victories but now he seemed more fruitful of excuses. The Prime Minister, deciding to deny him any more, ordered that a convoy of the very best tanks that could be made available should be rushed to him; the risk of taking them through the Mediterranean, now no longer under our control, would have to be accepted. Wavell and the army must, for once, be given some superior weapons.

They did not seem, at home, to be all that superior to anything.

At the end of August there were 408 cruisers on charge in the UK; less than half of them were fit for service; six weeks earlier there had been 1441 Infantry and cruiser tanks of which 391 were out of action. No improvement was detectable. The Prime Minister, perhaps understandably fogged by having constantly to remember the difference between an A 13 Mk III, an A 15 Mk VI and an Infantry Tank Mk III, demanded, in a Minute to the War Office of 29 June, that they all be given names, as Matilda and Valentine already had. With uncharacteristic archness he wrote, 'A 22 has an alias, I think'.

The Tiger convoy was given the highest of priorities. Wavell's assertion that he had men enough for six tank regiments but precious few tanks and that another armoured division had reached Rommel gave every justification for taking risks. Only Dill, of all the Chiefs of Staff, opposed the sending; he needed them all, he said, because of the shortage of tanks for home defence. He was brushed aside and, to mark his displeasure, Mr Churchill added another shipfull of cruisers. He signalled Wavell on 22 April that 307 of 'our best tanks' were about to leave. Along with them would go forty-three Hurricanes for the equally outmatched RAF.

The convoy of five fast ships passed Gibraltar on 6 May under escort of HMSs *Queen Elizabeth, Naiad* and *Fiji*. Air attack was incessant. One ship, *Empire Song*, struck a mine and exploded; *New Zealand Star* hit another but was able to continue. The battle for Crete was warming up as the convoy reached Alexandria. Willing hands unloaded the new machines, reduced by the loss of *Empire Song* to 238, but still enough to turn the scales as soon as they could be rushed up to their waiting crews. What emerged fell short of expectations. There were certainly sixty-seven of the new cruisers, henceforth to be called Crusader; admittedly their Liberty engines had been designed in 1917, the same year as their Wilson epicyclic gear boxes and their Christie suspensions, but they were at least new. The remaining cruisers, A 13s, had an average of 700 miles, half their track life, behind them. The 135 Matildas were in worse shape, many of them needing 48 man-hours in the workshops before they were fit for use, and of the twenty-one light Vickers Mk VIb eight needed a complete overhaul. Such was the response to Mr Churchill's order to Ismay of 22 April that he wanted 'large numbers of our best tanks' to go to Wavell.

It was impossible to ask General Beresford-Peirse, commanding the operation known as 'Battleaxe', to wait for all these things to be done. Rommel was reckoned to have 300 German tanks to Wavell's

200, mostly the Mk III and IV of about 22 tons apiece. In fact he had less than 200 of which only a half were heavies. They proved sufficient, when combined with carefully arranged minefields, the 50 mm gun and a few 88s. On 15 June, the earliest possible date, Beresford-Peirse put in his attack on the strongly defended Halfaya Pass region. It failed at all points. There is no need to set out the whole dismal story in detail. Half the British armour was knocked out, partly by enemy action and partly by what were called 'mechanical casualties'. Five Crusaders were lost because, through shortage of wireless sets, they did not receive the order to withdraw when it was spotted that they were heading straight for an A/T battery. The German casualties were negligible. A bearer party carried the reputation of General Beresford-Peirse to join that of other senior officers in the desert graveyard. It was not the fault of the brave tank crews or the regimental officers. Unsound strategy, little grasp of tactics appropriate to desert warfare and sheer bad workmanship in the factories lost what Mr Churchill called the Army of the Nile its initiative and its confidence.

This last was the most serious factor of all. Certainly since Crécy it had never been the tradition to put British soldiers into the field with inferior weapons in their hands. True, there had been exceptions – the bayonets that bent in the Sudan, the bored-out field guns of South Africa and the absence of any equivalent of the German minenwerfer at the end of 1914 are examples. Likewise, during the other war there had been periods when pilots of the RFC had been sent up in machines that stood no chance against their better-equipped enemies. All these, however, had been short-lived episodes. In Hitler's war it had become almost standard practice to put a half-trained army into battle with tools that men had come to expect to turn in their hands. Fulsome things, many of them deserved, have been written about the performance of British factory workers after Dunkirk. There were still some who would have been none the worse for a hanging. It is often said, by people who ought to know, that until Russia was dragged into the war Communist influence in the factories was strong and baneful. This can never be proved or disproved but it seems clear that once Russia was involved standards improved.

There was, however, some relief at hand. President Roosevelt agreed to let his comrade have first sixty and then another 200 of the new American light tank named after the Confederate cavalry General J. E. B. Stuart. The design was not better than that of the Crusader but there was one important difference, best illustrated by a story long current, even if apocryphal. In British factories, the tale goes, each half-made machine was neighboured by a bench with a vice. When a part arrived that did not precisely fit it was put into the vice and worked over with a file until it was more or less the right size. In American factories there were no benches. If a component was imperfect it was rejected and another supplied. The yarn rings true. First to get three 'Honeys', as the Stuart came to be called, were the Greys, the last regiment of horse and still sitting disconsolately in Palestine. They were captivated by it. The Stuart's 37mm gun was smaller than the 2-pdr but its shot had an armour-piercing cap that made it as effective. The tank's radius of action, however, was no more than 40 miles.

Less captivated was the Army of the Nile, back where they had started and looking distrustfully at their few remaining tanks. The infantry and artillery wanted nothing more to do with armour. The RAF despised the lot of them.

On 18 June, 1941, a second unheartening anniversary of Waterloo, 'Battleaxe' petered out. Four days later Hitler decided to turn on his friend Stalin and invaded Russia. The entire concept of the war altered at a stroke, from miniature to mural. If an eastern front could be recreated and kept in being then perhaps 1918 might come again, ending, this time, in a Compiègne without a Brest Litovsk. For several months to come this was a matter more for hope than anticipation.

While the fighting men were doing everything possible to combat the superior German weapons, a decision was being taken at home that came near to ruining all chances for the future. Lord Weir, of the Tank Board, as Director-General of Aircraft Production in 1918, had had to do with the coming of the Liberty engine. In its day it had been a very good piece of machinery but that day was long past. Only because nothing better had been developed during the locust years was the Liberty even considered as a power unit for tanks in 1940; everybody realized that it was tantamount to putting the engine of a Sopwith Camel into a Spitfire. In spite of constant reports from the Middle East that the thing was utterly unreliable Lord Weir and Sir James Lithgow insisted that it 'had proved its reliability' and that the troubles were caused only by sand which affected engines of all kind. The War Office expressed scepticism but was over-ruled and in May, 1941, the Tank Board formally adopted it as the engine for future cruisers. No member had enough knowledge or conviction to prevent this. When the Mission in the United States reported that the Ford Company was willing to make a V8 engine of equal or greater power they were brushed off. The Fords had not been tested; as soon as they became available Rolls Royce Meteor engines would be ready for tank use; anyway, a third type of engine would only complicate matters. Years were to pass during which the Army would have to put up with tanks that might in other respects be fairly good but whose power units could always be trusted to let them down. In a Grand Remonstrance drawn up in 1944 to rebut some of the charges levelled at the General Staff by the Select Committee on National Expenditure the War Office said bluntly that the Liberty engine had been forced upon them by these two gentlemen. On the evidence of the Tank Board Minutes the War Office had the right of it. A joint Ministry of Supply and War Office Mission had recommended adoption of the Ford engine. The Tank Board had refused its acceptance. Few decisions can have led to so much waste and damage. Instead of the Ford an order was placed with Leyland for 14,000 Liberties.

One man, at least, was under no illusions. General Macready, Assistant CIGS, set out his feelings on paper, in a note to the Tank Board dated 4 September, 1941: 'For a period tanks which are approaching obsolescence owing to lack of armour or weapon power would have to continue to be accepted by the Army.... It is still necessary to equip some armoured divisions with Infantry tanks which have neither the necessary performance nor weapon power for carrying out their role effectively against modern German tanks.' Lack of armour and weapons were, of course, mere additions to the untrustworthy engines. It is just as well that these things were hidden from Martel's young men. They had worries enough of their own. When Mr Bartlett of Vauxhalls was summoned before the Board for one of his regular carpetings about the performance of the Churchills he observed that it was not entirely the fault of the manufacturers. There had been a great deal of mishandling by drivers, many of whom had never before managed so much as a lorry. He may well have had a point. Men, or lack of them, also worried Macready. He put the army's requirements for 1943 at 20,000 tanks but remarked gloomily that he did not see how the number of armoured divisions could be kept up to anything like their war establishments. Time was to prove him right.

CHAPTER NINE
Treading Water

Back in the island two armies were still building. P. J. Grigg, still the top civilian at the War Office of which he would one day be head, spoke dismissively of divisions returned from France as having 'the bonds of discipline very much weakened by their experiences'. This observation, had it been known, would have come as a surprise to the subjects of it. Discipline had held firm throughout the army's ordeal and had, if anything, been tempered to a wartime hardness. Grigg was, however, on stronger ground when he wrote of how the army had to be sorted, organized and trained for a role entirely different from that for which it had been prepared in the years up to 1940.

First, it was plainly unavoidable that a large force should be permanently in readiness to deal with any invader. This engrossed very large numbers of Anti-Aircraft Command who would otherwise have been trained for future expeditions. In time much of their work was taken over by girls of the ATS and veterans of the Home Guard, but that time was still distant. Mr Churchill had a clear mind on the subject. Even before he became Prime Minister he had been chairman of the Military Co-ordination Committee – Pownall's 'Crazy Gang' – but there he was no more than *primus inter pares*. Upon his elevation he gave orders that many of the newly-raised infantry battalions be converted into either armour or artillery.

Martel made no bones about the fact that he was raising a private army, but it was intended only as an interim measure. To begin with he set about the Military Secretary, whose Department controlled all promotions and postings of officers. By gentle persuasion he extracted an agreement that the Military Secretary would keep his hands off the RAC. Martel, in consultation with his own people, would decide who should stay and who should go, who should have the commands and who should serve on the Staffs. This was a considerable achievement. It was particularly successful in the higher reaches of command. Among Martel's divisional commanders were Major-Generals Horrocks, Dempsey, Hobart and Leese.

The appearance of the last named, a Guardsman, is quickly explained. Martel's business was men – finding men, organizing men and training them. Being what he was he would no doubt have preferred to be running the mechanical side of things but in war one does what one is told. By April, 1941, there were, at home, five armoured divisions and three Army Tank Brigades. It was not enough and there could be no guarantee that recruits of the quality needed would continue to appear. As has been mentioned earlier the conscript-designate was permitted to choose where he wanted to go. The choice was not binding on the Ministry of Labour and National Service but it was honoured more often than not. The pick of the crop, understandably after the Battle of Britain, wanted to serve with the RAF; the Royal Navy, for traditional reasons, came next. The army got the leavings; and the leavings of the leavings went to the infantry. This is another tradition of the English. Line regiments take what they can get. They are, after all, only the point of the spear and take most of the casualties. The cream of infantry was, as it had long been, the Brigade of Guards. Martel cast covetous eyes on it.

The Guards, though quintessentially foot soldiers, had proved versatile before. A Guards Camel Regiment had served in the Sudan in General Gordon's day. Under Haig the Guards Division had furnished its own machine-gun battalions, trench mortar batteries and half a dozen things besides. A Guards Armoured Division might be a two-fold blessing. It ought to be a formation of exceptional quality and in addition it should attract young men who wanted to serve with the best and most famous names of all. The War Office, where a strong Guards element existed, was not at all enthusiastic. To make such a division, it seemed, Guardsmen would have to be subjected to instruction from lesser breeds and that was not to be thought of. Not so very long ago, within the memory of some still serving, King's Regulations had contained many paragraphs of a complicated kind on the subject of Guards Generals, the object being to ensure that they should never be sub-

ject to the indignity of being ordered about by linesmen. There
would be no objection to Guardsmen who wished to don greasy
overalls and get their hands dirty joining the tanks but they must
first leave the Brigade and sign on with the RAC. Martel explained
that that was not at all the thing he had in mind. The Guards
Armoured Division would be a private army inside a private army,
trained and commanded by proper Guards officers and NCOs and
nobody else. There would be no question of a Corporal of Horse
becoming a Corporal of Tanks. Martel, the veteran boxer, wore his
opponents down by skilful ring-craft and in April, 1941, permission
was given to him for the creation of his new ideal. The argument
about the wisdom or unwisdom of taking away a large proportion of
superior infantry has gone on ever since.

The young men present in the ranks, however, had no such misgivings. The Household Cavalry in particular jumped at it, for their
part in the war so far had been negligible and looked like diminish-
ing. Sir Oliver Leese was a popular figure and volunteers practically
queued up to join. Being Guardsmen, they set themselves the task
of doing all that the RAC could do, but better and with their usual
appearance of making it all look ridiculously easy. In early June the
first of them left for the training regiments and, says Martel, 'It was
quite exhilarating to see the intense keenness with which they attended these classes'. Very soon they were running their own training centre. They made only one condition. In accordance with
ancient custom a Guardsman belonged to his regiment. A Grena-
dier could not, in any circumstances, become a Coldstreamer, and
so on. Martel found this vexing, but it was a small price to pay. Here
he had troops who, when fully instructed, ought to be better than
any Panzer Grenadiers. Better, indeed, than any other tankmen on
earth.

That done, he cast his net wider still. A number of single battalions, most of them newly raised, had been converted to armour,
but Martel wanted more than battalions. He decided to take over an
entire Division. Why the 42nd (East Lancashire) Territorials who
had once been commanded by Hugh Elles drew the short straw is
not clear, but it was upon them that the choice fell. The Division
had a famous record in the other war and had fought manfully in
France. By mid-1941 the word Territorial had ceased to have much
meaning, for, in addition to cross-posting with the regular battalions of its regiments, the Division was now made up in large part
of young conscripts. In 1941 these were, in the main, of good qual-

ity. Before very long, however, wastage had compelled the enlistment of men of poor physique who had to be sent to special development centres to bring them up even to the unexacting standards laid down for recruits.

For immediate purposes the 42nd had a place in the scheme of things for repelling invaders and the War Office was unenthusiastic about letting it go. Eventually a compromise was reached. Its old weapons would be left at centres where they could be picked up again fairly quickly in case of need. Until that happened they would wear the black beret with the mailed fist emblem and learn about clutches and carburettors. The first brigade was set to its new task as soon as the Guards had vacated the training establishments.

All of this fell in with the wishes of the Prime Minister. He is accused by Grigg of 'clamping down approval on those models of tanks which could most quickly be produced in substantial numbers without too much regard to their intrinsic qualities'. Mr Churchill might have replied that, when under immediate threat, a horse-pistol in the hand is of more use than a machine-gun on the drawing-board. Had he been blessed with divine knowledge that there would be no invasion he might have taken different decisions. There was, however, no denying that the army would soon be cluttered up with obsolete and jerry-built machines. Nearly 2,000 of the worthless Covenanter appeared before the tap could be turned off.

The Prime Minister, with enormous experience of the subject behind him, was always a friend to the tank but his demand in April, 1941, for what he called a 'Tank Parliament' was received with modified rapture. The word 'Parliament' probably caused the trouble. Parliaments are assemblies of equals, few of its members being persons of outstanding quality, where the prize goes to the loudest voice. Nothing could sound less agreeable to well-disciplined and well-mannered officers of varying status. Loyalty, as the army understands it, means accepting without question the views of those set in authority even when one may strongly disagree with them. Careers of professional soldiers would not benefit from displays of unconventional virtuosity.

The first colloquy took place, by order, at 10 Downing Street on 5 May. Those summoned included the CIGS, his Assistant, and General Pope, all speaking for the War Office. Martel and his divisional commanders represented the army in the field and Admiral Brown with General Crawford the Ministry of Supply. The agenda included the organization of armoured divisions, their mechanical efficiency and plans for the campaigns of 1943. Russia has not yet been invaded but there is reason to suppose that Enigma had given the Prime Minister advance warning of what was about to happen. It is a matter of record that he passed the warning to Stalin who regarded it as just another capitalist trick.

Martel disliked the whole idea and for one clear reason. The 11th Armoured Division, entirely made up of Yeomanry regiments, was commanded by General Hobart whose ideas were not always those of the Commander, Royal Armoured Corps. Even worse, Martel knew Hobart to be on terms with Mr Churchill and suspected things to be going on behind his back. This was the subject of some rather tart correspondence between them. Hobart was the only dissentient; apart from him the armoured generals were pretty much of one mind about the things that needed doing and the methods to be adopted. Martel, in his writings, often uses the expression 'to clear my mind'. He intended that the Parliament should do exactly that and when called to speak immediately after the Prime Minister had opened the meeting he did so. 'Everybody realizes that we are stretched to the limit of our resources at the moment, but the fact remains that unless we carry out certain preparatory steps now we shall not be ready to deal the final blow when the opportunity occurs in one, two or three years time.' He pooh-poohed the idea that the war could be won by bombing alone. 'We have far greater industrial resources than Germany and if we set about it there is nothing to prevent us building a fleet of tanks which are one step ahead of Germany in armour protection and guns. We know from our experience in this war that the Germans will not face superior tanks, so that is the line to pursue.' Privately he had no such faith in the Ministry of Supply which, 'would very likely fail us'. He left the meeting with a feeling that it had all been a great waste of everybody's time.

Brooke attended the next meeting in June and spoke sensibly. His subject was spare parts or, more accurately, their absence. This petty business seems to have been brushed aside both by the Prime Minister and the new Minister of Supply, Lord Beaverbrook. In later writings Brooke complained that neither had listened to him, with the result that chaos prevailed in Egypt which literally brought operations to a standstill. The first Tank Parliament was on a Monday. On the Saturday Brooke went with Martel to Luton to find out how the Churchill tank was coming along. He seemed pleased with what he saw. Tanks were now being built on motor-car principles and this one promised extraordinarily well. The demonstrations of anti-tank weapons at Larkhill and Netheravon were less encouraging. The 2-pdr, 6-pdr, 75mm, Bofors and 3.7 anti-aircraft gun were all put through their paces, but Brooke, a gunner by trade, saw much room for improvement.

One gun was missing. The 3″ AA gun had started life in the Navy before the First War and was now obsolete so far as aircraft were concerned. In November, 1941, a captured German weapon was, brought to Colonel Berry, Chief Mechanical Engineer to 13 Corps, for examination. 'I could not believe my eyes. It was a British 3″ AA gun manufactured by Vickers and fitted to a Russian gun-carriage. It was a very effective and powerful weapon. Clearly it had been sent to Russia, captured by the Germans, serviced, and sent to the Middle East. When the 3″ guns in London were replaced by the 3.7″ guns, several hundred 3″ guns became redundant. If these had been fitted to 25-pounder gun carriages and rushed out to the Middle East the whole course of the war would have been changed.' It was common knowledge that the Navy needed every gun it could lay hands on for its defensively equipped merchant ships but it should have been possible to exempt these. Presumably, as usual, it was nobody's business. The Army must put up with whatever the other services did not want. Efforts were indeed made to use the 3.7 gun in an anti-tank role, as Rommel used his 88s, but it was a heavy and cumbersome weapon ill adapted for the purpose. The simple 3″ would have been a Godsend.

The Eighth Army no longer had an effective anti-tank weapon, not counting the purely defensive mine of which a stock had been locally made. Only the field guns, encadred in their regular batteries or darting about in tank-hunting 'Jock Columns', could knock holes in the armour of the Panzers Mk III and IV. Colonel Berry, who later became Chief Mechanical Engineer to the Army, wrote of the 2-pdr: 'The War Office considered that it was a very good gun. I never came across a single officer or man in the desert who agreed with that view. . . . It was simply too small to prove effective against German armour at over 600 yards. As an anti-tank gun it was virtually useless in the desert. . . . I listened in to an OC of an anti-tank battery reporting that his shots were bouncing off thirty German tanks that were attacking him and that this was probably the last that would be heard of him. It was.' The gun still fired an un-capped shot that tended to break up on impact. When the APBC (Armour Piercing Ballistic Cap) – equipped rounds arrived perform-ance improved, but they only arrived with General Montgomery.

Although the possibilities of the 3″ gun were obvious they had not escaped notice by the War Office. The suggestion that it be tried out in a tank seems to have come from Pope, judging by an oblique reference in one of Stern's Minutes. Not to anybody's surprise this did not work. The gun was far too big for any existing turret. The idea of using it as a towed anti-tank weapon might have been expected to strike the artillery branch but does not seem to have done so.

There was another wheel to the coach, about the seventh, that was based at The Grange, Knockholt, near Sevenoaks, and went by the name of the Armaments Design Department. Its Head was a Naval Officer, Commander Rowland Stokes-Rees, commonly called 'Rosie'. He and Stern kept up an animated correspondence upon the subject of tank guns but it was purely academic. The 'Dear Rosie' 'Dear Bertie' letters show that neither of them had much time for higher authority. Whether it was cause and effect is uncertain but some very odd weapons were produced during the days when armour suddenly became fashionable as an arm to destroy invaders. When the 7th Buffs were converted into 141st RAC the first machines to reach them were remarkable. A number of obsolete tanks had been fitted out with a miscellany of antique naval guns mounted *en barbette*. They looked imposing but it was wiser not to fire them. When the piece recoiled, as guns do, the breech would have squashed any crew member who might happen to be in its path. Before long all of them were withdrawn.

There are anti-tank weapons deserving of mention before turning to other things. Major Jefferis and his researchers were installed in a country house called The Firs at Whitchurch and were working on a number of them. The Sticky Bomb was used in the brief Syrian campaign but was not highly regarded and soon disappeared. After work on the projectile for the 2-pdr, which often broke up on impact for want of a cap, attention was turned to mines. Land mines, originally under the forgotten name of 'Fougasses', were not new. Lord Kitchener had used them in combination with barbed wire to cover his block-houses during the later stages of the Boer War. The original had been simplicity itself. A hole in the ground was filled with a powder charge tamped down with rocks. Through this was inserted an old rifle, muzzle downwards, with a trip wire attached to the trigger. It worked surprisingly well. In 1918 quite effective minefields had been extemporised from artillery shells or mortar bombs. By late 1941 the factories had begun to turn out fairly sophisticated affairs designed to slay infantry or tanks according to the users' wishes. They were not a substitute for some small infantry weapon. Jefferis' Shoulder Gun, the first 29mm spigot mortar, had its trials before the summer was out. It still needed a lot of work before it became the PIAT.

The A 22 tank, the Churchill, was to carry the heavy end of armoured warfare for a long time and its beginnings have been described. Stern had not been alone in seeing the need for a heavy tank and in the first days of the war Woolwich Arsenal, the builders of Matilda II, had been bidden to design one. The first design, the A 20, had not been so very different from TOG; it too broke down on its first appearance in June, 1940, with gear-box trouble. The machine was turned over to Vauxhall, the British end of General Motors, largely because the engine was their Bedford twin-six. Vauxhall, helped by Kenchington, were asked to refine the whole thing and get it into production as quickly as they could. With amazing speed they turned out a pilot model, the one mentioned by Martel, before 1940 was out. An order was immediately given for the building of 500 of them and, as this was plainly beyond the capacity of a single firm, a syndicate was formed. It comprised the Birmingham Carriage and Wagon Co, Broom & Wade, Metropolitan Cammell, Charles Roberts, Leyland, Dennis, Newton Chambers, Gloucester Railway Carriage Co and the Belfast shipyard Harland & Wolff.

Everything was done in a great rush, with the inevitable consequences. The transmission, called the Merritt-Brown, was the work of a brilliant young engineer, Dr Merritt, who had been working on the subject for the last couple of years. The construction was composite, an inner skin of ½-inch mild steel with armour plating bolted on. Although the demand for a tank that could be carried by rail made it narrower than could be wished the inside was surprisingly roomy. The first models were armed with the 2-pdr, the only tank gun then in production. Churchill nearly went the way of Covenanter, for the first models, made by firms completely unfamiliar with tank building, were as unreliable as most other British tanks. So bad were some of them that dropping the whole thing was seriously suggested. It was Beaverbrook who saved Churchill the first time. He gave his personal and dynamic attention to the makers and standards improved. All the same, though it went through many Marks and was used for all manner of purposes, Churchill never came near to being the perfect heavy tank. It was better made than Crusader, faint praise though that is, but it over-heated just as badly. The first of the 500 were delivered in June, 1941, the month of Hitler's invasion of Russia. Large numbers were sent to our strange and exigent ally; as the Red Army had better tanks of its own, they ended up, for the most part, on the quieter sectors of that long front. The army tank brigades for which the machine had been intended had to wait for them. Because of the diversions to the East further orders were placed, bringing the total on the order books to 4,000.

Among the first recipients of the early Churchills were the 7th Buffs, now re-christened 141st RAC. Because they lacked experience in their new weapons, and possibly because their defects were known to the manufacturers, Major Raikes was sent to live with them for some weeks. Eastbourne was fascinated by the sight of Major and Mrs Raikes doing their shopping in a tank. Raikes explained that he was obliged to clock up a certain number of miles and had no other way of doing it.

The other 1941 tank was still the Valentine. The Company's historian does not mention, as General Pope does, that it got off to a bad start. The 48th RAC at Castle Martin suffered 100 broken track-pins in a week and 'the question of tracks for the Infantry Tank Mk III was so critical that every effort was needed to enable them to operate, which they cannot now do'. The efforts succeeded. It was, however, popular with crews because of its reliability and ease of maintenance; the Canadian Pacific Railway built some 1400 under licence, nearly all of them going to Russia, for the Valentine was the only tank of which they demanded more. From the makers of the T 34, probably the best tank in the world, this was a compliment. Because it was there in late 1940 Valentine was for some time the backbone of the armoured divisions at home even though it was never the kind of tank they needed.

By the time of Russia's unwilling entry Martel had quite a useful force coming along. The 6th, 9th, 11th, Guards and 42nd Armoured Divisions, though ill-equipped, had made great strides in training. Behind these were five Army Tank Brigades and five more armoured brigades not yet encadred in higher formations. Training was carried out on a large scale, beginning with the great Exercise Bumper in September, 1941, when two entire Corps, along with the 9th and 11th Armoured Divisions, simulated a landing on the East Coast and were taken on by two other Corps, one of them Canadian with its own armoured division and two army tank brigades. The exercise taught much, but it was a pity that the RAF, busy with its own affairs, did not take a more active share. The lesson that a tank without an aircraft is a bat without a ball had still to be learned. In this the Germans and the Russians were still far ahead. All the same, something was emerging, some idea however imperfect of how a campaign should be fought under modern conditions. The use of the Support Group (originally Pivot Group), the armoured division's own lorried infantry and towed 25-pdrs, was beginning to be grasped. As in the other war, tanks could take but they could not hold ground. The 2-pdr was good enough, just, to punch a hole in another tank but it could not deal with anti-tank batteries. A proportion of the cruisers, about 10%, were provided with a small howitzer for that aspect of their work. Repairs and recovery were still dimly understood. By the end of the war REME counted more heads than the entire Regular Army of 1939. But REME and tank transporters were still some way off.

That REME was overdue is made plain in the Prime Minister's various telegrams of this time. 'I am shocked to see that one month later (after asking for proposals for improvement) we still have 25% of Infantry tanks out of order and that out of 400 cruiser tanks no fewer than 157 are unfit for action.' This was on 19 August. The month before had shown 391 out of 1441 being hors de combat. By the end of August the improvement was not remarkable. Out of 408 cruisers 'there are actually more unfit for service than fit. The proportion of unfit is getting worse every week'. It was bad enough at home with all the resources of civilian industry on call. In Egypt and Libya, lacking these advantages, it was a hundred times worse. It does not seem that the armour of the Afrika Korps was afflicted to anything like the same extent. German tanks were made by firms that had for years specialised in tank-building and nothing else. It was not a mere variant on the motor car industry. The Crusader could have been a good cruiser for its day had more care been taken over its construction. Valentine was a victim to better workmanship. Its manganese track, better by far than the Ford iron used in the others, carried it for long distances over rough ground; its engine, transmission and suspension gave little trouble and it could be trusted to carry its crew on to their objective. Once there, however, it often delivered them into the hands of their enemies. Its armour and weapons were no better than Matilda's, its bogie-wheels were unprotected and vulnerable and its speed, about 15 mph with luck, was not much more than half that of Crusader. Valentine was a stop-gap, suitable for use only under carefully chosen conditions until something fitter for battle turned up. This did not happen for nearly two more years. The Valentine remained in service far too long because there was nothing better.

When the next round of desert battles began the army had not merely to make do with poor quality weapons; it lost some of its best leaders. Major-General Vyvyan Pope, like all good officers, wanted a command and he had earned one. In September, 1941, he was sent out to Egypt as commander-designate of the Corps upon which the fate of the battle would probably depend. Like Justice Tilly he died, this time in an air crash, before he could take over. Brigadier Combe had been captured with General Neame; Brigadier Rimington had died of wounds and the number of senior officers left who really understood the art of armoured warfare was pitifully few. General Wavell went to India, his place being taken by the previous incumbent there, General Auchinleck. His inheritance was not to be envied.

CHAPTER TEN
'The Deep, Deep Russian Snow'
German song title c. 1942

In the days not long ago when Josef Stalin had been giving Adolf Hitler all possible help towards smashing the British Empire he had sent a delegation of his tank experts to find out what the Germans were doing in such matters. It was met by General Guderian who told of it after the war in his book. Guderian asserts that Hitler ordered all the Wehrmacht had to be shown to the Russians, holding back nothing. When the visitors were told that Panzer IV, weighing just 23 tons, was the biggest thing that Germany possessed they flatly refused to believe it. Hitler may, just this once, have been telling the literal truth but he displayed some economy of the candour due to an ally. Trials had just been suspended on a 65-ton monster named the VK 6501 and Dr Henschel was working on something smaller but still bigger than the Pz IV. The VK 3001H was a 32-tonner carrying a 75 mm gun. Even had the Russians been told of this it would not have worried them unduly. Their own T34 was better in every way.

The subject of the war on the Russian front is so vast that no description of it can be attempted here. Even an adequate sketch would fill not merely a book but a whole shelf of books. Suffice it that the German army put into the field at the beginning 121 divisions of which seventeen were armoured and twelve motorized. Hitler, of course, hoped for a quick victory before the onset of winter and counted on two things – first, the reduction in numbers and quality in the Russian officer corps following upon the 'purges' of 1938; second, a firm belief that the rank and file would refuse to fight, at any rate to fight very hard, for a system as rotten as Communism. In this second he miscalculated badly. Whatever the merits or otherwise of the system under which he lived, the Russian soldier was as brave, loyal and tough as any man living. Hitler hoped for a smash-and-grab raid: he got the Great Patriotic War. And, as soon became manifest, Russian tank designers and engineers were streets ahead of all others. German intelligence had failed badly; it is hard to advance any reason. Martel knew, from his 1936 visit, what was up the Russian sleeve, even if some of the details had been kept from him. There was no excuse for German ignorance of either the 47-ton KVI or of the T 34, justly classed as a cruiser, for, at 30 tons, it was faster than the Crusader at 20. Its 76.2 gun was the most powerful weapon yet mounted on tracks and the machine was reliable enough to have driven by road during trials from its factory in Kharkov round a course taking in Moscow, Smolensk and Kiev. This was the kind of thing for which Mr Christie had designed his suspension and it worked. Like the Germans, the Russians comprehended the use of aircraft and tanks as a single team, but they did not go about it in the same way. There were no dive-bombers in the Russian service; their place was filled by the Stormovik, an armoured fighter-bomber by which they set great store. Armoured aeroplanes were nothing new; the RAF had tried them out in 1918. The advantages spoke for themselves but performance suffered too much for the experiment to be worth while. Martel was sceptical about the claims made for the Stormovik but it was undeniably a useful partner to the T 34.

At the time of the invasion it was reckoned that the Russian army could field about 21,000 tanks of one kind or another. Though the machines were head and shoulders above anything else at the time the doctrines for their use were not. At least half of them were kept in the old way for infantry support. To this extent, but no further, the Russian army resembled the French. Nevertheless the first brush with the T 34 came as a very rude shock to the Wehrmacht. Within hours it was obvious that their machines were outclassed and the German engineers must be put to work without losing a moment to furnish something bigger and better than the Pz Mk IV. A Commission of tank designers, tank builders and representatives of the Ordnance Department was quickly put together and sent to Russia where it examined the few Russian machines that had been knocked out. It arrived on 20 November, the Tank Corps' Cambrai Day.

The speed with which the German Commission produced results and the speed with which Russia moved its tank factories safely behind the Urals are feats which make all British efforts seem pitiful. By the summer of 1942 the prototype Tiger was running. It was not a new design, it was too heavy, too slow and its armour lacked the ballistic efficiency of the Russian. In England, no doubt, another year would have have been wasted in trying to make something of it. The Germans, never people to reinforce failure, ditched it and looked for something better. In September, 1942 they found it. Ten months after inspecting broken T 34s, the MAN Company showed off their VK3002 on the testing ground at Nuremburg. An immediate order for delivery of 500 a month was placed and the tank was renamed Panther. Daimler, Henschel and several other firms were taken off their current work and set to Panther production.

The driving force behind all this was Hitler himself, with 'his beloved Porsche' – the words are Guderian's – for technician. The Führer's imagination was allowed to run riot. In March, 1942, he had demanded a tank of 100 tons weight; it was to be ready for the Spring offensive of the following year and the MAN people were also to make 'flats' on which to carry it. At the same time the engineers Grote and Hacker were ordered to design another which would be ten times the size of the first. Imbecilities like this apart, Hitler did his cause good service by forcing the rearming of his Panzer IVs with the long, high velocity L70 version of the 75 in place of the shorter L42. This greatly increased its killing range. Dr Porsche was sufficiently interesting to the British Government for a post-war enquiry into his activities to be ordered. The Report does not show him as the bogeyman of then current belief. The Doctor was never able to repeat the success of the Volkswagen that had won Hitler's good opinion of him. Most of his tank designs were either impractical, like the petrol-electric Tiger with a range of 30 miles, or they needed to be re-worked by either the Henschel or the Krupp firms. With his Führer breathing down his neck, Dr Porsche can hardly be blamed for having lost the mark of genius. There is a passage in the official report on AFVs in the Mediterranean Theatre which would have caused him pain. 'With Tiger the Germans lost the priceless quality of reliability ... and none of their models have since approached Allied standards.' The second part was a little premature but the first was true. Tiger crews had to accustom themselves to breakdowns; they were not on the British scale, nor anywhere near it, but the Germans, unaccustomed to such things, became indignant; they christened Tiger 'the furniture van'. To its enemies it still looked, and was, very formidable indeed. Slow, perhaps, in

moving its great gun on the mounting but deadly to the smaller deni-
zens of the jungle.

All this affected the Desert Army hardly at all as General Auchinleck took over. Great things were anticipated of him, and Mr Churchill sent the famous message that he expected soon to see results
that would rank with Blenheim and Waterloo. The Eighth Army, as
it was now called, would have its days of glory, but not yet. Nor was
it to be the most glorious period in the career of its first commander,
General Sir Alan Cunningham, the victor of Abyssinia. His army
was divided into two Corps of unequal strength, bearing the numbers 13 and 30. The plan was simple, though the battle became intricate. Cunningham's right hand, 13 Corps, comprising an army tank
brigade and two divisions, was to take Rommel by the throat. His
left, the three armoured brigades which, along with 7th Armoured
Division, made up 30 Corps, would ride round from the south and
stab him in the back. At the same time Tobruk garrison would
emerge and harry the Axis troops as they retreated. On the face of
things it all seemed entirely within the bounds of the possible. The
RAF, with more than 1,000 aircraft, could, as the French had once
been accustomed to say, 'nettoyer le ciel'. The army was equally well
off in point of tanks, with 756 of them fit for duty. About 400 of
them were Matildas and Valentines, obsolescent but still fairly trustworthy for infantry work; the cruisers numbered 336, of which 195
were Stuarts and the rest mainly Crusaders or worse. In reserve
were 200 more. The enemy now counted three German divisions,
15th and 21st Panzer, along with 90th Light. Between them they
were reckoned to own 558 tanks. This is Mr Churchill's figure. Captain Liddell Hart put it at 249, a third of them light machines, plus
146 Italian M 13s.

It was a kind of Crécy in reverse. The English armour looked as if
it should swamp the German defenders. These, however, now
owned the 1941 equivalent of the 1346 long-bow. It was the high-
velocity 50 mm anti-tank gun, long in the barrel and throwing a 4-lb
projectile that no English armour could withstand. In case that was
not enough, Rommel commanded some 30-odd of the fearsome 88s,
which were to remain for the rest of the war the best tank-killers of
them all. His own German armour included 174 Panzers III and
IV, each carrying a 75. There were vague recollections of how three
small cruisers had seen off the *Graf Spee* but it was a false analogy.
Exeter, Ajax and *Achilles* had been fine ships manned by highly
trained professionals. Cunningham's formations, for the most part,

were not. The ordinary divisions of 13 Corps, 4th Indian (a third of its infantry and all its gunners British) and the New Zealanders, were very good indeed. So was his artillery. In the early stages of the battle the 1st Army Tank Brigade, Matildas and Valentines, was unemployed. The remainder of the fourteen armoured regiments included every regular unit of the RTR. These nine were charged with the duty of seeking out and destroying the German and Italian armour. To accomplish this they still had on charge, mixed in with the newer machines, twenty-six old A 10s and a number of A13s. They were to cover a lot of ground.

The attack began on 18 November in pouring rain. The tankmen, mostly very young, can hardly have failed to know the handicap they carried, no matter what the figures might say. Once again Napoleon's dictum about concentrating to fight was set aside and the three armoured brigades of 30 Corps drove forward in separate entities. The German command could have wished for nothing better. Rommel had concentrated his main battle into a single block and as each brigade of 30 Corps drove up it was destroyed seriatim. By the evening of 22 November the Corps had lost two-thirds of its tanks and the Germans had numerical as well as qualitative superiority. A withdrawal of 20 miles followed at once. The mechanized cavalry in particular had demonstrated that a change from horse to tank had not affected their philosophy. Every fault for which the Duke had cursed them in the Peninsula was repeated; wild, hopeless charges against well placed guns could have only one end. Not that they were alone to blame. Infantry commanders, unequipped with decent anti-tank weapons of their own, were constantly calling for the tanks to come and help. The RAF could do nothing. It was not trained or equipped for tank-smashing and the mêlée in any event made it impossible to tell who was who, even though British tanks, as in 1918, now carried red and white stripes. Fortunately the rain made the German airfields unusable or matters might have been even worse.

On 13 Corps' front affairs were better, with Freyberg's New Zealanders carrying all before them. When Rommel decided that his time had come to move out he beat up the rear areas and took many prisoners but on reaching the Egyptian frontier his columns came up against the 4th Indian Division. This experienced formation gave him nothing for his comfort and by the 26th the Axis forces were streaming back to Bardia. General Cunningham, however, seemed to have lost his nerve and wanted to call the whole thing off.

Another fine reputation was carried to the grave-yard as Auchinleck himself took the battle by the scruff. Having ordered the attack to continue, he removed Cunningham and replaced him with his own deputy Chief of Staff, Neil Ritchie.

As some elements of the New Zealanders reached Tobruk, Rommel in his turn struck back. His tanks, attacked in the flank by 120 others from the 7th Armoured Division, repulsed a New Zealand brigade but made little headway. By the last days of November the Afrika Korps and its Italian ancillaries had begun a general retreat to the Gazala line. In a letter to the *Daily Telegraph*, published on 5 June, 1981, Sir John Langford-Holt told of how in 1948, as a young MP, he asked Mr Churchill whom he reckoned our greatest General of the war. His answer 'was immediate and definite – Auchinleck.' 'Operation Crusader' was certainly the moment when he stood on the heights.

General Martel may have been reckoned more of a technician than a commander but he pointed out the lessons 'Crusader' had taught. Hobart's all-armoured ideas were wrong and demonstrably so. The Germans avoided tank-to-tank slugging matches whenever they could and sought to lure the British armour on to themselves when hull-down or, better still, on to the guns. The place for artillery was of more importance than seemed generally understood. It should advance under tank protection and provide the punch when attacked. Mobile infantry and anti-tank guns were needed to protect the artillery. The old principles were still sound and tanks, against serious opposition, were not invincible. France in 1940 had been a freak. Yet it was from France that the lesson had come. In the last battles of the Hundred Years' War, at Formigny and Chatillon, the new French artillery had routed the English archers, the anti-tank gunners of their day. So it would have to be again.

Then, on 7 December, 1941, with both sides glaring at each other and wondering what to do next, came cataclysmic news. The Japanese had taken leave of their senses and bombed Pearl Harbor. For Mr Churchill, and not for him alone, it was the lifting of a dark shadow. The outcome of the war, though not its duration, could no longer be in doubt.

CHAPTER ELEVEN

General January, General February and General Motors

The day that was to live in infamy brought both similarities with and contrasts to its equivalent in 1917. Then, after the meeting between Lord Kitchener and Mr Schwab of Bethlehem Steel, all the power of American factories had been put at the disposal of a Britain still rich enough to pay for them. The results had not always been happy. Much of the material supplied had been of poor quality, as the 'dud' shells lying about on the Somme battlefields had shown. When the American armies took the field they were unable to provide themselves with much needed weapons and relied heavily upon France and Britain. Every artillery piece, for example, and every combat aircraft came from one or the other, as did their tanks. The Mk VIII machine, an Anglo-US collaboration, might have been the sovereign weapon in the unfought campaign of 1919. Since there was no demand for it, numbers of them were left to rust at the Aberdeen Proving Ground in Maryland.

The American story was much the same as the British, though possibly even worse. In 1919 the Tank Corps was disbanded as having no future use. During the rich years before the Depression a few experimental machines were made but nobody was greatly interested. Mr Christie tried hard to sell his products, but nobody wanted them. Captain Patton had gone back to the cavalry. In 1927, the same year as in Britain, the cavalry, instigated by General MacArthur, was bidden to study the subject. In 1920 anything to do with tanks had been turned over to the infantry under the National Defense Act of that year. The cavalry were therefore forbidden to use the word 'tank' and told to speak instead of 'combat cars'.

By 1934 some light machines, close copies of the Vickers 6-tonner, had come out of the Rock Island Arsenal and three years later a model known as the M1 Combat Car was taken into service. Its 7-cylinder Continental engine gave it a good turn of speed but the armour was negligible and the weapons only a brace of machine-guns. The Light Tank Mk 2A – the forbidden word was now permitted – looked at first glance much like the Renault FT17. By 1940 it was as obsolete as any Vickers Light. American officers were well aware of this and set themselves to study the events of the campaign in France.

The result was the Light Tank M3, with 38 mm of armour all over and 51 mm in front. Early models were riveted in the old way but this soon gave place to a welded turret of better ballistic shape. The main armament was a 37 mm gun, not quite as good as the 2-pdr but nearly so. The most important factor in M3 was that it was designed for mass production by the automobile industry, something that had never happened in England. It had also two pieces of refined technique peculiar to the US – a gyro-stabiliser for the gun and, in later models, a power-operated turret. The last Marks looked very different from the early ones. The Stuart, to give it its proper name, was an excellent small tank, about the same weight as a Crusader but much faster and more trustworthy.

The between-wars story of the US medium tank is much the same. In 1928 – the year the Russian 5-Year Plan included tanks – Mr Christie, faint but pursuing, presented his new model to the Ordnance Board. Two years later they tried it out, making it run for 200 miles on wheels only, 140 more on tracks at 20 mph and fording a stream 3 feet deep. All these things it did in fine style. The engine was our old friend the 1917 Liberty. The Ordnance Department thought well enough of it to order five. Christie actually made nine, two being ordered by Russia and two by Poland. As the Poles did not pay up, the US army took them over. Then followed a series of furious quarrels, much like those of Stern and the War Office. Christie, sensibly, set great store by a low silhouette and wanted no turrets (the latest Swedish tank closely resembles his) but the US War Office, like War Offices everywhere, wanted to keep to the things it was used to. No American tank of Hitler's war used Christie's suspension. Nor did they order any heavy tanks at all. It is hard to understand why. One would somehow expect that America would have refused to allow other powers to build the biggest machines in the world. But so it was.

16. Nuffield Cruisers: The A13

17. Nuffield Cruisers: The A15 Crusader

18. Degradation. The Crusader gun-tower

19. The same, as a bulldozer

20. The rudest mechanical of them all! The Covenanter Mk IV

21. The runner-up: A Cavalier

22. The next stage: The A20

23. An early Churchill: The Mk II

24. The much better Mk VI

25. The fate of some Mk IIIs. Dieppe, 1942

26. More, and worse

27. A Churchill in the wrong hands

28. The Empire's own tanks. A Canadian Ram

29. The Skink: A Canadian Anti-Aircraft tank

30. The Australian Sentinel

M3 GENERAL GRANT

31. 'England's Last Hope'. The U.S. Grant

32. Australian-manned Sentinels in New Guinea

33. Surplus to establishment. The unwanted Harry Hopkins

34. More failures. A Centaur Mk III

When the British Purchasing Commission arrived in America in 1940 it was told, reasonably enough, that it must buy US tanks or nothing. On offer were the Stuart and a prototype of the M3 Medium. All offended against one of the War Office canons, for they had a high silhouette. It could not be helped. Contracts were placed in November, 1940, for a number of M3 Mediums, henceforth to be called Lee, in addition to a number of Stuarts. The Lee was far from being a perfect design, for its main armament was mounted in a turret on the side, recalling to old hands the sponsons of an earlier age. The armament was, however, formidable – a 75 mm gun, derived from the original soixante-quinze of the 1890s but of far higher velocity. This would kill any panzer yet known, even though it might be difficult to manoeuvre into a good firing position. There was also a 37 mm in the turret. To show that Blue and Gray were now reconciled the anglicised version was called the Grant. Either was far better than anything yet produced in the British factories. Originally both tanks had the old-style riveted armour but America took more quickly to the welding process. By 1942 the Lee had reached its 5th Mark and thenceforth welding became standard practice. Users as well as makers appreciated its advantages. The official report on AFVs in the Mediterranean Theatre tells of rivets 'flying about like bullets' when a tank was hit.

These were the tanks with which America entered the war. During 1941 the total British output amounted to 4,841: the German figure, according to Guderian, was 2,875. Most of the British machines were the now obsolete Matildas and Valentines and a good proportion of the rest the useless Covenanters. At the so-called Victory Conference of September, 1941, it was agreed that Britain required 11,500 tanks from American factories, all of them cruisers. As those factories were still far from geared up for quantity production it would be a long time before they arrived. Before 1941 was out a new machine would be taking over from Lee and Grant. Continuing the tale of the Civil War, it was to be called the Sherman. Nameless save for the unglamorous M7 was another very serviceable weapon, the first self-propelled gun since Major Wilson's scandalously neglected equipment of 1916 and Sir Noel Birch's gun of the 1920s. To the British army it would be known as the Priest and its 105 mm howitzer would be a powerful addition to the armoury.

Though a few half-hearted attempts were made to produce something heavier, it was not a matter of much interest. The Tank Board note of 12 September, 1942, records that 'The Staffs (British and

US) are agreed that the requirement for heavily armoured tanks employed in an assault role is more likely to be met by the development of components for a tank of relatively small dimensions than by proceeding with the development of a large dimensional heavy assault tank. Moreover, the Staff are agreed that operational bridging requirements as well as other tactical considerations prohibit the use in the field (except in small numbers) of tanks weighing more than 40 tons (British) fully loaded.' The American taste was, as the Report says, for an 'all purpose' tank. The point was stretched to allow 'as an urgent project, the development of a small heavily armoured assault tank which may eventually replace the Valentine'. It appeared, as a prototype, too late for the war. 'Urgency' is a relative thing.

The task of the Purchasing Mission was not easy. The Americans seemed well disposed, but many, following their Ambassador, Joseph Kennedy, were convinced that Britain would soon have to surrender and it would be pointless to supply weapons for Hitler. The President, however, took another view and had a substantial following. The difficulties remained great. American tank doctrine, based upon experiences with little Renaults in the Meuse-Argonne, was very different from that of the British who remembered the Hindenburg Line. The Chairman's Report tells of it: 'In the American view armoured divisions will not normally be employed in fighting enemy tank formations. The latter will either be dealt with by self-propelled guns or tank-destroyers.... The role of the armoured force is to deal with the enemy communications and to attack infantry, artillery, etc, from the rear. In normal circumstances a heavily defended position will not be attacked by tanks but by other means such as air, artillery and infantry.' This was of first importance and for several reasons. Since no American tank was intended to mix it with a German it had no need to be of comparable size. The medium kind, Lees, Grants and Shermans, would be quite good enough. From time to time prototypes of a heavy tank were made but they were not followed through. The second point was armament. If tanks were to beat up batteries and battalions they would need, not solid shot, but high explosive. The short 75 sufficed for the purpose, even though it had slight armour-piercing capability. For the next couple of years this served well. The British cruisers were so bad that Americans were gratefully accepted, even though they did not accord with British ideas.

The Canadian General Staff were brought in at the beginning of the business. Already the Montreal Locomotive Company was at work on a Canadian tank called the Ram, which closely resembled the Grant, except for the fact that it had a turret. No Ram was ever used in action as a tank but a number of them earned a place in the Order of Battle in France when cut down to the armoured troop carriers called Kangaroos or, under the name Sexton, as SP field artillery.

Australia decided to go her own way and turned out at home an excellent medium tank that owed nothing to anybody. The Sentinel was Australian designed and Australian built, with three Cadillac engines arranged in a clover-leaf pattern. Sixty-five of them came out of the factories, a fine feat of engineering by a country of small manufacturing capacity.

The Mission had something to offer in exchange. A Matilda II was taken to be shown off and it attracted more interest than admiration. The Americans, quite rightly, pointed out that it was under-engined and under almost everything else. It did, however, have a power traverse new to the US designers. This was adopted at once. Mr Carr, the Mission's tank-designer, had comments to make about the Grant. In particular, the tracks were too smooth and had a poor grip in mud. 'Grousers' could be fitted but it was a slow and tedious business. Mr Carr and the American designers worked together on making something better. Then came the matter of turrets. One British article of faith was that this was the proper and only place for the wireless. The Americans disagreed. As, at this stage of the war, the British were still cash customers, they had their way on this point. You may tell a Grant (British) from a Lee (American) by the bulge at the back of the turret.

To one man on the American side a great debt is owed. With all this tinkering going on, Colonel (soon to be General) Barnes became impatient and demanded that a freeze be put on it all. Without that, he explained, the manufacturers would never be able to get started. The DRAC's Progress Report praises Colonel Barnes: 'A disastrous situation might have arisen in the Middle East had he listened.' But for his brusqueness there would have been no Grants for Auchinleck.

CHAPTER TWELVE

'The Sands of the Desert
Were Sodden Red'

Vitaï Lampada – SIR HENRY NEWBOLT

By the end of 1941 the Eighth Army was back in Benghazi and the 2nd South African Division, helped by the 1st Army Tank Brigade, had stormed Bardia. The garrison of Halfya Pass, overcome by hunger and thirst, surrendered on 18 January. In consequence of the Royal Navy meeting with a series of misfortunes this more or less coincided with loss of command at sea and some useful tank reinforcements reached Rommel in his safe ringside corner at Agheila.

Though General Ritchie did not enjoy the confidence of his two Corps Commanders, he was kept in his post. Whether Auchinleck would have done better to have taken it upon himself at this stage must be a matter upon which opinions may differ. He can hardly have forgotten that two years earlier Lord Gort had come under fierce criticism for doing exactly that. The 1st Armoured Division, mostly Crusaders and newly arrived, relieved the weary 7th on 6 January. Thirty-eight Valentines of 8th RTR were sent up from Bardia to join the 4th Indian Division near Benghazi a few days later. Another new formation, the 2nd Armoured Brigade with 150 tanks, continued its training some 90 miles in the rear.

Rommel began his come-back on 21 January, moving in a compact body of armoured fighting vehicles. Neither side could make any claim to being master of the air. On the 23rd he reached Antelat and encountered the 2nd Armoured Brigade arriving piecemeal from its training area. The three units comprising it were taken on in turn and smashed, mostly by the long 50 mm guns. By nightfall its 150 tanks were reduced to eighty. The Valentines of 8th RTR, which had only just reached Benghazi after an 85-mile drive across the desert, were immediately sent back on their travels, this time over the 74-mile route to Barce. The manganese steel tracks and good Vickers workmanship stood up to it well; of thirty-eight starters thirty-two arrived intact. It was not only track damage that put tanks hors de combat. Philip Guedalla, temporarily disguised in air force blue, was told that in a journey of 100 miles any tank would ingest about 20 lbs of sand. A single teaspoonful could wreck an engine. Filters mattered quite as much as track-pins.

The Afrika Korps was engaged not in a mere raid, as GHQ suspected, but in an all-out offensive. The Panzers soon drove through the 1st Armoured Division, leaving it with only thirty runners, and reached Msus. Then they swung towards Benghazi. A prompt withdrawal followed, and that not of the most orderly. By 5 February the Eighth Army, baffled and uneasy, was back on the old Gazala line. Rommel had hardly moved. It seems faintly absurd now that, when his tanks were scouring the desert for abandoned British petrol dumps, he was sitting upon the enormous Libyan oil fields.

For a month there was little in the way of combat save for 'Jock Column' activity, a new variation on the old style trench raid. Sometimes it came off, sometimes not. For example, when a large column unexpectedly bumped into sixty Panzers all of its thirteen Matildas were destroyed. They managed, however, to knock out several of the enemy before succumbing. A long period of building up strength followed for both sides.

For all the gallant efforts of the Royal Navy and the RAF, convoys were now reaching Rommel as never before. By early June he counted 280 tanks, all Panzers III and IV, in addition to the almost useless Italian M 13s, along with a plenitude of powerful anti-tank guns and forty-eight of the lethal dual-purpose 88s. On paper the reinforced British armoured forces were far greater than this. By early June Auchinleck had no less than fourteen armoured units of one kind and another with 850 tanks and another 120 in reserve. Far and away the best of these were 167 Grants whose 75 mm guns could see off any of the Panzers. The first of the 6-pdrs had also arrived though there had been little time for training men to use them. In two matters Rommel was better equipped. His tank transporters were well organized and followed hard on the heels of the Panzers, extricating and repairing them with great skill. The other factor seems small but was not. Petrol, on the British side, was carried in flimsy 4-gallon tins, incapable of being refilled, liable to split when tossed about and given to exploding when left out in the African sun where they shone like heliographs. The Germans used the stout Jerrican which lasted for ever and could take unlimited punishment. It made a considerable difference.

Auchinleck was under great pressure to do something, for the affairs of the Allies were not prospering. In Russia the Germans had failed to reach Moscow before winter, but they had survived and were on the offensive again. Singapore had gone and the Americans had had their own near-Dunkirk at Corregidor. Some sort of victory was essential. In the desert each side was planning an attack with the object of destroying the other's armour. Rommel got in first. On the morning of 27 May he had 200 tanks out of the 550 he now owned south of Bir Hakim, the left end of the British line. From there he set out northwards in three columns. Before breakfast time he had overrun the 3rd Indian Motorized Brigade and then he set about 4th Armoured. HQ 7th Armoured Division was scattered and a tank battle with the new American machines followed. They came as an unpleasant surprise and the Panzer crews learned for the first time how it felt to be shot up from distances at which they could not reply. Rommel brought out his sovereign weapon. Three batteries of 88s restored the situation and drove 4th Armoured back 20 miles to El Adem. Once again his superior generalship would bring re-sults. When the 22nd Armoured Brigade was thrown in to help out the Valentines of 4th RTR, both were knocked to pieces by the 21st Panzer Division. Only the 25-pdrs of the Support Group of 1st Armoured Division did any damage. By evening Rommel was 3 miles short of Acroma, leaving a third of his tanks behind him. Most of them had fallen to the Grants. For the moment he broke off the charge and took up a defensive position west of the point on the map called Knightsbridge. There he waited to be attacked. As none came for some days he paid off an old score. 150th Brigade of the 50th (Northumbrian) division, his old enemies of Arras, were isolated in what was called a box. With them were a few Valentines and 6-pdrs. Rommel put most of his force into the attack and met with a recep-tion that would have pleased but not surprised Martel. 'Yard by yard the German–Italian units fought their way forward against the toughest resistance imaginable. The defence was conducted with marked skill and as usual the British fought to the end.' As at Arras he called up the dive-bombers. No help came from Ritchie and 150th Brigade, along with two squadrons of 44th RTR, went under. The job took most of the Afrika Korps and an Italian division the best part of three days. Two RTR battalions, 7th (also ex-Arras) and 8th, made brave attempts to intervene but the 88s were too much for them. When the attack came it failed dismally.

Rommel then turned upon the Free French at Bir Hakim. This time it was Verdun rather than Sedan and resistance lasted for nine days. Having overcome it, and after various ploys, Rommel went to ground in the place known to history as The Cauldron. There Ritchie attacked him. The attack was ill planned, ill co-ordinated and ill executed. By the time this had become understood the 400 tanks with which it had started were reduced to 170. This put the two armoured forces into a rough numerical equality. It also showed that Matildas and Valentines had no place in the battles of 1942. The 4th and 7th RTR began with seventy; they came out with twelve. The 22nd Armoured Brigade lost sixty tanks out of 156. No praise can be too high for men who, knowing their probable fate of being 'brewed up', went back in again and again.

Confused and confusing tank battles swept to and fro across the desert during the next days. On 12 June new tanks had been brought up sufficient to raise the British total to 330. By nightfall half of them had been destroyed in the now customary way. Two days later, his tanks down to fifty cruisers and twenty mixed Matildas and Valentines, Ritchie ordered a complete withdrawal. The South African Official History calls it a 'sauve qui peut'. It is hard to contradict this. Rommel turned on Tobruk.

Hard measure has been meted out to General Klopper, the South African officer commanding the garrison. His country, with a white population less than half that of London, had put into the field two excellent divisions which had seen some of the hardest fighting of any. It was all very well to trumpet about last men and last rounds but, with command of the sea gone, Tobruk had little real importance. It can only be conjecture, but it would not be surprising if Klopper felt his country to have taken enough casualties already and that he would not serve posterity by incurring a lot more to no purpose. Tobruk was never a fortress in any sense. The Australians had made it seem like one, but that is Australia's way. There was hard enough fighting before the place went under. What remained of 4th and 7th RTR fought it out to the end; when the last Matilda had been destroyed they continued the fight on foot with revolvers as their fathers had done in 1918. On 20 June, 1942, Rommel became master of Tobruk. The Eighth Army fell back to the Alamein line.

Another Australian, Sir Richard (later Lord) Casey had something to say about it. As Minister of State in the Middle East he was an inspired choice; in youth he had served in both Gallipoli and France with the AIF, won the DSO and MC and had ended up on the Staff of General Sir John Monash after which he had become a diplomat of high degree. Such credentials were unique. Casey has left it on record that much telegraphing went on between Cairo and the War Office during February and March about the relative fighting value of British and German tanks. By May the conclusion had been reached that it was necessary to put up three British tanks to cope with two Germans. On 20 June a further report propounded that this was too optimistic. The German tanks were so much faster and hit so much harder that a superiority of 3 to 1 was needed to make anything like a fair fight of it. This reflected the general opinion and it is hard to blame Auchinleck for any unenthusiasm about forcing a battle before something better in the way of weapons had reached him. This was mid-1942. It may be instructive to remember it when we reach mid-1944.

CHAPTER THIRTEEN
The Third Year of Creation

Martel, determined to learn at first hand all that a commander of new armoured forces ought to know, spent the greater part of December, 1941, and January, 1942, in the desert, watching every move and making careful notes. It was unlucky that he left a day or two before Rommel went on the rampage. Had he only remained a little longer he would have seen what happened to an army when its communications broke down and the battle was left to fight itself rather than in accordance with the wishes of commanders. The Libyan desert was probably the worst place in the world where this could happen. Two and a half thousand years before, an army of 50,000 men, led by Cambyses, King of Persia, had completely disappeared somewhere in these parts. One piece of desert looks much like another and tight control was needed to prevent a repetition.

Martel's problem was two-fold. There was plainly a lot of desert fighting to be done before the final stages of the war would be reached and his armoured formations would have to master its techniques. Nevertheless it was not in deserts that the last rounds would take place and his soldiers must, in addition, learn how they would have to carry out their business in the more enclosed conditions of Europe. It would be asking a lot of them.

The 'Bumper' exercise had convinced him that armour had its limitations and that it must work closely with guns and infantry of its own. Nothing he had seen in Libya had persuaded him otherwise. There were, however, strong voices which could not be ignored that said different. Hobart remained the odd man out amongst his commanders, still insisting that the all-armoured idea was the key to victory. From outside the RAC another expert, now removed to the very different ambience of AA Command, said the same. General Pile had watched 'Bumper' and was unimpressed. The air, he asserted, was being completely ignored and the armour was being placed under infantry commanders, 1918 fashion, instead of being used as a tank army. He complained about the number of unarmoured vehicles cluttering the place up; Martel could have told him that when Rommel cut past Bir Hakim some 10,000 of these had formed part of his train. Both Pile and Hobart had, or were believed to have, Mr Churchill's ear. It was not merely the trumpet that was giving an uncertain sound; a large part of the brass section was doing the same along with some of the woodwinds.

The conductor pressed sturdily on. The idea of the RAF allotting squadrons to the army which would have nothing with which to occupy themselves between land battles was hardly realistic. Martel's view, which events were to justify, was that a senior RAF officer should be permanently at Army HQ as air commander in the same way that General Uniacke had been artillery commander in 1918. Nor was he going to be humbugged by the War Office Committee set up to produce an official doctrine for armoured warfare. Each of Martel's officers was given beforehand written answers to the questions he was bound to be asked. 'General Hobart, of course, gave his own views, but the answers of all the other witnesses was so unanimous that the final report of the committee was quite harmless.'

Martel's conclusions, unaltered by what he had just seen, were firm. The armoured divisions did not contain too few tanks; they had too many. As things stood, the drills worked rather in this fashion. Two armoured brigades would attack, possibly side by side. An ordinary division would follow behind and take over the captured positions. Its leading troops would be under orders of a divisional HQ a long way back and not subject to the armoured division's commander. The consequences were obvious – time lost, signals delayed or corrupt, orders misunderstood or plain disagreement upon what was needed. A far better organization would be to give the armoured General sufficient foot and guns, especially anti-tank guns, of his own so that he might run the whole battle and not merely a part of it. The best arrangement would be for the armoured division to have its armoured car regiment for the essential purpose of reconnaissance, a brigade of three tank regiments, a motor battalion plus a complete lorried infantry brigade, a couple of regiments of field artillery, another of anti-tank guns and the usual, indispensable, Sappers. Martel avers that all save Hobart agreed with him.

The second half of 1941 gave promise of better things in the way of equipment. Vickers were now providing only a small proportion of the army's tanks and were able to spare Commander E. R. Micklem to go to the Ministry of Supply as head of the department of tank production. He proved a great asset. By the time of his move the Company was turning out only Valentines and a little machine called Tetrarch designed to be air-portable. Even at this early stage such things were being seriously mooted. Pile tells of a meeting with Lord Beaverbrook in which the Minister demanded a tank capable of going into an aeroplane. When told that the 70-tonner of his dreams was out of the question he settled for 'an outsize tank with a huge gun in it'. Tetrarch was nothing like that but its flying days would come.

Under Micklem, however, more serious things were afoot. At long last a really good cruiser tank seemed to be taking shape. The Cromwell, named perhaps for one of the few skilful commanders produced by the English cavalry, was to have a Rolls-Royce Meteor aero-engine and would be vastly more powerful than anything that had gone before. Martel would have been more than human had he not remembered his brushing-off a few years earlier over the Napier Lion engine. At last it was becoming accepted that, as with the Wright radial engine fitted to the Grants, there was nothing impossible about making a modern engine that would drive either aeroplane or tank. Meteor was only another name for the Spitfire's Merlin.

Though two full years were to pass before it saw battle, Cromwell was the White Hope from mid-1942 onwards. There is amongst the Tank Board papers a letter from General Macready to Sir George Usher dated 27 May that makes this clear: 'A hundred 6-pdr Cromwell tanks might well make all the difference between success or failure in a battle or even in a campaign.' He was perfectly right. In the following August Sir George had a row with Commander Micklem, then recently appointed Chairman of the Tank Board, and resigned. In his valediction he wrote: 'By resigning I have protested against a defective system which cannot provide the Army with its fighting requirements.' He told General Weeks that he ought to do the same. Weeks replied that nobody had the right to resign in wartime but four senior officials followed Usher. The Select Committee's

Report charged the War Office with 'lack of urgency' over cruiser production, implying that the Staff were quite happy to leave it to the Americans. The reply was an indignant denial but it conceded that 'there may have been an unfavourable general atmosphere created to some extent throughout industry and, for that matter, throughout the British forces by these various development troubles'. A rare example of War Office litotes. The fact remains that no Cromwell was to appear for a very long time. The reasons will presently be explained.

Cromwell or no Cromwell, it was to America that we should have to look for the next cruiser tanks and Pratt, promoted Major-General for the purpose, was appointed to liaise with the US authorities. He made one discovery which intrigued Martel and explained the odd arrangement by which the Grant carried its main armament on one side only. When British designers set about planning a tank they began with a mock-up of the fighting body. That done, the engineers were bidden to put it on tracks and insert an engine where it would not be in the way. The Americans, determined that, whatever faults it might have, their machine would work, began at the other end. First they built a chassis, then they fitted it out with a reliable engine, transmission and suspension; only when that was done did they turn to the fighting part. For Americans it was the gun, not the engine, for which a place had to be found where it would not interfere with the working of the machine. Hence the sponson. The Grant was awkward to manoeuvre but it seldom broke down. To begin with the Americans employed radial aircraft engines which were air-cooled and thus avoided a lot of complicated plumbing. They worked surprisingly well, even in the desert. When piston rings wore out, as they quickly did, it was no great matter to change the complete engine.

The first Sherman appeared in October, 1941. It was, of course, an American design but the hand of Pratt could be discerned. The placing of radio equipment in the turret rather than in the hull was the result of his suggestion, as was the 2″ smoke mortar. By the end of the war more Shermans had been made than all the other British and American models put together. All told some 50,000 were produced. Most of them came from the huge Detroit Factory set up by William S. Knudsen, the Chief of War Production.

The entry of America brought not merely an ally but a new enemy. As usual matters began disastrously. The 18th Division, intended to reinforce Auchinleck, was diverted to Singapore where it practically piled arms and marched into captivity. The small garrison of Burma received an accretion of strength early in February, 1942, with the arrival of the 7th Hussars and 2nd RTR, all with Stuarts. In the course of the next eleven weeks, during a long and thoroughly disagreeable retreat, every tank was lost, the last ones being destroyed by their crews before they were able to escape on foot across the Chindwin. There were few lessons in armoured warfare to be learned, only that the Stuarts were excellent little tanks, many of them having covered some 2,500 miles without a breakdown. It was very different from the desert. Nobody hated the Italians and Rommel was positively well-liked. In the course of his Jeb Stuart-style ride during 'Crusader' he had swept up to a Casualty Clearing Station and had stopped to chat with some of the patients. All of them reckoned him to be on the wrong side. No such warmth was ever felt about any Japanese – a vile enemy who could hardly be considered human.

The litany of disasters continued. There is an old army saying that to do nothing is to do something positively wrong. The Dieppe raid casts doubt upon the truth of this. Russia needed encouragement and the Canadians were chafing for something to do but this was hardly of assistance to either. It was a repetition of the plan for a landing on the Flanders coast, prepared in 1917 but abandoned. On that occasion, knowing that tanks would have to mount a sea wall, it had all been carefully worked out and appropriate equipment in the shape of wheeled ramps provided. This was not repeated at Dieppe. Apart from more heroism and more names to be carved on the War Memorials, it did nothing but furnish the Germans with a number of the latest Churchills with which they could play to their hearts' content. Russia was in sore need of relief for, as von Manstein put it, 'the whole front was tottering . . . and the German army crossed the Don on a broad front'. Dieppe was little for their comfort.

CHAPTER FOURTEEN
Much Ado About Rather Little

After the loss of Tobruk and the 'Gazala gallop', Mr Churchill had to suffer all the indignities vis-à-vis President Roosevelt of a school-boy waiting outside the headmaster's study. The President was magnanimous; 300 new Shermans, about to be handed over to the 1st US Armoured Division, should be taken from them and sent at once to the Middle East. Auchinleck could have used them in June, 1942. On the 24th he relieved Ritchie and took command of the Eighth Army once more. It was not before time.

Some ten months before the battle usually called First Alamein General Sir James Marshall-Cornwall, GOC British Troops Egypt, had been given a special job to do. With the 2nd South African and 5th Indian divisions at his disposal he was to build a Torres Vedras position between El Alamein and the Qattara Depression, a distance of about 40 miles. Colonel Ray, the South African CRE, was put in charge of the work largely because his sappers were miners from the Rand who knew all about explosives. Within a month they had blas-ted out of the limestone rock a chain of machine-gun posts and underground shelters. They were about to come in useful. Auchin-leck let Rommel have Mersa Matruh and established himself amongst the Springbok's works.

What followed was a battle much like those which had proved the best value to the British army for a long time past. The Duke had begun it at Bussaco and again at Waterloo; Kitchener had copied it at Omdurman. Haig had never had the opportunity. The plan was simple enough. Dig yourself in and force your enemy to attack on your ground. When he has had a good hammering move out and see him off. The Eighth Army was too worn out with lack of sleep to perform the whole play but Auchinleck managed the greater part of it. For the first time for far too long it was the voice of the guns that rose authoritatively over everything. Every piece, field and medium – and a medium battery has the fire-power of a cruiser – that the army could scrape together was put into action. The result was devastating. The Afrika Korps had never been hit like this before and it did not like it. Not content with giving them a hammering, Auchinleck spoofed Rommel as Marlborough at Ramillies had spoofed Villeroi, keeping his Germans dashing from one end of the front to the other. They were the only troops who mattered, for the Italians had had enough. The pursuit did not amount to much for the means were lacking and the armour in particular was on its last legs.

It was 'the Auk's' final appearance in the desert. His dismissal, of course, came from the Prime Minister but the driving force was General Smuts. The loss of his good division in Tobruk hurt terribly and he blamed Auchinleck squarely for it. Before the month of August was out a new Army commander had arrived. He was Hobart's brother-in-law, General Bernard Montgomery. Though it can hardly have seemed like it at the time, Auchinleck's removal from the desert and return to India was a service to the cause in more ways than one. He knew the Indian Army as did no other man and the task that awaited him, of making it fit to take on and beat the Japanese, could not have been carried out by any other, save only for Slim. And the need for Slim was not in Delhi.

An attempt had been made to produce an Indian Armoured Corps and a formation called the Indian Armoured Division was already in Iraq. It was, perhaps, not the arm of the service for which the Indian sepoy, by upbringing and tradition, was best suited, but the thing had to be done. Sooner or later a powerful and fairly modern army would have to go back into Burma and the British one was already feeling the shortage of manpower. The huge AA Command at home was becoming increasingly dependent on the girls of the ATS and the part-timers of the Home Guard. India must help itself.

It would not be an easy matter. The Indian Army was, as it rightly insisted, the biggest volunteer force in the world. Its best was the equal of any, but it had grown to such an extent that a large part had to be of lesser quality. The famous regiments of horse and foot were long established father-to-son family businesses, but, as Lord Kitchener had found long ago, they made up an aggregation of units rather than a modern army. There was no reserve organization; as gaps appeared in the ranks they were filled not by time-expired soldiers but by new young men. It was hard enough to keep the old regiments up to establishment. To raise a new corps of a completely different kind seemed near to impossible. When the Canadians began to raise an armoured formation they found their best crews from among the tractor drivers of the prairie provinces. The best of the English seemed to come from long-distance lorry drivers. Neither abounded among the martial races of India. Sikh taxi drivers were not quite the same thing.

Martel was sent there in October, 1942, to advise on what ought to be done. The start was not encouraging. The IAC training Centre at Lucknow housed some 2,000 men, but one glance was enough. These were not the kind the Corps needed. Contemporaneously with a great weeding out went an increase in pay for tank-men, from 18 rupees a month (about £1.25) to 33. Volunteers were sought from the RAC cadets at home to become the first new IAC officers and many old cavalry rissaldars and rissaldar-majors had to be found other jobs. For a newly-fledged subaltern to instruct English tank recruits is not the easiest thing in the world; to do the same to strangers in a strange tongue is harder still. As Martel observed, it had got to be done but it would take time. Most fortunately of this commodity there was plenty; there was little else, until he was able to secure some Valentines. These would serve well enough for now. The Japanese light tanks that had shown up in Burma were not formidable and a 2-pdr would do their business. Nor, as it seemed then, would any cry go up in the jungle for an infantry tank. There were plans for three armoured divisions, including the one in Iraq, plus three more army tank brigades, all on the UK model. The existing three armoured car regiments were encadred into a brigade so that they might train together and share common work-shop facilities, such as they were. When it became apparent that, as at home, the Navy and the Air Force had collared most of the trained technicians the plans had to be scaled down. An Armoured Fighting Vehicle School, run by RTR officers, was set up and did fine work. GHQ, India, was persuaded to take the matter seriously enough to set up an AFV Directorate and Martel left the country persuaded that, with ordinary luck, the Indian Army ought to have an efficient armoured corps in a year's time. It would take far longer to sort out the chaotic arrangements for spares and repairs, but the Home Army had little enough to boast about on that score.

Martel came home with much to think about. A quick visit to the Burma front in December, 1942, and the first days of 1943 had served to convince him that Eastern Army, as it was then called, was not tank-minded. The 150 Stuarts lost during the retreat had won golden opinions; many people said that but for their presence the army would have been destroyed. Their methods of work, however, had been forced upon them by circumstances and had not been of their choosing. Forcing Japanese road-blocks behind the retreating troops, carrying wounded and exhausted infantrymen wherever room could be found and serving as the only artillery available had been all very well, but tanks could do more than this.

At home there had been some changes. The private army had not actually gone public but some of its shares had changed hands. The change came with the army tank brigades, the heavy infantry of the new model. As they would be obliged to work closely with infantry of the traditional kind it no longer made sense for the armoured element once it had become a going concern to be under a commander with no authority over the unarmoured part. The armoured divisions at home (Guards, 6th, 9th, 11th and 42nd) would remain more or less as they were, but five infantry divisions would each absorb an army tank brigade as part of the divisional establishment. The Canadian Army, uninterested in deserts and with its eyes on Europe, preferred to stay as it was. Cloth-model exercises for senior commanders continued fairly regularly and a common doctrine for the RAC was worked out.

In June, 1942, a sensible move was made towards improving both quality and quantity of the army's weapons. Stern, you may remember, had furiously criticized a system by which the best civilian brains had been shut out of military affairs. By chance there was one man available with high credentials on both sides of the fence. Ronald Weeks was that rare creature, a captain of industry and a General of Territorials, a director of Pilkington's Glass and other important companies with DSO and MC ribbons on his jacket. His appointment as Deputy CIGS with responsibility for the structure and equipment of the Army was the work of P. J. Grigg and it was a most far-sighted one. Henceforth it would be Weeks who would have the last word about what the army needed and he could, and did, stand over the Ministry of Supply with a stick until it was delivered. To assist him he was given a research branch, various scientific advisers, seats on the Army Council and Supply Council and a number of Operational Research Groups to act as connecting files between the field army and the factories. The appointment was long overdue, but it made an immense difference. At last proper research by trained scientists was carried out both on our own weapons and captured ones. 'Weapons Development' became, under Weeks, an acceptable sub-department of the War Office and from then on the days of the 'dud' tank seemed to be over. At any rate until the existing ones had been used up.

Martel did not share P. J.'s enthusiasm for Weeks. 'In spite of the good work which he carried out the fact that he knew very little about tanks and lacked military knowledge were, of course, a great handicap over this work. Although we led the world in this type of heavy tank up to 1942, with our Matilda and Churchill tanks, we now fell right behind on this side. The appointment of a regular officer would have been far better.' Praise, however, came from 'one of the Corps Commanders concerned in the Overlord assault' – Grigg does not name him – and from General Montgomery who remarked that he doubted whether the War Office had ever sent an army overseas so well equipped as the one fighting now in Normandy. On tanks Martel, and quite a number of participants, took another view. It all centred on one matter. Whatever may have been produced, the army still had no battle tank; cruisers were not a substitute.

Though Martel knew nothing about it, a decision of a thoroughly bad kind had been taken and the Board's mistaken dogma accepted. It is set out in a letter to Stern bearing the date 11 September, 1942, over the signature of Oliver Lyttelton, then Minister of Production: 'The US Technical Mission under General Barnes plus our representative prohibit the use in the field of tanks weighing more than 40 tons.' The need, it seems, was for an 'all-purpose tank'. Though no such thing was ever likely to exist a Tank Design HQ was set up to produce plans. Stern, outraged, wrote to the Prime Minister setting out the absolute need for heavy machines. 'TOG is the only tank in sight carrying a 17-pdr and heavy face-hardened plate. A day is bound to come when once more there will be an urgent call for heavy assault tanks and then once more we shall fail. Imaginative planning has been sabotaged.' No reply appears in Stern's papers. D'Eyncourt added his weight, inquiring, 'How much treasure has been wasted in the manufacturing of thousands of Mk IV 'I' tanks?' (The first name for the Churchill.) The various Notes in the Appendices to his History of the Second War suggest that Mr Churchill was, for whatever reason, kept much in the dark about these important matters. For example there is a letter from Stern to Lord Weir, Chairman of the Tank Board, of 19 May, 1941, saying that, 'The Prime Minister wishes to have a 3″ AA 20-cwt gun mounted on some track'. Mr Churchill's wishes seem to have been disregarded. There is a further note dated a month later telling of a meeting at Fosters in Lincoln where it was announced that a number of Rolls-Royce Merlin engines had been made available for TOG. Nothing more is heard of it. With such a power unit TOG might have been developed into something serviceable.

Sir Albert Stern, the only hornet capable of stinging Martel's 'Powers that be' into producing a tank fit for use in the assault of prepared positions, had stung too often. On 4 November, 1941, Sir William Rootes, Chairman of the Supply Council at the Ministry, sent him a curt letter announcing that the Special Vehicles Development Committee had exhausted its usefulness and was disbanded. He received the answer that might have been expected: 'Twenty years have been lost in the development of tanks in England. Who are the authorities proposing to put in charge of tank development? A Mr Hopkins, without knowledge or experience of tanks.' Sir Albert warmed to his work: 'The Armoured Fighting Vehicle position, both as to design and production and even more as to planning is, in my opinion, appalling.' In this there was much truth, but the war had to go on. As for Mr C. J. W. Hopkins, MBE, Stern was being unkind. He was a naval constructor in d'Eyncourt's old Directorate at the Admiralty and knew all there was to know about landing craft. In his capacity of Head of a Tank Board sub-committee he designed an amphibious tank. Commander Micklem, late RN, called it a waste of time and it was dismissed out of hand in April, 1941. Shortly afterwards Mr Hopkins bowed out from the Board and from history.

Along with better weapons for the field army went better leaders. The Corps Commanders in the desert had suffered the misfortunes that afflict most British generals unlucky enough to hold high commands early in a war. None of them were armoured men either by training or hastily acquired experience. The French in the 19th century had the expression *'un bon Général d'Afrique'* to describe a man good enough to chase Abd-el-Kader on a camel but not fit to take on Roon or Moltke. The British Army had produced a number of such *bons Généraux* and they had failed. At last there were men at hand who could take over from them. Two of Martel's armoured divisional commanders were given steps up and sent to try their hand against

Rommel. Oliver Leese gave up his Guards Armoured Division and took over 30 Corps: Brian Horrocks, CO of the 2nd Middlesex on the way to Dunkirk, relinquished the 6th for 13 Corps. The diggers in the grave-yards of Generals' reputations in the desert still had vacancies but for neither of these. Of deserts they knew little or nothing but they had seen service in France, learned the lessons of that inglorious but instructive campaign and had been working at it ever since.

CHAPTER FIFTEEN
Last Round in the Arena

Posterity can learn much about an army from the work of cartoonists who knew it intimately and had the skill to put it on paper. Bruce Bairnsfather's 'Old Bill' was the archetype of the men who had served Sir Douglas Haig. Everybody who had been there knew him; 'Old Bill' was utterly genuine, the embodiment of the Regular Army that had almost been wiped out at Ypres. Bairnsfather, of course, drew officers, frequently visiting Cox's Bank and being told that they were overdrawn. There was, however, no commissioned equivalent who appeared regularly. It was different with the Eighth Army. Jon's 'Two Types' were as recognizable to their contemporaries as ever 'Old Bill' had been and it is not surprising that one of them should have been a tankman. The Fair Type, with his beret, flowing moustache, corduroy trousers and the sambhur-skin boots known as 'brothel creepers' – not that there were any brothels to creep in – was just as familiar. The tank was no longer an oddity; it was part of the landscape.

When Alexander and Montgomery arrived the army of the Two Types was down on its luck. Spring might have been in the air but its first days, coming at the end of a bitter winter, leave men drained of their vitality. Rommel had become a cult figure, much as du Guesclin had been to the Black Prince's men. The joke about the garbled signal from the SAS, 'FOR ROMMEL CAPTURED READ CAMEL RUPTURED', had an uncommonly long run. Things were, however, on the up grade. The Shermans would level the quality of tanks and the 6-pdr gun, whether in a Crusader or on the ground, would make a world of difference. Only the artillery remained as it had been, towed by 'Quads' which carried no armour and were reckoned highly combustible. It is no disparagement of General Montgomery to point out that his army had riches far beyond those of his predecessors.

The two Corps which made up the army, 13th and 30th, had changed places, 30 Corps now being the pivot on the north end, and 13, with most of the armour, lying to the south. A new formation, 10 Corps, had arrived from Palestine, but its debut had not been happy. On 25 March, at Mersa Matruh, it had been surrounded and made its way back to the Alamein position as best it could. Montgomery re-fashioned it into an armoured corps, the first of its kind, under new management. Into it went the 1st, 8th and 10th Armoured Divisions, the 9th Armoured Brigade, recently formed out of the cavalry regiments in Palestine, and the New Zealand Division of two brigades. This was to be his thunderbolt. Until the Shermans arrived, however, it must remain a thunderbolt under instruction. 10 Corps would have no hand in the first of the forthcoming battles.

13 Corps was, as Horrocks says, 'right out in the desert'. His front was lightly held by the 7th Armoured Division, made up of 122 Crusaders and Stuarts in what was little more than an outpost zone. The solid part was the 2nd New Zealand Division. The armoured punch, to be hurled at Rommel as soon as the Afrika Korps had driven through 7th Armoured, was a single brigade of sixty Grants. 'ELH', they were called – 'England's Last Hope'. Whatever the paper strength might suggest only these were fit to engage the Panzers III and IV of the 15th and 21st Divisions with their long 50 mm and now 75 mm guns. Rommel was reckoned to have some 200 tanks, thirty-seven being Panzer IVs which could take on Grants at ranges far beyond their reach. Everything depended upon ELH. The most encouraging thing was that the Germans were known to be short of petrol.

Alam Halfa was Horrocks' battle. With help from a Staff that included Hobart's nephew, a practitioner of much experience, he concluded that in order not to run out of fuel Rommel would, after crossing the Ragil Depression, wheel north, near to the southwestern tip of the Alam Halfa ridge, rather than take the more attractive but longer route to the east and Cairo. He seemed in no particular hurry to come on and by the time he arrived, late on 30 August, the workshops had brought in sufficient repaired Grants to make up a total of ninety-two.

A set-piece, unhurried, defensive battle gives time for refinements. The Meinertzhagen gambit, leaving a misleading map to be captured amid much theatricality, left General von Thoma with details, suitably doctored, of where vehicles could or could not go. Opinion seems divided as to whether he fell for it. Be that as it may, Rommel did exactly what Horrocks wished him to do. After halting his tanks for a fill-up, he swung off on a course that took his armour hard by the aiming posts that had been put out to mark the ranges of each kind of anti-tank gun. 149 Valentines of the 23rd Armoured Brigade moved out as arranged to the north of Ruweisat ridge; this, as the Navy say, crossed Rommel's 'T'.

The heart of the battle was a point, called 102, near the tip of Alam Halfa ridge. There the ninety-odd ELHs were ensconced in comfortable hull-down positions with the 75 mm gunners waiting in the sunshine. The experience was new to the Afrika Korps. Not only field artillery and 6-pdrs were setting about them, but British tanks were being dangerous. At one point, where the Panzers had made a dent, the Scots Greys in their new Grants, galloped down on them but, unlike their ancestors, they rallied in a disciplined way when ordered. Horrocks had firm instructions not to get mauled and he was obeying them as far as he could.

It was 7 September before Montgomery called the battle off. The Grants still stood fast, refusing to be lured out. When his tank losses passed the hundred mark Rommel drew away, each of his vehicles towing at least two others. There was no serious pursuit and for good reasons. The Afrika Korps had left its mark, with 13 Corps taking 1750 casualties and having had sixty-seven tanks of its own put out of action. Of these thirty-one were Grants, mostly belonging to the 4th County of London Yeomanry, but thirteen were capable of repair. It could have been a great deal worse and during the course of the battle cheering news came in. The 300 Shermans so rudely snatched from the US Army had arrived and were being ungreased.

It would have been perfectly possible for Horrocks to have chased the Germans from Himeimat Hill where they sat comfortably protected by a British minefield and with a grandstand view of all that was going on in 13 Corps' southern end. Montgomery forbade it. He had no objection to the Germans observing and reporting upon what they saw. Rather the reverse. When he had finished making dumps and pipe-lines and other things they would, with luck, persuade Rommel that the next attack would be coming in the south. He could not be expected to realize that they were all dummies.

Horrocks' *guet-apens* had been a complete success, but it was still only a curtain-raiser as had been the first stages of Bussaco and Waterloo. The next act must find the British armour seeking out and destroying its German counterpart as it had never done before. This would certainly demand the cavalry spirit demonstrated to extreme lengths, but not by heroic charges into the middle of mine-fields. Mines, from being a kind of optional extra, had become one of the most important factors in a desert battle. Much study had gone into the laying and the clearing of them.

Mining in the desert was, inevitably, a most useful way of containing the activities of enemy armour. The Italians had begun it back in the Wavell days with a device known to the British army as the Thermos bomb. In appearance it resembled a large vacuum flask and it was a most intricate piece of work. Large numbers of them were assembled in a cylindrical container which was dropped from an aircraft. The container burst open on impact scattering the bombs over a wide area. Each was then activated by a small oil cylinder which ruptured upon hitting the ground releasing the oil into a second cylinder and thus activating the explosive charge. They were quite effective, but, being complicated and expensive, they dwindled away after a while. The conventional buried mines used to defend the fortified camps were much like the early British mine, being oblong in shape and touched off by any weight that might fall upon the rocking lid. Against armour they were not very effective. It was the Germans, with their ancient traditions of man-traps and spring-guns, who introduced the first really destructive affairs.

The earliest and most lethal was the Teller mine, used in large quantities by the Afrika Korps. This was a dumpy cylinder containing several pounds of explosive and was exploded by a detonator screwed into the top. The Teller was powerful enough to blow a Dingo armoured car to pieces and even against a tank it could be completely disabling. Fortunately for the Sappers, whose business it was to clear the fields of them, it needed a heavy weight to set it off. A man could walk through a minefield with impunity unless he had the misfortune to disturb an S-mine. This was a typically German device, bottle shaped and packed with several hundred ball-bearings. Once buried in the sand, only a triple prong showed above the surface. When this was touched two explosions followed; the first shot the bomb waist high and the second exploded it, blow-ing the victim to rags. The only defence was to drop flat as soon as the first charge went off. During the weeks of relative inactivity which Montgomery was using to improve training, Colonel Hecker, Rommel's Chief Engineer, put all his available labour to work. The best estimate is that nearly half a million mines were put down. Only 4% were S mines; the rest were mostly Tellers but much thickened up with Italian, French and British anti-tank mines, the last of these having been turned out in Egyptian factories. It was loathed by both sides as being by far the least reliable of them all. The fields were planned with ingenuity worthy of a better cause. Usually the maze began with a couple of lines without any markings on the ground; behind them were weapon pits and sangars that could hold small garrisons to keep the obstacles covered by fire. Behind them again there lay anything up to three or four miles of desert before the next collection was reached. Transverse belts made sure that intruders who had got through the first line were boxed in. Then came the main belts, complete with ingenious traps prominently displayed; drive round these and you would have a gun waiting for you. The whole business had been carefully worked out.

With the enormous amount of land covered it was obviously impracticable to think of any extensive clearing. The best that could be managed was to clear lanes or gaps of a standard size. It was fixed at 24 feet, enough for two tanks abreast. A School of Mine Clearance was established by Brigadier Kisch, the Chief Engineer of Eighth Army, to work out drills for this.

Among Sir Albert Stern's papers there is a letter written after the war by Lord Justice Cohen, Chairman of the Royal Commission on Awards to Inventors. In it he tells of how a South African Sapper named du Toit came up with a contraption he had designed for the purpose of destroying mines where they lay and which he demonstrated in model form to Auchinleck. It was to be mounted on the front of a tank and consisted of a number of lengths of chain whirled around a shaft which would beat the ground ahead and touch off any mine that might be there. Auchinleck was sufficiently taken by the idea to have du Toit sent to England to show his idea to Martel who was known to be reviving the tank-rollers that had been brought out at the end of 1918. The flail was obviously superior and a few were mounted on Matildas and sent to Montgomery.

The principal remover of mines, however, remained the unprotected Sapper. By the time of Alam Halfa a number of mine-detectors of the kind now sold in shops to treasure-seekers were in their hands. The inventors were two Polish officers. The machine, operated by a battery and looking like a Hoover, was whisked over the sand with a stethoscope attachment plugged into the users' ears. When it gave out a high pitched whine he called up his No 2 who placed a small wire cage over the mine. The next man unscrewed the detonator and dug it up.

The standard gap was eight yards wide and marked by T-shaped pickets. A quarter of a mile separated the gaps. When the right moment came bicycle lamps showing red and green were mounted on the pickets showing the tanks the safe path through. When possible mine-clearing was done at night but as often as not it had to be carried out by day and attracted both artillery and machine-gun fire. There are pleasanter jobs.

Mine-laying, on the British side, was exclusively Sapper business, though instruction was given at the School to Pioneer platoons and others sufficient for them to be able to extricate themselves should they find that they had wandered into danger. The British mine was an Egyptian-made improved version of the pre-war Mk 2 and less devastating than the Teller. Nevertheless it served its purpose well enough. The laying was always done under cover of darkness and called for considerable expertise. The Sapper officer's last job, an absolute one that could not be scamped, was to deliver an accurate map showing exactly where each new field was. One weakness was obvious, though nothing could be done about it. Gaps were wide enough to allow the passage of no more than a tank at a time. If a single one should become disabled before it had gone through then the gap was out of action. This was to have dire results. When the time should come for Montgomery to strike, everything would depend upon the speed with which his 10th Corps could be through and clear. The 88s and the long 75s mounted on Rommel's Mk IVs – 'a devil of gun' one RTR officer called it – would be the next obstacles to be overcome.

General Montgomery claims to have foreseen pretty clearly the shape that the battle from which came his title would take. This makes one matter perplexing. To pierce the minefields and clear paths for the infantry called for heavy tanks that could absorb punishment. Valentines and Matildas, designed long before such things were thought of, were altogether too frail for the purpose; some of them might get through but most were doomed before they started. There was a tank in existence that stood far more of a chance. The Churchill had already gone through three Marks and about half of the 4,000 originally ordered were in service. The latest version carried a 6-pdr and, with all its faults, the 40-tonner would have been able to offer more resistance to both mine and gun than either of its smaller sisters. The question poses itself as to why it was not there, save for a few sent to be tried out. More will appear about this later but the answer is tolerably certain. The Churchill, the only infantry tank that was not hopelessly obsolete, was distrusted. It had never overcome the original bad reputation that early models had earned and the General Staff simply dared not expose it to battle. Montgomery, whatever headdress he affected, was not really a tank man. As will appear later, he was known to have no interest in heavy machines; had he asked for Churchills his demand would certainly have been met. He made no such request and his thinking tallied with that of the War Office. When the first 4,000 had been delivered there were no plans for ordering any more. The Churchill was certainly a mule among tanks, lacking both past and future. For all that, it is fair to suppose that it could have tackled minefields and guns with more hope of getting through than attended upon either Matilda or Valentine.

Mines, as a general rule, knocked out tanks by breaking their tracks and suspension units. They were seldom fatal to the occupants. Fire was another matter. An inquiry held to find out why British tanks seemed to 'brew up' so easily produced an unexpected answer. It had nothing to do with the qualities of petrol or diesel fuel. The commonest cause of fire came from red-hot splinters penetrating the tank's ammunition and setting off the cordite. A lightly armoured storage bin went some way towards improving the crews' chances of survival.

The Second Battle of Alamein accorded with every classic military principle save only one. Economy of force, usually taken in the British service to mean that a boy can perfectly well do a man's job, was not conspicuous. The enemy forces were made up of eight infantry and four armoured divisions with a ration strength of some 96,000; about half of these were Germans. In tanks they possessed between 500 and 600 in about the same proportion, though the German element was slightly the bigger. Against these the Eighth Army fielded seven infantry divisions, most of them experienced and of the highest quality, three armoured divisions and seven armoured brigades, one of them commanded by Kenchington on his release from tank making. His Brigade, three inexperienced Regiments with a mixed collection of Grants, Shermans and

Matildas, was fairly typical of the whole, though it suffered more harshly than most. The armoured formations mustered ten RTR battalions, seven regiments of regular cavalry and the same number of English county Yeomanries. 30 Corps had its own tank brigade, three battalions of Valentines each under command of the infantry division with which it was working.

There was a small Churchill presence. Two samples had been sent to Auchinleck for evaluation at the end of 1941. The manner of their shipping did no credit to anybody. Both had been lashed down on an open well-deck, unlocked, ungreased and without so much as a tarpaulin to protect them. After three months at sea they arrived; the floors were awash with salt water, rust marks stretched up the walls for nine inches and the damage to the electrical gear, including the turret-operating mechanism, was immense. The radio in each case was ruined. As Auchinleck pointed out, no American tank was ever put aboard without every crevice being filled up with masking tape. Nobody from either the makers or the RAOC had looked at them, apart from a Staff Sergeant who noticed that one of them was not properly greased up but did nothing about it. A furious Prime Minister asked Mr Justice Singleton to investigate. When his report arrived, six months later, Mr Churchill sent a Minute to General Ismay: 'Alas, I am too busy to chase these rabbits as they deserve, and no one else will do anything.'

What happened to the pair during the next nine months is not clear. As they needed at least a fortnight's work before they could even run they were probably pushed to the back of the workshops where more urgent matters were demanding all the skilled labour available. At some point they were joined by four more; all would have been of the early and unsatisfactory Marks. Only once were they sent into battle, on 26 October, 1942. The troop was named 'Kingforce', after its commander, Major King. A first was knocked out immediately by a direct hit from an 88; the other two retired hurt with their guns disabled. One is said to have been knocked out by a friendly 6-pdr. It was hardly a fair test but no demand for more Churchills went up. Nor was any attempt made by the authorities in the UK to force them upon the Eighth Army. The tank enjoyed so bad a reputation that the General Staff had never wished to see them sent out in the first place. As we have the advantage of knowing what could not then have been known it is fair to speculate upon what a hundred or two Churchills might or might not have achieved. But it can never be more than speculation. The improved models of late

1942 with their 6-pdrs ought to have justified themselves. The last arrived Crusaders mounted the 6-pdr but the majority still carried only the 2-pdr which was now reckoned a pop-gun and had been supplied to infantry battalions. It was rather like Arras again. The fast, vulnerable cruiser carried the punch; the better-armoured infantry tank had hardly any.

All told, the army contained 1114 tanks of one kind or another with 434 of the best being the fist of 10 Corps. The ones that mattered were the 287 Shermans and 128 Grants. With them, for the first time, worked the self-propelled guns. To many old hands it seemed that Hobart's Royal Tank Artillery had arrived, for the 75s of the American machines were really field pieces and the track-mounted 105s of 11th RHA (HAC) were unarguably medium artillery. These last went by the name of 'Priests', following the curious nomenclature begun by 121st Field Regiment: their Valentine-mounted 25-pdrs, a makeshift of limited value, were known by the strange name of 'Bishops'. The Priest was an excellent equipment; it could not display all its virtuosity during its debut because the crews had hardly seen it before going into action. And US artillery techniques were still based upon what the French had taught them in 1918 the language was different from that of Larkhill, with 'mils' instead of degrees and other things that only a gunner could explain. As another example of how the army was coalescing behind its armour, the Scorpions used at Alamein, ex-Matildas, were driven by volunteer crews from the RE.

Ancillaries for the fighting machines now existed as never before. Six Transporter Companies brought new and repaired tanks right into the battle zone. Further back the REME, still just forming and not yet in the Army List, were putting themselves together from picked mechanics belonging to the RASC, the RAOC and a few from the RE. They could do everything for a tank except build one. Co-ordinating them all was the Tank Reorganization Group, whose business it was to bring tanks from the dockside to whatever place, including the battle area, happened to be calling for them. There were also the oddities. The 8th Armoured Division had never been properly formed; its HQ was sent to Horrocks in order to keep up a flow of spoof signal traffic for the benefit of 21st Panzer; in this it worked very well. Also in 13 Corps area were two other small and unusual units. 124th RTR was in charge of the dummy tanks; the 211th Field Park Company RE, not normally regarded as shock troops, furnished a device of their own invention, the Snail. It was an ordinary 3-ton lorry with its engine doctored so as to leave a trail of diesel oil behind it. This showed up beautifully in the moonlight and served to mark the lanes cleared by Sappers through the mine-fields. Because men need to eat and drink and feed their guns and vehicles, armies working in the desert are limited in size. To satisfy the needs of Montgomery's men and their machinery, thirty-six General Transport Companies RASC, with a load-carrying capacity of more than 10,000 tons shuttled between railhead and the forward area. In the wings, additional to all these and waiting for a job that never came, was a Brigade of Fuller's tank-mounted search-lights. Their contribution was to furnish the three Matildas that carried du Toit's mine-clearing flail.

One principle of war that was respected and gave due reward was surprise. Though it was obvious that attack was imminent and any almanack could have given the date of the full moon, Rommel took off for Berlin and did not return until 25 October. His locum, General von Stumme, displayed virtuosity if little else in trying to hold a 40-mile front by spreading his formations thinly along its entire length. The minefields between him and Montgomery were formidable indeed, but they could not be kept permanently covered by fire.

The battle began many days before the first soldier made a move. Rommel, as was known, was living mainly upon the spoils of Tobruk and his petrol was running low. The Navy and the RAF kept it so. For a fortnight, beginning on 9 October, bombers went for his airfields, dumps, transport, batteries and minefields and harried his Italian ports. Fighter planes based in Egypt cleaned the sky of the Luftwaffe and the Italian Air Force. That done, it was the turn of the Royal Regiment. For the first time since Haig's day 1,000 guns lifted up their voices in chorus; a desert moon made Fuller's lights unnecessary and after a 20-minute pounding the assault troops moved out at 10 pm. This time the leaders were infantry, with, hard on their heels, small parties of Sappers whose task was to make straight the way through the minefields.

30 Corps in the north carried the heavy end. Its Divisions, made up of Australian, New Zealand and South African infantry, were probably the best in the world; the born-again 51st (Highland) was coming along well and had a score to pay off. By 7 am on 24 October, after a stiff fight, they held Miteira Ridge and waited while the gaps were made ready for the two armoured divisions, the 1st and 10th. Further to the south, Horrocks' 13 Corps had made little

headway and, by order, discontinued its attack. Horrocks' task was to keep the 21st Panzer Division on his front and out of mischief for as long as possible; this was the reason for the deception plan and it worked for a fair time. Once his infantry had stopped, the 7th Armoured Division, under Harding, was to go north and join the others. Montgomery had decided that the training of his troops was far from perfect and he wanted no tank v tank battles that could be avoided. Anti-tank guns, of which he had plenty, did that sort of thing better. The armoured formations should use the speed of their cruisers to cut in behind Rommel, straddle his supply lines, wreck his transport and, using their own guns and infantry, make ready to deal with the German armour when it came racing back.

General von Stumme was killed on 25 October at the crisis of the battle. Everything turned upon the quick making of paths through the minefields and this was not going according to plan. The 'Scorpions', du Toit's flailing chains mounted on surplus Matildas, constantly failed to arrive or, having done so, broke down shortly after they had started work. There was nothing like enough mine detectors and Sappers were reduced to prodding Teller mines with bayonets. Montgomery, urged on by Freyberg, ordered that priority be given to the northern gaps. Through these were to pass 10 Corps, under Lumsden. The two divisions – Briggs's 1st and Gatehouse's 10th – were commanded by experienced officers who were held in high respect, men quite as good as any German general. Their first attempt to burst through had ended in chaos, tanks, Sappers and infantry all jumbled together with each cursing the other roundly. Many tanks had been lost either on uncleared mines or by enemy anti-tank gunfire. The Sherwood Rangers alone lost sixteen, half Crusaders and half Grants, before they were called back. A mass of vehicles, armoured and unarmoured alike, milled around the eastern edge of the minefield. Dawn came up behind as the last of the tanks disengaged.

Things had gone no better in Horrocks's bailiwick. The 7th Armoured Division ran on to mines and yet more mines, some of them uncharted. Again infantry and tanks cursed each other, the former claiming that they had cleared lanes but still the tanks would not go through, and the latter observing that the infantry could neither read a map nor deal with anti-tank guns. Matters did not look conspicuously cheerful when the moment came for Montgomery to assert himself. When both Briggs and Gatehouse told their Corps Commander, Lumsden, that further advance was impossible he and Leese paid a joint visit to Army HQ in the early hours of 25 October. De Guingand, Montgomery's Chief of Staff, was worried enough to commit the sacrilege of waking the Army Commander. Montgomery spoke quietly but firmly. Far from calling anything off, the operation would proceed as planned. There followed a broad hint that any commander who hesitated would be replaced on the spot. None of the distinguished officers concerned would have been influenced by threats. They were disciplined men and they obeyed orders.

A week of hard slogging followed of which there are plenty of descriptions available. For the purposes of this book there is no need to follow it in detail. It was not until just after dawn on 2 November that Horrocks's Intelligence Officer came running to his caravan to announce that the leading troops were through and that the Royals and the 4th South African Armoured Car Regiment were having a wonderful time shooting up streams of transport heading westward.

It had been a testing period for the tanks and it was not over. At about the same time as Horrocks was receiving his news the biggest tank battle yet seen in the desert was coming to its climax. The 9th Armoured Brigade had been made a part of the 2nd New Zealand Division in order to try out Martel's new organization. In practice it had been employed in much the same way as usual. At dawn on 2 November, having been held up by Rommel's artillery and air, it found itself looking down the barrels of a screen of anti-tank guns on the Rahman track instead of being behind them. Before this had been taken in the Brigade was attacked by what remained of the German armour. In the fight that followed the guns of the Panzers and the 88s slaughtered eighty-seven tanks. Horrocks saw them later, all burnt out. The 9th Brigade, however, still fought on, knocking out several Germans and gaining time for the arrival of the 1st Armoured Division. The battle that followed, known as Tell el Aqqaqir, was expensive to both sides, but the Eighth Army could afford the loss. Next day the Afrika Korps limped away with twenty-four of their original ninety Panzers. The Italians, who never had a chance in their M 13s, sensibly took off away from the sunrise.

After some fighting in the south, mainly carried out by the 4th Indian Division, the pursuit began. Montgomery still mustered 600 tanks, the enemy about 100, eighty of them Italian.

It was not, of course, anything like an all-tank affair. At the end of the battle Horrocks went to seek out General Morshead whose 9th

Australian Division had not merely almost destroyed the German 16th Division but had also tied down the formidable 15th Panzer and 90th Light Divisions for a critical period, taking many casualties in the process. Morshead, known to his Diggers as 'Ming the Merciless', replied as only an Australian could: 'Thank you, General. The boys were interested.' It had indeed been an interesting battle. If great Powers have to fight each other there can be no better place than uninhabited deserts. No roads, rivers, forests, towns nor even what the Russian communiqués called 'inhabited localities' got in the way. Against the tank a simple weapon had proved deadly and stultifying. Whether mines would be as important in Europe remained an unanswered question, but much thought would have to be given to the problem. Had they been used in 1940 as they had been even in 1918 matters in France might have fallen out differently.

The Eighth Army set out for Tripoli and the rain began to fall, laying the dust in the arena. You will not need to be reminded that it is the Latin word for sand. It had provided a magnificent theatre for scenes of armoured warfare but the play was nearly over. In the battles to come the scenario would be very different.

A decision taken now came near to ruining the Allies' chances in Normandy. The Director-General of Artillery, Campbell Clarke, had sent to North Africa the first of his 17-pdr dual-purpose guns. The Army Commander was either not told of this or was unimpressed. When Colonel Blagden, a temporary adviser to the Tank Board, submitted a cable to the War Office Montgomery signed it. 'The 75mm gun is all we require.' No British-made tank could handle our answer to the 88. When it was almost too late the gun was put into some Shermans.

CHAPTER SIXTEEN

'Without Tools He is Nothing'
THOMAS CARLYLE

There are several groups of people who may fairly claim that, but for them, the war would have been lost. Fighter Command in 1940, Bomber Command subsequently and the Royal Navy from beginning to end could all make out convincing cases should they want to. A group, however, of which little is known in this country has every right to join them. A Russian engineer named Tsigankov, leader of a team at the Kharkov factory, designed the tank which saved his country and possibly the Allies.

The T 34, you will remember, was a Christie and the best of them. There was far more to it than a superior kind of suspension. To begin with it had a powerful diesel engine tailor-made for the purpose and not a mere adaptation of some other. It was rated at 500 bhp, nearly thrice that of the Matilda. Its armour was not merely thick but far more sensibly designed than anyone else's. From the first Bronze Age smiths onwards it had been tolerably obvious that a curved surface deflects missiles better than a flat one. The tank pioneers hardly needed to be told this but they had to use the materials available to them; this meant flat plates or nothing. The 1918 tanks had used them and won. Nobody in the following years would bother to look further. The tanks of 1939 were no improvement, as Stern bitterly remarked. Even the German designers of the pre-war years had not bothered themselves greatly on this score. Very possibly they felt it unnecessary.

The Russians took another view. Since before 1812 they had been over-invaded and each time had lost their natural advantages of space and snow because their enemies were better equipped than they. This time it would be different. The tanks they had sent to Spain had not caused much of a stir and the war with Finland had raised no eyebrows at the sight of any weapons in the Soviet armoury that looked like world-beaters. Not impossibly this was deliberate. The best Russian tanks were made for Russian conditions. The T 34, by mid-1941, had been modified by experience. It now had welded armour projecting over the tracks and keeping them as safe as ingenuity could manage. The tracks themselves were unusually wide, with small-pitched links and floating pins. Thus the T 34 could cross mud and snow impassable to anything else yet known. The whole tank was streamlined as the carapace of a tortoise is streamlined and shells that would have penetrated other tanks' armour of the same thickness merely ricocheted off. Then there was its gun. There was no nonsense about starting with a small weapon and working upwards. The T 34 began life with a long-barrelled 76.2, more powerful even than Rommel's long 75 and a year before it. The tank lacked refinements but it was strong, simple and reliable. The names of Engineers Koszkin and Morozov who helped with it deserve remembrance.

The first appearance of the T 34 had been in October, 1941, in the last stages of the battle for Moscow. A single brigade, crewed largely by instructors and students from the Kharkov Training School, had charged Guderian's 4th Panzer Division and shocked it. Guderian wrote of 'grievous casualties' and of 'the vast superiority of the T 34 to our tanks'. When it became plain that an entire Panzer Division had been practically destroyed by smaller numbers Guderian admitted that the Red Army now had tank superiority. But for the T 34 it is highly probable that Moscow would have gone under. The road to the Caucasus would have been open and beyond the Caucasus lay the Persian oil. With that captured or destroyed, it would be difficult to see how Britain could have continued in the war. The armies kept idle in Persia and Iraq could hardly have delayed the Germans for long. German engineers, as mentioned earlier, went furiously to work upon bigger and better tanks of their own. The Russians set about designing a T 34 with a gun almost as big as an 88. These activities took up much of the year between Guderian's discomfiture and the Battle of Alamein.

Back in the UK an army was pondering about how to invade Hitler's dominions, something that, with US partnership, was now a certainty. Martel still headed the RAC but he was by no means a dictator. There were always voices, sometimes loud ones, proclaiming that he was going about things in the wrong way. Hobart never disguised his feelings and Pile, though still Commander-in-Chief of AA Command, added his weight to the 'all-armoured' school. If that were not enough there was the problem of manpower. Events had shown that the planned number of armoured divisions and Army Tank Brigades simply could not be kept up. Nor was it merely an inability to raise more. It was proving impossible to keep in existence all those already raised. The 8th Armoured Division, in the Middle East, never became a reality and quietly ceased to exist. The 10th, after Alamein, was withdrawn to the Lebanon and dwindled. The 42nd, the ex-East Lancashire Division, lingered on until 1943 when it was disbanded. The 1st and 7th remained with the Eighth Army; all that was left at home was the Guards, the 6th, the 9th and 11th Armoured Divisions along with the five Army Tank Brigades. The intergration of these with infantry divisions, tried out by Montgomery with the 2nd New Zealand, had not worked and was abandoned.

On the matériel side Martel's visit to the desert had taught him useful things and he passed them on. The Valentine, for want of skirting-plates, suffered needless casualties by having its bogey-wheels shot away; neither it nor Matilda should now be exposed on a battlefield. Whatever question marks might hang over the Churchill it was upon this machine that slogging matches of the future must depend. It had shown up fairly well at Alamein. The one used as a HQ vehicle by a Brigade in the 7th Armoured Division had kept out everything fired at it most satisfactorily. The only casualty had fallen to an 88. The Churchill and the Cromwell – as strange a juxtaposition of names as Stuart and Grant – would be the tanks of the next campaigns along with those provided by the Americans. Churchill was ready by the autumn of 1942 but Cromwell was not. An interim model, the A 24 or Cavalier, had got to the pilot stage by January, 1942, merely to produce something better than the Crusader during the period when every Rolls Royce Meteor engine was needed by the RAF. When the flying service was glutted with them some might be spared for the designed A 27 which would bear the Cromwell name. Cavalier had little to commend it; the Liberty engine and Wilson epicyclic gear-box were still the 1917 models. The entire machine, of which 500 had been ordered, turned out to be even worse than Crusader in point of reliability. Once again the Ministry of Supply had furnished the army with a weapon that would be a danger only to our own side. The machine did not go into service. The Birmingham Carriage and Wagon Company was invited to take over Cromwell and agreed to do so. It was explained that they would probably have to wait a long time for Meteor engines and for the time being they might as well turn out something capable of using either the old or the new. The result, the A27L – for Liberty – was first called Cromwell 2 but later Centaur. The first of a total of 950 emerged at the end of 1942.

The General Staff was more angered at this than by almost anything else. They had been told that the Liberty-engined Centaur would be 'a very close second best to the Cromwell. So unreliable did it prove in operations at home that it has been condemned as a gun tank'. It took up 17% of all British tank output during 1943: the Churchill accounted for 15% only. A few Centaurs were provided with a turret containing a pair of 20 mm high-angle guns and were described as Anti-Aircraft tanks. They do not appear to have operated in that capacity. The last ninety or so were armed with the 95 mm howitzer and handed over to the Royal Marines who did not want them. This was the best the Ministry could do in response to a War Office demand that Crusader production be stopped because the Staff was 'under no illusions about it being obsolete and unacceptable'. When it became past argument that Centaur was 'inadequate' production was 'cut to a minimum'. Its story may as well be rounded off here although it means making a leap in time. 200 Crusaders were put into store with the idea that, when invasion came, they could be turned into armoured bulldozers. So badly were they prepared that when, early in 1944, the demand for their services came, each one needed several hundreds of hours work on it before being serviceable. To replace them 200 AA Centaurs were ordered to be converted because 'it will hold together the labour force at Nuffield Mechanization until Neptune and Tortoise is sufficiently [sic] to absorb the labour'. Neptune was a landing craft that never saw the sea; the story of Tortoise must wait its turn.

An extra anti-tank weapon had arrived by a devious route. In December, 1938, not long after Munich, a Czech arms manufacturer named Frantisek Janacek had turned up in England. He went at once to the BSA Company at Small Heath with whom he had had dealings before and explained that he and his father had been working on a new type of armour-piercing ammunition for the Czech army; now they were anxious that Britain and France should have it. BSA, under Mr Leek, knew Janacek's reputation and gave him the facilities he needed. On the evening before the Germans marched into the Janacek factory, an Englishman employed there – his name has not survived – packed the prototypes into suitcases and drove them in his own car to the British Legation from whence they were smuggled to London. He then went back to recover some missing drawings; these he drove out of the country, carefully timing his arrival at the frontier post to coincide with a broadcast of one of Hitler's more animating speeches to which the guards were dutifully listening. The War Office was uninterested but Mr Leek was favourably impressed. Some months later the Janacek projectile was fired from a specially adapted 2-pdr and 'whipped through armour-plating at a considerable range'. The shot had a band, or 'skirting', near the middle which was squeezed flat during its passage through an unrifled barrel. High velocity was thus obtained and, with a core of tungsten carbide, a material of great hardness, it would go through any known armour. Tungsten was hard to come by – the Germans when trying the same thing ran out of it – but the performance of the Janacek projectile was so impressive that, says the BSA historian, the Government set up special factories for it. By mid-1942 the weapon was being produced in quantity and designs were in hand for 6-pdr and 17-pdr versions. The converted 2-pdrs, with their new ingredient, were known as Littlejohn guns. Apart from obvious uses they provided the punch for the Tetrarch light tanks used by the airborne forces. The velocity, however, wore out barrels uncomfortably soon.

Planning for the North African landings began in July, 1942. They required a substantial part of Martel's armoured force plus a contribution from the US. The British element was made up of General Keightley's 6th Armoured Division – a mixture of Valentines and 6-pdr Crusaders – and two Army Tank Brigades, Grants and Churchills. These last were under suspended sentence; if they did not put up a better performance than anybody expected they would join Covenanter and the rest in the knacker's yard.

From the tank point of view the Tunisian campaign was most instructive. The country over which it was fought marked a kind of half-way house, for it was neither empty desert nor heavily built-up like mainland Europe. It began well enough; the French decided not to offer much resistance and soon accepted Admiral Darlan's orders to down tools. The three landings, American at Casablanca and Oran and a joint Anglo-American one at Algiers, began on 8 November and fighting ended, probably by chance, on the anniversary of Armistice Day. Then the Germans began to arrive, mostly by air and at a surprising rate. The real battle for Tunis began with the Allies caught off balance. Their first priority had been to snatch such airfields as they could and the transports were loaded with the light troops best fitted for such a task. Rain had begun to come down on the Eighth Army as it headed towards Tripoli, but it was a cooling shower beside the rain that fell on General Anderson's First. By Christmas, 1942, it was bogged down around Medjez el Bab, 30 miles south-west of Tunis. By mid-February, 1943, Rommel was in the Mareth Line facing east and a new army under von Arnim was looking in the opposite direction at Anderson.

Strategically the German situation was hopeless, but it was not the Wehrmacht's form to cower in bunkers and wait for the end. Patton, still far away, was the oldest tank practitioner still in the business, for he had commanded a battalion of Renault FT17s in the Argonne before most of the crews on either side had been born. General Fredendall lacked this experience and his troops were going into their first battle. As yet the US 1st Armored Division was not up to the style of the Afrika Korps and Rommel swept them off the Kasserine Pass without too much difficulty, knocking out 100 of their tanks in the process. Then he divided his force into two, one column making for First Army's communications at Thala and the other for Tebessa, the most likely junction with the advancing Eighth Army. It was his last throw. Once again it was the guns that did the most damage. Anderson had learned the painful lesson forced upon most British Generals of his day, that tanks were not invincible. This he repeated in his Christmas present list. He wanted, not the 11th Armoured Division, but another ordinary one; 17-pdrs and Vickers machine-guns; above all lots of Shermans since 'our existing tanks are tragically useless'. Montgomery took a different view. When Martel 'pressed hard to try to persuade him' to ask for Churchills as being just what he would need for his attack on the Mareth Line he refused; the cruisers would do perfectly well and in any event no infantry tank was any good against the kind of defences they had met at Alamein. Martel disagreed, saying that Churchills would have saved his old 50th Division a lot of casualties. Montgomery did not favour size and weight in an AFV. In a letter dated 17 January, 1946, the Commandant of the School of Tank Technology at Chertsey told Stern that 'I think the only opponent to the heavy assault tank is Monty himself'.

Stern, in his apologia for TOG, had pointed out long before that 'if extensive tank warfare continues it will be a design competition in the size and muzzle-velocity of the gun carried and also the defensive armouring'. The Germans were ahead in the competition and looked like staying there. Time's whirligig does bring about its revenges, though not very often. One of those rare occasions had arrived. The 36th Infantry Brigade, Territorials from Kent and Sussex, had been part of the 12th Division trounced by Rommel in France back in 1940. Resuscitated and refilled, it now formed part of the 78th Division in Tunisia. It was upon them, early in February, that there descended a dozen German tanks, two of them being of a size never seen before. This time the Brigade had something better than short Lee Enfields, and the Brigadier ('Swifty' Howlett of the Queen's Own Royal West Kents) had commanded a battalion at Doullens. He gave strict orders that no gun should open its mouth until he fired a Very light and this he withheld until the first monster was on his outpost line. The 6-pdrs opened up and five tanks, including the two Tigers, went down. One was dragged off by its friends and a Valentine was despatched to bring in the other. It was not man enough for the job and as it panted away a shell hit it fatally. Martel, hovering about to see what he could usefully learn, was soon on the spot. The corpse was far bigger than anything he had seen before, turning the scale at all of 60 tons, with a track of enormous width and a turret containing an 88 with an all-round traverse. The front had an armoured belt of 4 inches, the sides a thickness of 2½ and the turret something over 3. In spite of all that the 6-pdrs had holed it in five places, three times in the flanks and twice in the turret. 36 Brigade was not dissatisfied.

The Tiger, in fact, was not a new Russian-inspired tank as the Panther had been. It had begun life in 1937 when the Henschel company had been ordered to try its hand at making a machine in the 30-ton class as a possible successor to the Pz IV. The first prototype, called DWI – Durchbruchswagen, or 'breakthrough vehicle' – had appeared at the time of Munich but had been set aside to make room for something even bigger, a 65-tonner with the factory name of VK6501. This too was soon dropped and DWI resuscitated in a slightly larger form. There were several variants on the theme turned out in ones and twos by other factories before, in August, 1942, Hitler personally gave the prize to the final Henschel design. It turned the scale at about 55 tons and during the next two years about 1350 of them went into service. On its first public appearance it was far and away the most powerful weapon of its kind anywhere.

The Churchills, whatever Anderson might say, had done better than anyone had dared to expect. During Rommel's attack after Kasserine nine of them belonging to 25 Brigade had knocked out four Germans for the price of one. The cruisers of the 6th Armoured Division had fared less well. Anderson's Christmas present of Shermans had arrived more or less simultaneously with the Panzers and the crews were only just beginning to get their measure when they were pitchforked into a tank v tank battle. 'It was a great handicap to them,' wrote Martel. 'Taken as a whole, the troops did well under very difficult circumstances and the result was a great relief to everyone.' As praise it sounds limited.

General von Arnim, successor to Rommel who had gone home sick, became 'un bon Général d'Afrique' in his turn, hurling packets of twenty or thirty tanks at Montgomery's guns without any serious artillery plan to help them on their way. The British infantry, now equipped with a platoon of 6-pdrs to a battalion, were almost honorary gunners themselves and accounted for fifty-two. The quality of air support had also much improved. Before the Mareth battle the Allied air forces had kept at a respectable height, fighting the German aircraft and dropping bombs that did less harm than was hoped. Air Marshal Broadhurst changed all that, ordering his pilots to come in low and to go for the tanks. From then onwards the tanks' principal enemy came through the roof.

How Montgomery circumvented the Mareth Line is a story told in many books and does not call for repetition. Martel wrote of it with bitterness, again reminding that if only the Churchills had been there, as they could have been, his beloved Geordies might have broken through at the eastern end and would certainly have suffered far fewer casualties. Be that as it may, the 1st Armoured Division, carried 60 miles through the night on transporters, swept through in clouds of dust to El Hamma and von Arnim withdrew to his last line of defence. There were still some six weeks of hard fighting ahead for both Armies before the end came. The 6th Armoured division demonstrated how well it had been trained by a spectacular break-through from the Tunis direction towards Hammamet, driving completely behind the enemy position and denying them a chance to make any stand across the neck of the Cape Bon peninsula. Three days later General Alexander was able to report to the Prime Minister that the King's enemies in North Africa had been eliminated from the war.

Like all campaigns, it had its lessons. With the coming of the Sherman the Allies had, at last, a decent cruiser tank, though there was still much room for improvement. It was on the subject of infantry tanks that opinions differed, sometimes vehemently. The Churchill had a good cross-country capacity and could fight its way into most places. Its armour would keep out 50 mm shells but the 88 was death to it. To deal with these big guns was the job of other arms but it was surely not technically impossible to build something that would stand some chance of survival against them. Whether it was worth the effort of building Tigers of our own was highly arguable and was duly argued. Martel was still pressing for something of the kind but all we had either *in esse* or *in posse* was TOG 2.

He returned home in mid-February with no job to do. During his spell in India and Burma the appointment of Commander RAC had been abolished. All that remained was an Adviser at GHQ Home Forces, an appointment of Major-General's rank; it was given to the sometime GOC 30 Corps, General Norrie. Martel was unemployed. In April, 1943, a task was found for which he had unique qualifications. General Martel went back to Russia as Head of the Military Mission. It must have felt like banishment to the saltmines with so much yet to be done at home, but Martel had all the soldierly virtues and made no complaint beyond remarking that 'it was not a very attractive post'. With him out of the way, and saddled unfairly with much of the blame for the useless tanks, power in all matters pertaining to armour went to General Alan Brooke. It also gave the chance of a last fling to Martel's professional opponent. Just before he left for the East he learned that General Hobart, relieved of command of the 11th Armoured Division on grounds of age and health, was promptly given a new command. On the face of it the 79th Armoured Division was just one more formation of a kind now familiar. In fact it was nothing of the kind. Hobart's task, in which he delighted, was to study the ways in which tanks could break the Atlantic Wall. Compared to this the breaking of the Hindenburg Line would have been a simple affair. Whether it could be done at all was an open question. The only precedent, the failure at Dieppe, was hardly encouraging.

Tunisia saved the Churchill from the scrap-yard. It had never been all that highly regarded and production had been planned to end in the summer of 1943 after some 4,000 had been made. The good reports that came back from Anderson after the last battles went to the War Cabinet, which decided to order another 1,000. A proportion was to be made with thicker armour, whatever the cost in speed, and efforts were to be made to up-gun it by putting in either a 75 or a 95 mm howitzer. In time both versions appeared.

The end of the campaigns in Africa also ended a definite and important period in the development of armoured warfare. The desert battles had been, in the main, affairs of tank v tank and for this work the weapon needed was a gun of good armour-piercing ability. Then, in the words of the War Office, 'As the Germans developed their vast resources of anti-tank defences in North Africa came the need for mounting in our tanks a powerful HE weapon to subjugate the anti-tank defences.' This is a matter of first importance and explains much. After North Africa British doctrine on the employment of armoured forces came closer than before to the American dogmas. It was not the job of a tank to fight another tank; therefore, this truth being accepted, it no longer needed a tank-smashing gun of its own. Paper and performance do not always tally. In July, 1942, during Auchinleck's last days, the War Office had asked the Ministry to investigate the possibility of mounting a 17-pdr in the Sherman. Almost by return came the usual *non possumus*. A year later the request was repeated; this time ways of doing the thing had, apparently, been found. An order was placed for 2,000 Shermans – the much sought after Firefly of 1944 – to be so equipped. What happened is unclear; the only certainty is that the order was never carried out.

Common justice to that much abused body the General Staff demands mention of a circumstance that could be repeated regularly on every few pages from now onwards. No sooner had the invasion scare passed and the United States come into the war than all went into reverse and, in the words of the War Office reply to the Select Committee, 'successive invasion dates were held up to the General Staff as their beacon light'. Each time, inevitably, the cry went up that lots of tanks must be ready, with trained and experienced crews, to embark for whatever part of the coast of Europe happened for the moment to be in favour. Add to that, 'The Ministry of Supply has laid down from time to time the necessity of keeping obsolescent types of tank in production in order to preserve manufacturing capacity' and you may feel that the soldiers merit a little sympathy. That said, one still remembers that the big German tanks could slaughter any British or American one from a safe distance and that nothing useful was being done to redress the balance.

Everybody had a finger in this particular pie. In April, 1943, a

General Staff requirement was submitted to the Cabinet; it laid down that 60% of tanks should be armed with a 75 or similar gun that would fire an HE shell and still retain a reasonable anti-tank performance. At a meeting of the Defence Committee (Supply) on the 20th of the same month Lord Cherwell attacked the present Mark of 75 as being inadequate for either purpose. The Prime Minister agreed that he remained unconvinced and wanted to know when the new, long-barrelled, high-velocity model would be available. Nobody could tell him. A further meeting took place in May when it was agreed that 30% of all tanks should be converted to the 75 and the proportion of close support machines with the 95 mm howitzer should go up from ten to twenty. The HV 75 must be hurried along. Thus, apart from any 17-pdr Shermans that might pop up, no tank existed after four years at war that was fit to go into a tank battle. It is hard to find any excuse. Tiger no longer held any secrets. Not only were the Tunisian corpses available for inspection, in Sicily another specimen was captured wholly undamaged. Officially the Tiger was disparaged. The paper called 'German and British Tank Armament Policy' insists that 'British users would not accept ... the cramped fighting space which the Germans and Russians appear to accept'. One may question how far tank crews would have agreed with this. That apart, its gun was too long and badly balanced. Nobody in high places feared the Tiger. That was the business of men in the ranks. Nobody had the heart to remind the Ministry of what it had said (in a note to General Macready) as long ago as September, 1941: 'By June, 1943, we ought to be manufacturing tanks considerably superior to the Mk IV Infantry and Mk VII Cruisers carrying, say, 3" 17-pounders and with heavier armour.' Indeed they ought. What they had done appears in a pencilled note in the margin of the Tank Board Statement of Policy dated February, 1943. The text reads: 'Every endeavour will be made to improve the general reliability and working life of the Liberty engine.' The anonymous penciller commented: 'Have not been done in 3 years. What hope now?' The Board went on with a resolution 'To cause the appropriate authority to proceed with development of armoured aircraft'. It would not have been difficult to think of matters that pressed harder. Rival Government Departments dote on motes and beams.

In a tale of such failure to provide the Army's needs it is as impossible as it is pointless to seek scapegoats. The Board, on 19 February, 1943, laid down that 'a weapon of the 17-pdr SP gun on a Valentine or Vanguard (an improved Valentine) should be designed with a view to going into production in place of the Valentine or Vanguard tank as soon as possible'. Within days the War Office asserted that it needed no assault tanks at present but it could use some Valentines as SP artillery. Vickers made some hundreds of them, under the name of Archer. As a tank-destroyer it had its limitations since the gun was so long in proportion to the chassis that it had to be installed pointing backwards. This, at least, kept the driver alert. If he stayed in his seat when it fired the recoil would decapitate him. Though no substitute for the Firefly, the Archer had its uses.

Notwithstanding that the Defence Committee had laid it down that no research or development should take place in 1942 that could not produce something serviceable in 1944 work of a sort went on. The General Staff, insisting that development 'should be pressed forward with all urgency', gave a clear call for what the army needed: 'a definite requirement for at least a proportion of super-heavy tanks with powerful armament'. Speed was not of first importance. 15 mph on roads and 9 across country would serve. TOG, which might have been made to fill the bill, was 'not suitable for adoption'. 200 Churchills were to be given heavier armour and Vauxhall were put to work on a super-Churchill. It emerged just too late for the war, under the name of Black Prince – a slow 50-ton machine with a 17-pdr. By then it was out-dated by the Comet and its successor and only six were made. The survivor stands, with other monuments, in the RAC Museum. To confuse students further, the name Black Prince was also given to a proposed radio-controlled tank – the kind of thing proposed by General Birch in the '30s – that never saw the light of day. Vickers were set to work upon bigger and better Valentines, under the names of Valiant and Vanguard.

In spite of the fact that the improvements in enemy equipment had made them little better than coffin-ships, the Matildas and Valentines still came out of the factories. Production of the former continued until August, 1943, by which date just under 3,000 had gone into service. Valentine had an even longer run. The last of the 8,275 made emerged in June, 1944, just before D-day. It is hard to find any justification for such wasted labour. They should have been scrapped long before.

There remained one demonstration of how British designers, should they feel so disposed, could think big once the 40-ton rule had been quietly dropped. Sir Miles Thomas, of Nuffield Mechanization, started it all off. In a letter of 6 August, 1943, to Commander Micklem, Chairman of the Tank Board, he raised again something that had been regularly under discussion since the previous April. There ought, surely, to be a small assault tank, very heavily armoured and carrying a 6-pdr. Micklem agreed, but the General Staff did not. What was wanted, said the War Office, was something very much bigger and carrying at least a 75. That, said Thomas, meant a completely different concept of vehicle, something with a weight of more than 65 tons, most of it armour. The Staff did not really want it but this was the moment when the Nuffield cruisers were going out of production and work was needed to keep the labour force together. All that was left to them was the unwanted landing craft called Neptune; they would gladly build an equally unwanted super-tank. It was given the name Tortoise. Hitler was personally designing something similar, with Porsche's aid, which they called 'Hummel' – 'Bumble Bee'. A Tortoise mock-up was put on show just before Christmas, 1943. General Briggs inspected it and observed that it could only be justified provided it could carry a 3' 7" AA gun; this had been proved effective as an A/T weapon but it was too big and awkward for regular use. To keep Nuffields happy he ordered a 'soft hull' mock-up. This emerged on 25 February, 1944, and, in Briggs's absence, an order was given for twenty-five Tortoises, to be delivered in September, 1945. That done, the Board went back to discussing the future of the unemployed light tank called Harry Hopkins.

It is hard to understand how sensible and experienced men could have been persuaded to take Tortoise seriously. It was of 76 tons weight – 4 tons less than TOG – and its 32 pdr gun (a modified 3.7) drooped when travelling on to a pair of crutches resembling those that hold up the booms of sailing boats. In speed Tortoise and TOG went neck and neck. Tortoise, however, had one characteristic all its own. TOG had a big, roomy turret that could accommodate any gun within reason and give no cause for complaint by crews as Germans and Russians were said to have voiced. Tortoise had no turret at all. To aim the great gun it was necessary to back and fill with the whole machine until Tortoise was pointed in the right direction. Fortunately it was as late in coming as it was graceless in design and the war was over before the first specimen appeared. Of the six made you may see the only survivor in Bovington's elephants' graveyard. No doubt producing it kept the Nuffield workers together. Perhaps they might have been more usefully employed in putting 17-pdr turrets on Shermans. The War Office ordered these a few days after Briggs's visit to the Tortoise mock-up. What happened is unclear; nothing like 2,000 Fireflies were available in June, 1944. Many participants called them the only tank worth having in Normandy. Tortoise was not the same thing. Nor was the Mk VIII Light Tank named Harry Hopkins. When the Board ordered 100 of these they were duly turned out; that done, they went into store. None was issued to units. That should hardly cause surprise. Nobody had any use for a small white elephant.

CHAPTER SEVENTEEN

Mountains and Rivers

Martel's banishment to Russia began on 4 April, 1943, with a very cold high-altitude flight to Moscow. The Foreign Office had advised him, unsurprisingly, that suavity was the key to getting along with our quasi-allies but Martel, who had done course and distance before, was unpersuaded. The British officers on the spot gave counsel of a different kind. It was better to stand no nonsense.

There was something of a mystery, still unresolved, about what had become of all the tanks sent to Russia in 1942 by way of Persia. The best figures available show that 5,238 had gone from the US, 4,260 from the UK and 1,220 from Canada. Most of them, that is to say all but Valentines and Shermans, had been rejected as unfit for combat; one cannot blame the Russians too much had they regarded the Matildas and Crusaders as having been specially built as part of an Imperialist plot to do down the Red Army. Martel had audience both of Stalin and Marshal Vassiliesky which seem to have gone well enough. He was, at any rate, promised a battlefield tour early in May; when he returned they would meet again. The tour began with a visit to GHQ of the 1st Guards Army. The Army Commander, without visible reluctance, showed the party that half of the operations map that covered the enemy dispositions. Martel asked civilly through the interpreter to be shown where the Russian army was. That brought a flat refusal. Such things were never discussed. Martel, the once Combined Services welter-weight champion, either lost his temper or affected very convincingly to do so. Did the Russians imagine that an officer of his seniority had travelled so far merely to endure tomfoolery of this kind? The name of Stalin was mentioned. At that the covering of the half-map was ripped off and all became sweetness and light. It was well worth while for the Russians to cultivate Martel. For one thing he was able to hand out Intelligence reports, presumably based upon Ultra decrypts, which were of the greatest value once the first one had proved right. All the same one cannot avoid a suspicion that much was kept from the guests. Martel reckoned the Russians, though brave and hardy, to be second-rate in technique: 'One of our Middle East armies would have completely outclassed any army on either side on the Russian front.' He did, however, write with approval of the Russians organization for armoured formations and their employment in conjunction with the unarmoured. Their thinking was much the same as his, but shortage of wheeled transport always handicapped them. The habit of using the heavy KV tanks in their proper role of infantry support in attacks on the strongest positions was plainly right; likewise the use of T34s either on the flanks or in assaults on the less strongly held places. A Russian Armoured Corps was, he found, about equal to a British Armoured Division: it comprehended some 200 tanks, three brigades of lorried infantry, a motorcycle and a reconnaissance battalion along with the usual complement of engineers, A/T guns, AA guns and signals. After their great victory at Stalingrad the Russians became, in Martel's view, far too pleased with themselves. When they spoke of attacking the score or so of German Panzer divisions still in being he told them brutally that they would be hit for six. The Russians were at first greatly affronted; Martel again explained that success in Africa had always come about by encouraging the adversary to waste his strength in the minefields and upon the guns before hurling oneself upon him. The Russians, calming down, explained that such talk was all very well, but during the two previous summers the Panzers had always broken through. Much sensible discussion followed and Martel's point seemed to be gained. When the mighty German attack at Kursk, on both sides of a salient, came on 5 July the northern horn broke against well-sited Russian defences. The gains in the south were hemmed in by strongly held 'haunches' (Martel's word) and the attack ended with failure and retreat. One must not exaggerate Martel's part in the affair, but it was far from negligible. His reward was to be recalled and replaced by a RAF officer who, in the nature of things, knew little or nothing about armoured warfare. His advice was not needed.

At almost exactly the same time, on 10 July, 1943, the Allies invaded Sicily. The combined forces of Britain, Canada and the US included some 600 tanks, every one of them a Sherman. This, once again, demonstrates the quality of War Office thinking during the design years. The Sherman was a cruiser, quite fast and with a shell-firing gun, but not heavily armoured, an indifferent performer on hills and with the habit of bursting into flames when hit. The Churchill was heavier, stronger and a better climber. Although designed for clearing ways for infantry, its present gun was useless for anything but driving holes in another tank. The German infantry were far better equipped than the British in the ways that mattered. The belt-fed Spandau was better than the magazine-fed Bren; the 4″ mortar was longer-reaching and heavier charged than our 3″; to the multi-barrelled Nebelwerfer we had no equivalent; even the 9 mm Schmeisser machine-pistol was far better made than the Sten. The infantry was going to need all the help it could get. In his interim report of 3 August General Alexander wrote that 'Progress may be slow but the country must be seen to be believed. Only a few mountain roads which pass through gorges and round cliffs, which are easily defended and more easily demolished.' The sands of the desert had grown cold. No more scores of tanks wheeling and charging like so many Arab *harkas* in a Beau Geste film or Mongol hordes. From now on it would be back to the twos and threes. Now it would be a matter of roads and bridges and rivers and railway lines; villages could be bombed into near-impassable obstacles and to mines would have to be added demolitions. Roads clinging to mountain sides can be quickly blasted away, leaving nothing behind. To all this, of course, was added the customary hindrances of guns and other tanks. Only overhead could things be said to have improved. The Mediterranean Air Force made up from the RAF, the SAAF and the USAAF had more than mere superiority. Its domination of the skies was now so near absolute that men no longer had to enquire whether a formation was 'ours' or 'theirs'. Once, not so very long before, the answer had been a foregone conclusion. By the summer of 1943 it was that again, but with a difference.

There were new arts for tankmen to learn as well as old ones to forget. For the first time tanks had to be loaded into the various kinds of landing craft and, after a sea-crossing not enjoyed by all, be driven off them on to a beach. This was seldom, if ever, unaccompanied by bomb and shell. There were rivers to be crossed. The tanks of 1919, or some of them, could have sailed over under their own power where no bridge existed but the art had been lost. Instead, Sappers had ingenious ploys. In a smallish river that did not run too fast they would shovel in earth enough to make what in Africa is called a 'drift'; that done, two layers of coconut matting topped with another of rabbit wire made a surprisingly effective crossing point. There is nothing that the Sappers cannot do.

All the same it was another reminder of the arts that had been forgotten. Twenty years or more earlier Major Martel, RE, as he then was, had demonstrated his 'stepping stone' bridge made out of crates resembling the cribs used in the breaking of the Hindenburg Line. They might have proved very useful.

The first Brigade ashore, the 231st from Malta, encountered little resistance. This was just as well. The parachute troops ordered to grab the Primasole bridge had been, for the most part, dropped too early by inexperienced American pilots and more had drowned than had landed. The few survivors seized their objective and waited for the tanks. When they arrived and began to clatter across, the 88s opened up. One by one the Shermans were knocked out and, in the words of the *Daily Telegraph*'s experienced correspondent Christopher Buckley, 'the first half-mile of road beyond the bridge became such a shambles of shattered vehicles and wounded and dying men as I have seldom seen in war'. He and the other correspondents had expected a tank battle in the Catania plain, and its 'openness and extreme flatness seemed to promise that our tanks would be able to operate with some freedom there, as they had done in the desert'. All concerned had failed to understand how little cover the anti-tank gun in skilled hands needs to do its work. Buckley tells of how for some days afterwards senior officers kept telling him that 'of course, this is not tank country'. He had witnessed almost every battle since the Spanish Civil War and was a better judge than most. If the assertion were true then nowhere in Western Europe was 'tank country'. This he refused to believe.

The demonstrable fact was that tanks alone were seldom likely to break through anything much. It was co-operation with the air, the guns and the foot that would produce results. The Durham Light Infantry, under cover of a regular barrage, finally did the job. The hardest nut of the whole campaign, the hill-town of Centuripe, was cracked by the 78th Division brought over specially from Tunisia for the operation. It was an old-fashioned battle which demanded all the skill and determination that county infantry regiments could produce. Sicily did nothing to inspire confidence in tanks among their own crews. 'The hardest, the bloodiest and above all the most disillusioning campaign in which the Brigade had served during the war' was the verdict of the 23rd Armoured Brigade. Some moral effect still remained. It is told again by Christopher Buckley: 'What a solidly comforting thing a tank, especially if it be a Sherman, is to the man on foot. I can well understand the argument that the presence of a few tanks in action again and again justifies itself even if the country is not really suitable for their employment. It justifies itself because of the fillip which it gives to the infantry. The feeling that "The tanks are there!" serves as an assurance to the men on the ground that they will not be speedily or easily overrun. And as our Shermans ground their way up the lane I felt that our landing could really be regarded as established.' This is an important point and nobody was better fitted than Buckley – writing after he had seen many landings – to make it. Only a few infantrymen at any one time saw the horror of mass 'brew-ups' as the guns took their toll. The mere fact that the tanks were there proved that the landing was no mere raid but a solid operation of much power. The Americans, with Kasserine as their equivalent of the 'Gazala Gallop' out of their systems, had likewise got back their confidence and Patton was teaching them their trade as they drove forward. But the desert days were gone for good and the dice were weighted against them. It was back to 1918, when Hugh Elles had spoken of them 'chipping in where they could'. That would be the pattern of the tanks' immediate future.

Tank tactics apart, 1918 was far away. The aspect presented by the new battlefield could hardly have been more different. No great swathes of country had been reduced to its primitive state; nor was the landscape dominated by monstrous belts of barbed wire. Wire was still in use, the Allies having given up the old double-apron fences for the more portable Dannert coils, but it was no longer ubiquitous. The main obstacle now was the all but invisible mine. The Teller and the S-mine were familiar and to them had now been added something that only a German could invent. The shoe mine, so small that it could hardly be spotted under a light covering, was designed simply to blow a man's foot off – which it did, most efficiently. Mere knowledge of their presence enforced caution. Nor was the Polish mine detector as reliable as before; the Germans had taken to putting wooden boxes around their infernal machines. Having thus deprecated one aspect of the German mentality, justice demands mention of another. The Italian Army had, for all practical purposes, bowed out of the war without taking a curtain call.

The Germans who remained fought like demons. The manner in which the men of the 1st Parachute Division and the Hermann Goering Division carried out their duties calls for high praise. Even the dimmest of them must have known in his heart that the cause was lost, but they set about the Allies' tanks with every weapon that came to hand. As no hand-held Panzerfaust had yet come into issue they rammed home-made Bangalore torpedoes under the tracks, though the Besas of the next tank could not miss. Snipers with telescopic sights picked off carelessly exposed heads and hands with all the skill of Conan Doyle's White Company. One way and another the 23rd Armoured Brigade lost twenty-five of its ninety-five Shermans. The total Allied loss came, Buckley says, to 103 against the German 260. Several of these were the dreaded Mk VI Tiger. It was a machine that blurred such distinction as remained between a tank and a self-propelled gun, for its 88 was factually a piece of medium artillery. The Tiger's best work was always carried out from a stationary position, preferably hull-down; once it started to move, in country such as this, it became a liability, for its bulk could not be hidden, it would have collapsed most bridges and, as Tunisia had shown, the 6-pdr could penetrate its skin. BSA, who made the Littlejohn projectile, insisted that it could do the same. Every tank now had many enemies. Mines under the floor, shells through the walls and, soon, air-launched rockets through the roof. In spite of all this many people in the Allied camp, like the Germans on meeting the T34, wanted Tigers of their own. Designers in both countries were bidden to think about it. What success they had will appear in due time.

The Sicilian campaign lasted exactly thirty-eight days. Most of the German troops escaped across the Straits of Messina in a small Dunkirk of their own, largely thanks to the mines and demolitions they left behind them. The last ones took off on 16 August. On 3 September the first elements of the British Army landed on the mainland of Europe across the same straits. The disembarkation, on a lovely day of high Italian summer, was not spoiled by any rough behaviour. 'I do not suppose that in the history of the world there has ever been a case of an invading army being met by its opponents on the shores of their native land with a touching of caps and requests to "Carry your bag, sir?"' The Eighth Army made tea on the beach, while men in green uniforms helped to unload the guns, tanks, petrol, stores and the rest. Anxious enquiries were made about the propriety of tipping them. Jon published a cartoon showing a poster of Mussolini replaced by one reading *'Viva Due Tipe'*.

Six days later the Fifth Army landed in the Bay of Salerno. Their welcome was less cordial.

CHAPTER EIGHTEEN

'The Doctrine of the Strenuous Life'

THEODORE ROOSEVELT, 1899

By the time of the Italian invasion armoured affairs at home had undergone a change. The great plans of the past for a dozen or so armoured divisions all operational at the same time had evaporated. The 1st was broken up after Mareth, the 10th packed off to Lebanon and the 42nd disbanded at home. The 6th, plus two Army Tank Brigades, was still in North Africa refitting. The 7th, with one armoured brigade and part of another, was in Italy. At home remained the Guards, 9th and 11th Armoured Divisions awaiting the last invasion of them all.

On the equipment side the Sherman was king and looked like remaining so. Valentines continued to be made until the Spring of 1944, but, apart from specialized armour, there was no longer a place for this good and well-liked machine. By the time production ceased Vickers had made 2,515 of its various Marks. The Company now had only two tanks in its catalogue – the 7-ton Tetrarch which, with its 2-pdr Littlejohn gun, was going to the airborne forces and the last of the light tanks, Harry Hopkins, that nobody wanted. The figures show an odd state of affairs. In 1941 British factories had turned out 4,841 tanks of all kinds. The German figure, given by Guderian in his book, was 2,875. In 1942 the figures were 8,611 against 5,673 and in 1943 7,476 against 11,897. For the first year a third of the UK output had come from Vickers; in 1942 this had dropped to a quarter. As Vickers made everything from battleships to leathercloth for seats this is hardly remarkable. What is remarkable is the difference between the numbers produced and those that saw battle. The Covenanters, Cavaliers and Centaurs had been a heavy self-inflicted wound. It is creditable to the motor industry, in alliance with the railway workshops, that they turned out so many. It was not their fault that the War Office did not know what it wanted and that designs were so often faulty. It was their fault, the fault of the factory management, that so much bad workmanship had been allowed to pass uncorrected. By mid-1943, however, better times were in store. The Cromwell was the best designed tank yet, its engine was a Rolls – prised from a grudging RAF – and its gun ought to have been better than that of the Sherman. The Grants and Lees that had become surplus to establishment were packed off East, some to the Indian Armoured Corps and the rest to Australia where desert battles against the Japanese seemed not impossible. 'Much wants more' is one of life's immutable laws. Having got Grants they all demanded Shermans. The US industry set itself out to oblige.

Though the British Army was completely dependent on America for its cruiser tanks, the Tank Board and industry had not entirely abandoned the struggle. It was firmly demanded of designers that any new ideas should not go beyond developing existing types: leaps into the dark would disorganize production. Thus the Cromwell was a development of the Crusader, and so of the A9 and all the other early failures. That does not mean that it was a bad design; on the contrary, it was rather a good one. The troubles came with its constituent parts. Difficulties over the proper engine for it have already been mentioned but they were only one chapter in the book. Whoever thought up the name of Cromwell laid himself open to Third Form humour about Ironsides, for these were the cause of much tribulation. General Macready had written a long letter about them back in May, 1942, to Sir George Usher, not long before his resignation. The first batch from the factories had been fairly good, but the second was a disgrace. The Consett Iron Works had supplied the armour; it was so bad that all tanks equipped with it had to be marked with a red triangle showing that they were unfit for battle. It would be less than fair to condemn the makers out of hand; Consett had never pretended to be an armour-plate specialist and had been unenthusiastic about taking on the job. Nevertheless, 'From the War Office point of view this situation is about as grave as anything could be.' Macready had still more to say: 'The Army at present possesses practically no reliable cruisers of British make. Hundreds of Covenanters now in service cannot, or will not, be modified for a very long time, whilst Crusaders though, we hope, improved owing to recent modifications, are still rather under a cloud. The Infantry tank situation is even worse as we have approximately 1,000 Churchills which cannot be sent abroad.'

Cromwell needed more than its proper engine and decent armour from established armourers. There remained the matter of a gun. The design and production of a new piece purpose built for the new tank was entrusted to Vickers and once again the Company came up with something good. The 77 mm was in fact a short 17-pdr, capable of firing both armour-piercing and HE projectiles but easier to handle in a confined space and with a higher rate of fire. There was, however, a snag. When attempts were made to marry up tank and gun it was discovered that the turret ring was 7″ too small to accept the weapon. Nothing could be done about it. The Cromwell was set aside to be re-equipped with the much smaller 75. This may sound like a mere adjustment but it was not. Troubles with the mounting delayed production by a full year.

As the urgent need was to hurry into service some sort of tank with a 17-pdr or something of equal power the Birmingham Carriage and Wagon Company were bidden to make a bigger Cromwell without loss of time. Three specimens were lengthened, the centre of the hull was widened and another pair of bogie wheels was added to take up the extra weight. Stothert & Pitt built a big turret for it, mounting a 17-pdr. The result was what might have been expected. The weight was too much for the suspension and the thickness of the armour had to be reduced. The turret, which gave the machine a hydrocephalic appearance, turned very slowly and could carry little ammunition. There was no means of water-proofing with the consequence that the tank could not get its feet wet during any possible landing. The A30, inaptly called the Challenger, had to be abandoned. Only the Sherman remained as a possible mount for the tank-killing gun.

While all this wasted effort was going on, reports began to come in about Cromwell's stable companion. 'We had taken courage and ventured to send the Churchills to battle. Two years had made it a fairly serviceable weapon.' It kept out the 50 mm and the long 75 but, in Italy, its armour was found inadequate and its cross-country performance was hardly better than that of the Sherman. Thus spoke the Report on AFVs in the Mediterranean Theatre. It can scarcely be exaggeration to say that without the products of American factories the war would have been lost.

The Indian Armoured Corps tends to be overshadowed by others who operated nearer home. It deserves better. Like all formations of its kind it had got off to the kind of sticky start inevitable under the rushes of war. Its tasks were very different from those of the others. Sicily may truthfully be described as 'not tank country' but it is Paradise, in the original sense, when compared with the Arakan and the Chindwin Hill Tracts. Thick jungle bounded by mountain ranges, chaungs (waterways) commonly fringed with mangrove swamp that is almost impassable even on foot and a complete lack of roads render armoured warfare hardly practicable. There is no need of an enemy. When one is present, and that enemy is Japanese, one may put it even more strongly. In Malaya and during the first Burma campaign the Japanese soldier had demonstrated his skill in attack. At Rathedaung, on the tip of the Mayu peninsula, he had shown that he needed little tuition in the building of defensive works. The 'bunker' that Fourteenth Army came to know rather well was made of heavy logs covered with 4 or 5 feet of earth and camouflaged so skilfully that it could hardly be identified even when one was standing on it. The place was unimportant but the Indian Army, dejected after its early defeats, needed a tonic. The Army Commander – it was still called Eastern Army and not yet Fourteenth – was General Irwin whose last appearance in the war had been with de Gaulle at Dakar. He despatched the 14th Indian Division, eight brigades of Indian troops and one of British, along with a troop of Valentines to chase the Japanese out. General Slim, though not involved in the planning, objected strongly to so small a tank force, arguing that 'The more you have the fewer you lose'. He was over-ruled. In the first attack, on Donbaik at the end of February, 1942, he was proved right. Every tank was knocked out by the Japanese artillery. The next attack, by unaided infantry, failed equally completely. So strong were the bunkers that the Japanese, quite deliberately, waited until the assailants were on top of them, whereupon they brought down all the power of their artillery. Inside the bunkers they were perfectly safe. The attackers were not and took many casualties. The Japanese, like Kitchener at Omdurman, moved into the attack while their enemy was still reeling. How Generals Slim and Lomax retrieved a potentially disastrous situation is outside the scope of this book. You may learn of it and, unless you know it already, will find the story told by Slim in his *Defeat into Victory* instructive. Suffice it that the Indian Armoured Corps was not heartened by its initiation into battle.

It is unfortunate that as one drives from Chartwell to London the first noticeable object, in Westerham, is a statue of General Wolfe brandishing his sword. Mr Churchill passed it on every journey. He greatly admired Wolfe and in this he did well. There is, however, more needed to be a dashing and ever-victorious General than swashbuckling and noisy behaviour. This Wolfe had; unfortunately General Wingate, who lacked some necessary ballast, seems to have reminded the Prime Minister of the Westerham figure. From this came some good but more evil. General Slim, probably the most accomplished professional the war produced and certainly one of the most attractive personalities, had much to put up with as a result. In August, 1943, he assumed command of the newly-formed Fourteenth Army. It had a front 700 miles long extending from the Chinese border to the Bay of Bengal. Before him lay a wide belt of jungle, hills running in places to a couple of thousand feet or more, without railways, roads or even decent maps. For half the year during the monsoon it is trackless, the climate is not delicious, and it is rich in bug-borne diseases. Like the desert it is a place where great wars may be fought without bothering civilians but it is emphatically not tank country. In the course of time Slim's army overcame all these things; but, as every member of it would agree, it could not have been done without him. For a long while to come this was going to be infantry work, aided by such guns and sappers as could be had and further aided by a first-rate air force, part RAF and part USAAF. The tanks continued to be based on Ranchi, mastering their equipment and making themselves ready for the day when they would go back. Under this modest ex-Gurkha they knew that, next time, they would not be set an impossible task. The Grants were welcome, but the IAC still wanted Shermans.

As Slim was settling down to his new task Alexander, perhaps his only peer, was watching the disembarkation at Salerno. It began on 9 September in a strength of four divisions, half British and half US. There were no obliging little men in green to help them unload. Instead there were large numbers of men in grey, plentifully equipped with artillery, waiting for them in a different frame of mind. As the first elements walked ashore the Panzers swept down on to the kind of target of which their gunners dreamt. This time they encountered something new to them. The guns of the Fleet, throwing shells of a size that few soldiers knew, roared out in salvoes that made the earth quake under them and filled the air with reboant, deafening noise. The RAF and USAAF joined in and, by degrees and under great pressure from the enemy, a bridgehead was

slowly built up. The Germans used their tanks imaginatively, sometimes pushing them down to within a couple of furlongs of the
water's edge. As they later acknowledged, it was naval gunfire rather
than anything else that prevented them from throwing the invaders
back into the Mediterranean. Sea power should never be under-
rated.

The 7th Armoured Division took four days to disembark and
drive clear of the beaches; the only crossings were by narrow lanes
which gave way under the tracks and caused the machines to belly.
Eventually, on 22 September, it moved off on a two-brigade front,
one on either side of Vesuvius, heading for the River Volturno. For
the first time on the mainland it encountered the kind of conditions
that tanks in Europe would have to expect for the rest of the war. It
became road-bound. The great number of unarmoured vehicles
carrying infantry, towing guns or loaded down with petrol, ammunition and everything else, formed traffic jams of the kind for which
a Stuka pilot would have sold his soul. Happily for the Allies Stukas
were now only a memory. As the process of dragging (pushing
would have been a better word) the red-hot rake of war up the Italian peninsula was not going to be done by a great armoured charge
the 22nd Armoured Brigade was sent home at the end of the year,
save for a single battalion. The other brigade, the 4th, joined the
Eighth Army near Brindisi early in October. The country there-
abouts was less than ideal for them. Craggy mountains run down
sharply into a narrow coastal plain greatly cut up by small but deep
streams. For the first time bulldozers came into use as progress
without them was close to impossible. Again, an enemy presence
was hardly needed.

The end of 1943 marked the lowest point of the fortunes of the
tank. A couple of months later General Pile was invited to luncheon
at Chequers where he found a gloomy Prime Minister. Mr Churchill
complained about Anzio – this was the occasion of the much-quoted
remark about having arranged to throw a wild cat behind the
German lines but all that had happened was that a deflated whale
floated gently on to the shore – though he accepted responsibility for
it; he complained that the troops from North Africa had had to go to
Italy as we lacked the ships to send them anywhere else; finally he
said that we had too much armour – tanks were finished. Pile, the
old Tank man, was having none of that. He explained matters carefully and accurately. Tanks were not doing well in Italy, but they
were absolutely necessary. Foot and guns could break into a pos-

ition, but, unless the armour was then pushed through, another line would promptly be formed and another behind that; which is exactly what had been happening and the situation for which the geography of Italy might have been designed. Mr Churchill was not persuaded, muttering something about the gun being the master of the tank. Burma and the Appenines between them seemed to have reduced armour to an expensive irrelevance.

Another voice was grumbling, though the words were different and came from the wilderness. Sir Albert Stern, that unwearying if one-idea'd man, produced at the end of 1943 a paper headed 'Tanks 1944'. It began uncompromisingly: 'England produced no up-to-date battleworthy fighting tank for use in 1943. The pre-war Valentine and Matilda were obsolete; Crusader, Cavalier and Centaur were all unreliable with out-of-date Liberty engines (1917) from the museum of the last war. Cromwell, proclaimed in September, 1942, by Sir James Grigg as the best tank in the world, had not yet passed its acceptance tests. Even if it did pass it was already out-of-date for 1944, let alone for 1945, so far as armour and armament were concerned. The Churchill, including the new model heavy one, was equally outdated in design and under-gunned. The turret space did not permit of adaptation to anything bigger. The 17-pdr was 'an excellent weapon for defence, but 1944/45 should see our Armies in attack and the guns for attack require HE against anti-tank defences'. All of this was true; whether Stern rightly identified the cause must be a matter of opinion. He put it down, once more, to the failure of Government to seek the guidance of his Committee whose developments were 'sabotaged at every turn and the Committee dismissed before its developments were complete'. Their prototype had been approved by the Tank Representative of the General Staff who had told them that it met exactly their future requirements. That done, the matter was dropped. 'It is common knowledge that the General Staff is highly dissatisfied with the design of the British tanks available for 1944.' Anti-Stern feeling obviously ran strongly within the Ministry. When Sir Andrew Duncan was asked whether any member of his Committee had been consulted during the search for a counter to the Tiger he had answered, 'I do not suppose they have been, unless it was appropriate that they should be'. This neither was nor was meant to be conciliatory. Stern saw in it not merely an insult but a breach of duty. 'When others had obviously failed it would not have been waste of time to investigate these experiments carried out by serious and successful men, well known for their imagination, foresight, energy and achievement.' This may have economized a little on modesty but there was truth in it. The Board, however, had become weary of his Cassandra style, over-looking the fact that Cassandra had always been right. There is a Minute dated 4 August, 1942, the one rejecting TOG, which suggests that Sir Albert be invited to see the latest prototypes 'in the hope that this might serve to allay his fears'. It adds nastily that 'A single individual clearly cannot have at his call the wide range of experience and facilities available to the Ministry of Supply'. A short examination by Stern of the Cromwell prototype as it was in August, 1942, might have given him the opportunity for a well-expressed rejoinder to this. It was the Ministry, with all its experience and facilities, that had designed and made the wrong-sized gun for Cromwell's turret, or the wrong-sized turret for Cromwell's gun. Nor was the Churchill, about to be dropped until Tunisia saved it, much of an advertisement either.

The paper makes another and important point. All cruiser tank production had been handed over to Nuffield Mechanization and its associated companies and 'each successive type has been a mechanical failure and at the same time out-of-date'. Tank production, he asserted, 'falls into the category of heavy engineering. Yet the great mistake has been made and is still being made in this country of putting this work under the control of the motor-car industry.' The justification for this appeared to be that 'a similar policy of employing the motor trade for Tank design has been adopted in America'. This was something about which Stern knew a great deal more than most men. For the last period of the Kaiser's War he had been Allied Commissioner charged with the co-ordination of tank business with the US Government and the Treaty under which this had been done was his work. Since then his banking experience had added much to his understanding of American industry. His condemnation was made with an authority that few men could match. 'It is a complete fallacy to compare our light motor-car industry with such giants of industrial engineering as General Motors or Chryslers of America. These great firms, with their output of many types of heavy engineering, has each an annual production far exceeding even the great Ford Motor Company.' The Nuffield consortium cannot be blamed for not being members of this league; the burden laid upon them was an unfair one. Battle tanks are not variations on the Morris Cowley.

In spite of all these things changes were coming, although it would be a long time before any improvement became evident. Commander Micklem, now controller of tank design, was better fitted for the task than had been any of his predecessors. On leaving the Navy in 1919 at the age of 28 he had joined Vickers and for some years past had been General Manager of the Elswick Works where the Company's tanks were made. The excellent machines that were to appear just as the war ended bore his hall-mark and it was not his fault that they were so long delayed. The pity of it is that he and Stern, with an age gap of a dozen years between them, did not work better together, for their minds were never far apart. When, in 1944, the Ministry at last opened a professional tank factory, converting one no longer needed for making guns, it was Micklem more than any other man who provided the necessary push. Stern, of course, had been calling in vain for such action since he was first press-ganged into the business. And in 1946 it was Sir Robert Micklem, then Chairman of Vickers-Armstrong, who followed up Sir Albert's idea and pioneered the building of huge oil-tankers. On his untimely death in 1952 Micklem was succeeded by Sir Ronald Weeks, the last of a distinguished line of ex-officers. Vickers was, and possibly still is, almost an honorary Government Department.

Whether the Prime Minister's pessimism was drawn from the CIGS or vice versa cannot be known, but General Brooke was of the same mind. When Martel came back from Russia in the Spring of 1944 he naturally sought audience. Accounts of what tanks had done in the East and might do in the West fell on stony ground. 'He (Brooke) replied that he did not agree with me. He considered that the power of the tank was on the wane, and that the anti-tank gun had the measure of the tank.' Martel's further and anxious enquiries showed him that, three months before the invasion was due, the official view of the General Staff exactly tallied with this. He sat down and wrote a long and closely-reasoned paper setting out why the forthcoming battles must be decided by the tank arm and justifying his conclusions by telling of his recent experiences among the monsters. A copy went to General Montgomery. 'He told me that he had not time to discuss (my notes) with me and that he really wanted no advice on how to use armoured forces.' One cannot but feel lack of enthusiasm for Montgomery in Martel's writings, though he was too well-mannered to say as much. Telling of the Cromwell, he remarks that 'at last we had our cruiser tank right', but adds that 'we had fallen back on the infantry tank side. Our hopes that experimental models with really thick armour, and well gunned, would be made, had not been fulfilled. The statements from General Montgomery that he wanted nothing but cruiser tanks or one type of capital tank had naturally carried much weight. Although other commanders did not agree with these views, the CIGS was not prepared to over-rule them. Little was done about this really heavy infantry tank.' As a force Martel was spent. No job was found for him and in 1945 he retired from the army. Nor did his misfortunes end there. After his death his *DNB* entry was written by Captain Liddell Hart.

The task of contriving the means to crack open Albert Speer's Atlantic Wall clearly demanded something more than deluges of ex-plosive followed by an attempt to land an army of the traditional kind. Dieppe had given lessons of the 'how not to' variety and a lot of thought would have to be put into positive ideas. The man chosen to design and make the tools by which the job might be done was Gen-eral Hobart. Though not universally loved there was much of Wolfe in him; certainly more than in some of the other radicals who hap-pened to catch Mr Churchill's eye. The task was not unworthy of his talents. The bulk of an invading force could hardly travel other than by ship. The tides on the French coast are, for some reason, faster and bigger than on the English. The beaches below their high-water marks would be wired and comprehensively mined. There would, in some places, be sea-walls to be scaled. Every potential landing-site would be covered by fire from everything between small-arms and medium artillery. Once the crust had been penetrated the in-vaders would find little for their comfort. The roads that they would have to use would be cratered and mined; every river and stream would have had its bridges demolished. Bombed towns and villages would form their own obstacles. There are factors obvious to any-body who devotes a few minutes thought to the matter. One is less obvious, though it should have occurred quickly to anybody with even a tourist's knowledge of Normandy. The bocage country con-sists of small fields with boundaries unchanged since remote an-tiquity; they are divided by hedges and, over the centuries, these have developed firm banks several feet high. No two seem to be on the same level. They are not, in the current jargon, 'user friendly' to tanks. On the other hand, seeing that to cross them a tank must rear up and expose its underparts, they are just what an anti-tank gunner needs.

In his address to the Commons about Anzio Mr Churchill told the story of a sailor who, having saved a boy from drowning, was accosted by his mother demanding to know what had been done

35. Tank Marines. A Centaur with distinctive markings

36. Another 'dud'. The Original Challenger

37. The champion that might have been. The Cromwell

38. Invasion planning. The first Straussler equipment of 1941

39. Invasion planning. Churchill and landing craft at Inverary

SHERMAN FIREFLY

40. The only tank worth having in Normandy. The Sherman Firefly

41. A private enterprise offering: The Vickers Tetrarch

42. Tetrarch loaded into a Hamilcar glider

43. Tetrarch in Russian service

44. Success at last! A pilot model of the Comet

45. The Comet in business

46. Misguided zeal. The 80-ton Tortoise

47. Some Friends. The Russian T34

48. The Russian JS3

49. Some enemies. The Tiger II

50. The Jagdtiger

51. Tiger, Panther and King Tiger in captivity

with his cap. To be querulous about the omission of some device for bank-crossing when other and less tractable problems had been overcome may seem ungracious. Perhaps it is, but much ill came of it.

Hobart's command was called the 79th Armoured Division, but this was no more than a name. In fact it resembled not so much a divison as a part of the British equivalent to the Todt Organization. Only the landing craft were not Hobart's business. These, in succession to Fisher's 'Beetles' of 1915, were the charge of Sir Roger Keyes and, later, of Lord Louis Mountbatten.

It was as early as March, 1943, that the work had started. In the beginning the nucleus was the Brigade equipped with Fuller's Canal Defence Lights for which no use had been found. Like so many similar devices, the CDL would probably work well given that it could choose its own conditions. The machines, viewed from the side, made fine targets; from above they led aircraft to them and mud splashed over the lights soon reduced their efficacy. They were a luxury that could not be afforded, but for the time being they were kept in existence. Also not entirely new were the mine-clearers. Du Toit's Flail, the affair of whirling chains in front of a Matilda worked by a separate engine bolted on to the outside, deserved development. Another 1942 effort, the Valentine Snake, did not. A long pipe, packed with explosive and towed across a minefield until the moment for detonation came suggested hope rather than experience, though a few had been tried at Alamein. All these things would have stirred ancient memories among the men of 1918 who remained. The rollers they had pushed in front of their tanks for the same purpose had been disinterred by men unborn at their first appearance. They had still worked, but the Flail was better, even though it kicked sand or mud straight into the driver's eyes. As with most things, they became used to it. The Sherman Crab was the best of them all. The chains ran off the main engine at double the Flail's speed and were inside a protective housing. Nor did they require that the gun be unshipped. This might be important when waddling slowly up a beach with the chains roaring and thrashing. Crabs would work in groups of five, three flailing and the others watching for something at which to shoot. With the coming of the Crab it looked as if mine-sweeping had been worked out.

There were, however, other obstacles to be circumvented before a tank could walk across the beach and climb on to dry land. The geologists had suggested the next one. Many of the stretches of sand on the French side were not sand at all, not in the sense that the Eighth Army understood the word. A noticeable part of them contained, so they suspected, a proportion of something called blue clay, the last remnants of the forests that had flourished there in pre-historic times. Blue clay would, they thought, bog down any tank ever made and in order to make certain they needed samples of beach from every likely landing place. These were duly obtained and the suspicions became certainties. The geologists went to work again to ascertain whether any part of the English coast was similarly afflicted. The answer turned out to be that the same conditions existed at Brancaster in Norfolk and a Trials Wing was set up there to find out the antidote. There were, inevitably, more examples of misplaced ingenuity all devised for the purpose of laying some sort of carpet. The big wheel driven by a rocket was, not surprisingly, a failure; after much trial and error a vast roll of hessian stiffened up by tubular scaffolding and mounted on horns projecting from an early Mark of Churchill seemed to do the trick. It was taken into service under the name of Bobbin.

The Royal Engineers now had a long tradition of working with tanks and had never sniffed at them as the Royal Artillery had once done. The first mine-clearers had been manned by Sapper crews and the Corps was enthusiastic about collaboration in the business of demolishing obstacles from sea-walls to pill-boxes. To that end they were given tanks of their own. The AVRE, Armoured Vehicle Royal Engineers (a cut-down Churchill), became their particular charge. The 5th and 6th Assault Regiments RE came into being. Apart from machines for mine business they had another weapon. Its official name was the Petard but nobody ever called it by that. The Flying Dustbin was a spigot mortar that could throw a 25-lb explosive charge a matter of some eighty yards at which range it could shatter most things made of concrete. This was in addition to the usual sapper business of building bridges. In 1918 a bridge-laying tank had existed but had since been forgotten. For many years the Martel box-girder had been the standard equipment. The immediate need, however, was for something different. It was satisfied by a small box-girder bridge pivoted on the horns of the AVRE and capable of giving a way up sea-walls or across ditches. For wider obstacles there was the Ark, a larger version that could be carried on an AVRE once the turret had been removed. In addition to these affairs the Assault Regiments were provided with powerful blasting charges to be laid by hand and known as Beehives or General

Wades. Most useful of all the new tools was the armoured bulldozer for clearing away demolitions. To begin with they were ordinary machines of the construction industry. Thus equipped they should be capable of taking care of mines, wire, concrete emplacements, ditches and the mine-laced metal barriers on the tide-line that were known to exist. A final touch was the Bullshorn Plough built on to the bows of some of them in case the action of flailing bogged them down. It was not for nothing that General Hobart had begun his career with the Indian Sappers & Miners. The River Alde, in Suffolk, is a mile across at its widest point on the top of the tide and it made an admirable testing ground.

All these devices were to come into play once the tanks had made land. The flat-bottomed craft that would carry the first flight, disgorging them from its let-down ramp, would be certain of a rough passage both literally and metaphorically. To imagine that they would be able to run their bows gently ashore and allow the passengers to roll out dry-shod would have been foolishly optimistic. Some waterproofing of tanks had been carried out before the Sicilian landings but there was room for improvement. It was a matter to which the Germans had given much thought. With a tank of 56 tons and the bridges over Russian rivers few, far between and probably not up to such a weight, this had been highly necessary. 500 Tigers had been fitted out with a Schnorkel breathing apparatus which, in conjunction with various rubber plugs and an inflatable tube around the turret ring, enabled them to wade under twelve feet of water and stay submerged for more than two hours. Ingenious though this was, it fell short of what was needed for a Channel crossing.

When the way to do it was shown to him Hobart exclaimed that he could kick himself for not having thought of it unaided. Mr Nicholas Straussler had the answer. It was a variation on the Berthon folding boat that yachtsmen had known for decades. The tank – in the first place a Valentine – was compassed about by a folding canvas frame fitted under the hull and with its gunwales raised by tubes of compressed air. The tracks and suspension remained under water and made quite an effective ballast keel. Motive power was provided by two screws driven by the tank's own engine, as had been done by the Medium D in 1919. Once on firm ground the flick of a lever let out the air and lowered the skirts, thus enabling the tank to go about its ordinary business. The device came to be called the Duplex Drive – DD for short.

It was not a new arrival. There is, among the Tank Board papers, a letter dated 28 September, 1942, from Sir George Usher to the Minister in which he writes of 'Valentine Duplex tanks using the Strausslerized equipment'. 436 of them were ordered from the Metro-Cammell Company. At one of the Board's regular meetings on 24 September, 1943, General Weeks being recorded as present, it was resolved that all DD tanks should thereafter be Shermans. This may have slipped the General's memory. The first Valentines had been tested at Portsmouth but, as no further mention is made of them for a long time, they probably shared the fate of the unwanted Crusaders and went straight into store to await the day when they might have work found for them. In all probability those concerned with the business would by then have moved on.

In July, 1943, the first of the new series of trials were carried out at Fritton Decoy, in nearby Norfolk, and General Brooke was taken for a sail. He became an instant supporter and gave orders for 500 Shermans to be thus fitted out. General Weeks, his Deputy, is reputed to have said that Valentine would do perfectly well but, for the reasons above, this is doubtful. By comparison with Fritton Decoy the Serpentine is a maelstrom. The Navy, unimpressed, demanded evidence of seaworthiness and tests were carried out at Stokes Bay. Naval hauteur seemed justified when the first seven Valentines were put into a sea featuring waves some six inches high. The first one drifted away because its screws did not work; the Navy sent a launch to take the tank in tow and by rushing off at great speed sank it. Another jammed itself in the exit from the landing craft and went ignominiously home. The demonstration had been unconvincing but Hobart was certain that he had the heart of the matter. He was right. After much practice extending over a month the crews had attained so high a standard of performance that the time for getting a DD tank out and away was reduced to fifteen seconds.

All these things had existed in rudimentary shapes by the end of the First War. In addition there were two other forms of specialized armour then in being, one of which was re-animated and the other not. The flamethrower had first appeared in 1916, in the hands of the Germans at Douaumont. It had been a man-carried affair with a pressure-tank full of petrol on the operator's back and a hose-pipe in his hand. For a time it had been terrible, until its extreme shortness of range was noticed and riflemen picked off the wielders. Under the name of Lifebuoy it was revived in Burma for burning out Japanese bunkers. In that form there would have been no place for it in the British Liberation Army but when tank-carried it became something formidable. One battalion, 141st RAC and formerly 7th Buffs, was given the Crocodile, as it came to be called. It consisted of a Mk VII Churchill which towed behind it a 9-ton armoured trailer filled with 400 gallons of compressed gases, far more effective than mere petrol. This gave fuel for a hundred shots of one second duration with a maximum range of 120 yards. The makers, surprisingly, were Lagonda. Two more units were converted to Crocodiles later in the campaign once its effectiveness had become plain to see.

The Mk IX Tank of 1918, arriving just too late for war service, had been a genuine armoured troop carrier capable of transporting an infantry platoon with all its gear. Soon after the armistice it had been tried out with buoyancy tanks and a screw which drove it satisfactorily across rivers. That done, it went for scrap and oblivion. The army of 1944 landed in France with no armoured infantry transporter, apart from the little Bren carrier that was Carden's legacy. As the battles wore on and the need became plain a makeshift, named Kangaroo, was hurried out in the shape of old tanks, mostly Canadian Rams, stripped of their turrets. The Americans were longer-sighted. The Buffalo, used by the Marines in the Pacific, and designed for swamp rescues in Florida, was a tracked and amphibious vehicle open at the top but capable of a good turn of speed. In water it was propelled by an ingenious arrangement of its own tracks which could turn themselves into paddles. So useful was it that by September a British tank regiment acquired a stock of them for the attack on Walcheren and by the end of the year a complete Brigade had been formed. The Kangaroo was a Canadian brain-wave. So was the Churchill AVRE.

From all this it can be seen that much sound thought had gone into devising means of breaking through the Atlantic Wall. Far less had been devoted to furnishing the Allied armies with tanks fit to stand up to their enemies in battle. The customary excuse is that great superiority in artillery and its fire control, plus something like complete mastery of the air by the RAF and USAAF, made it unnecessary. It is true that the Typhoon could and did kill any German tank by means of its 60-lb rocket, but that was little comfort to the crews of the Shermans, Cromwells and Churchills pitted against Tigers and Panthers. Only one tank in the Anglo-American armoury was fit to take them on with any chance of success. The 17-pdr gun was now in service and for its particular purpose was reckoned as good as the 88. Those Shermans which had been converted to carry it – they were given the name Firefly – could shoot it out with the odds about level. Every other tank then in service was outranged by something in the order of 1,000 yards and could only hope to survive in single combat by calling up the air or the guns. This was hardly a State secret. The Tank Board had ordered the conversion of 2,100 Shermans to be carried out as long ago as December, 1943. By late July, 1944, just under one third of this number had been delivered. The country was cluttered up with tanks, most of them obsolete or useless for other reasons. Quite pointlessly, factories had wasted labour and materials in turning out about 100 of the light Harry Hopkins for which no use could be found, to say nothing of the Tortoise. When General Bradley was compelled to ask Montgomery for some Fireflies Montgomery felt obliged to refuse him. This was the great tank scandal. With the war nearly five years old and with the last two of them largely given over to planning the battles in Normandy it is beyond forgiveness. To estimate how many names appear upon the War Memorials of three countries because men in authority failed to grasp the obvious is not possible. One may reasonably ask why the only big gun we had could not also have been mounted on the heavier and better armoured Churchill. The answer is that, when designed, it was, by order, of such a width that it could be carried on ordinary railway trucks. This made it narrow for its length and the turret could not be remade to take anything bigger than the obsolete 6-pdr or the obsolescent 75. The Germans and the Russians did not make mistakes like this.

The Cromwell and, to a lesser extent, the Sherman were the greyhounds of the tank world. Once the crust had been broken and the German army was in retreat their speed would be invaluable for carrying out the old light cavalry function of cutting down fugitives and turning an orderly retreat into a rout. That time still lay in the future and for immediate purposes the need was for something more on the lines of a pit-terrier. One man, at least, perfectly understood this. In a Note circulated to all concerned as long ago as 23 April, 1943, Mr Churchill had minuted that it seemed 'of the highest importance to have some thicker armour for a proportion of our tanks. At least 200 and preferably 400 Churchills should be fitted with the heaviest armour possible, at a sacrifice of speed down to 8 or even 6 miles an hour or less . . . Pray let me have a report on the Stern tank or any other alternative that can be devised.' One may fairly ponder the suggestion that since British engineers seemed incapable of producing a Tiger or a KV they might have been put to work upon the improvement of TOG rather than having it scrapped out of hand. Ricardo's engine and Stern's cemented armour were both excellent; the weak link, the transmission, might well have been made strong by Merritt-Brown's system. And with a 17-pdr or, better still, a 3′ 7″ AA gun, TOG could have taken on Tiger or Panther at 2,000 yards, whereas the others had only the choices of getting out of the way or being destroyed. True, it would have been useless once the first battles were over but it might well have earned its feed during the break-in. The alternatives of which Mr Churchill had written came into existence on paper but by D Day the 50-ton Black Prince and the 76-ton Tortoise were not even in the trial stage. This was no great loss.

There is an aphorism, much in use at the time, that the antidote to a tank is another tank. It is, at best, half true. Ancient beliefs that war is an heroic contest between two sides, preferably fairly matched, and with the better man winning die hard. In practice it does not work like that. Big brothers beat up little brothers; little brothers do such damage as they can on the disengaged side. During the First War artillery had beaten up infantry who lacked the means of hitting back. This time it was tanks that did the beating up. It may be unchivalric but tanks are more usefully employed in smashing their enemy's supply columns, without which he can neither fight nor live, than in banging away at each other. This may be nobler but is seldom effective unless one side has very superior machines that can massacre rather than fight.

This was the doctrine of the US Army, plainly set out in many conversations with the Tank Mission. General Patton's Standing Orders for his Third Army spelt it plainly: 'The primary mission of armored units is the attacking of infantry and artillery. The enemy's rear is the happy hunting ground for armor. Use every means to get it there.' The US Army pinned its faith entirely on the Sherman; other tanks, such as the light Chaffee and the heavy Pershing, came too late to the battle to have any influence on it. For all that, when Patton spoke of armour he meant more than just Shermans. American military thinking had been dominated by the spirit of the chase; once the crust had been cracked speed would dictate the course of the last campaign. As the armies could not be other than road-bound something faster than a tank would be essential. These thoughts took shape in a series of heavy armoured cars; the Greyhound at 7 tons, the Staghound at 12 and the great Boarhound at 24 were, in fact, tanks on wheels, all capable of road speeds of at least 50 mph and every one of them carrying both cannon and machine-gun. The British had had something not so far behind in 1930 with the Crossley 6-wheeler. Like many other good things it had been dropped in favour of the cheap and puny. The British Army was grateful for the loan of Staghounds, some of which they burdened with Crusader turrets and a 75, since their own AEC armoured car was detested because of its height.

In this fashion the Allies prepared to invade Hitler's Fortress Europe, with great quantities of obsolescent fighting machines every one of which would be inferior to its opposite number in the same class. Only by sheer weight of numbers, should it be possible to bring them to bear, and by constant intervention by their air forces could they have any hope of victory, possibly even of survival, so long as the German armour was still able to do its work. This the crews would have to learn for themselves. The British element was already shrinking from lack of men even before the first casualties were taken. By the standards of 1918 the British Liberation Army was a small one. After five years of war it was still not 'highly scientific' and the War Office had failed in the duty to 'keep abreast or ahead of modern developments in every deparament of war material'. Events had not justified Captain Liddell Hart's 1931 dictum that 'The nation will no longer be used to swell the encumbered ranks of a vast conscript army but to furnish the materials for its mechanized spearhead'. The conscript army was not vast merely because the nation was running out of young men. The last two divisions formed, bearing the numbers 81 and 82 and both serving in Burma, were West African, the young men of Nigeria, the Gold Coast, Sierra Leone and the Gambia.

CHAPTER NINETEEN
Seconds Out of the Ring

In Italy the tank was very far from being master of the field. The attack across the Volturno in October, 1943, once more demonstrated how nearly right Mr Churchill had been when he remarked that they were finished. When loaded into landing craft, floated down to the river mouth and then driven north they succeeded in making a disembarkation a little way behind the German lines. Once ashore, however, they found the minefields and were hemmed in. Only the crossing higher up by American infantry saved them from destruction. The best that could be said was that the landing had diverted part of the German force that might otherwise have opposed the Americans. It had not been the intention of the planners.

Nor did things go better for them on the Eighth Army front. Buckley watched the Canadian infantry attack towards Ortona a week before Christmas. The artillery bombardment was as intense as any he had heard, and that was saying a lot. It ought to have blotted out the German machine-gunners and mortar positions but it did not. They merely burrowed down further. When the barrage lifted they emerged and mowed down the Canadians as their fathers had mown down the British infantry on the Somme. 'Where were the tanks? It was their task to give close fire support, and they were moving up behind the infantry. But in close, undulating country, thickly studded with trees, they lost touch. Sheering off to a flank they overran the enemy positions immediately opposed to them and made a good deal of ground. But they could not remain in position, because the infantry who should have been there to consolidate the ground which the tanks had won had all been killed. They had been killed by the German machine gunners, who in their turn should have been killed by our artillery. And so, the tanks being out on a flank in an exposed position had to be drawn back. But as they withdrew diagonally across the enemy's front, they were raked by fire from the anti-tank guns which had been newly brought up, and suffered further losses. This is a fair sample of how matters commonly fell out during the assaults on the German winter line. Buckley, by no means a debunker of British Generals, had this to say about it: 'Our celebrated genius for improvisation had kept us far too busy meeting, often in a hand-to-mouth manner, the needs of the day instead of planning for those of the day after tomorrow.' It was a criticism that could have been made far beyond the Italian theatre.

It was not until 23 May, after Cassino, that the tanks once more came into their own. On a morning of heavy rain some hundreds of Shermans, British and Canadian, massed for an attack up the Liri Valley and fell upon the Panzers. For two days the armour fought it out, with three Shermans for every Panzer III or IV. The War Office proportions of May, 1942, still held good. The German Order of Battle included a number of Tigers, though they took no part in it. Losses on both sides were heavy, but the battle ended with a German withdrawal and the Allies in full cry on the road to Rome. Kesselring as a last throw brought in his precious Panthers and launched them at the Americans who met them with artillery fire. This did the business and American vanguards entered the Eternal City two days before the Normandy landings began.

In March, 1944, Slim fought his Alam Halfa, at Imphal and Kohima in Assam. For Fourteenth Army it was harder pounding than it had been for the Eighth, as the place was not of Slim's choosing, nor had he superiority in anything but air. The tank side of this tremendous battle was of no great magnitude. The Japanese, by enormous efforts, had managed to get a number of their medium and light machines across some of the most daunting country imaginable, but they achieved little. The 3rd Dragoon Guards, with their Grants, broke them up, destroying four and bringing one back captive. Before the war 'Japanese' meant, by definition, something cheap, nasty and probably made of tin. The days of high technology were far away. Much of their equipment was, in fact, extremely good: gunners went green with envy when the optical sights of Japanese guns fell into their hands. In tanks, however, they were still far behind Europe and America. So far, in Burma, this did not greatly matter. It was an old-fashioned war where old-fashioned skills and virtues counted for everything. After Kohima, as after Alam Halfa, the worst was over and Slim was able to take the battle to his enemy. Much still remained to be done and a lot of ground to be covered before his tanks could be of significant importance.

By contrast with what was happening on the Russian front, all this was an affair of pygmies. The Panther of 45 tons and armed with the long 75 had been rushed into production as a counter-weight to the T34 and had made its first public appearance at the Kursk offensive of July 1943. Not even German factories were exempt from the consequences of rush jobs and during its early stages more Panthers dropped out of the line from mechanical breakdowns than from enemy action of all kinds. The causes of these were sought out and eliminated in a manner that British experts seemed incapable of matching, and, by June, 1944, the Panther was as reliable as a tank can be. This was to become painfully obvious in Normandy. Nor did the Panther series end with what may be called the standard type. Hard on its heel came Hitler's favourite tank, the one in which he took a personal interest. Jagdpanther – Hunting Panther – came out of the stables early in 1944. At 45 tons it was of about the same weight as a Churchill but it could travel twice as fast – 28 mph to 14 – and it mounted the powerful 88 by contrast with the Churchill's 75. The engine was a Maybach of 23 litres developing a brake horsepower of 700 at 3,000 rpm. The Churchill, you may remember, had a Bedford lorry engine of half that power. It can hardly be surprising that the Panther also carried 110 mm of armour to the Churchill's 88

The Jagdpanther was not the ultimate in German tanks. The Tiger, or Panzer VI, has already appeared and had a formidable reputation. Buckley remarked on it in Italy as being, for defensive purposes and in a hull-down position, 'the most nearly invincible tank in existence'. When it moved, however, its lack of speed and conspicuousness made it a target for anything fit to take it on. Tiger II was a new design, much of it coming from the brain of Dr Porsche. Its armour was the thickest known, 150 mm at the front and sloped much after the fashion of T34. Suspension was still as before, but some of the wheels were doubled, while the intervening axles carried spaced ones overlapping the others. This made for stability, though at the price of extra maintenance. The gearbox gave eight forward speeds with a pre-selector and the clutch was much the same as the Merritt-Brown. All this meant that the Tiger was surprisingly easy to control and a pleasure to drive. Its main armament was an 88 with an extra long barrel that would knock out anything the Allies could bring against it from a range of more than 2,000 yards. The Churchill would be lucky to disable it as a couple of furlongs. Altogether Tiger II's 56 tons contained more wickedness and good engineering than most people thought possible. The Big Cats between them would certainly become lords of the steppe as soon as the Spring arrived.

One marvels at the German capacity for producing great numbers of fine tanks (Guderian's figure for 1943 was 11,897) when Bomber Command and the US 8th Air Force were doing their best to stop them. More remarkable still was the Russian feat in bodily moving entire factories beyond the Urals and still keeping up production. It makes the explanations, or excuses, of the Ministry of Supply and the War Office between them seem a little unconvincing.

The Russians' summer campaign of 1944 began with something like a certainty of eventual victory and would plainly be a series of offensive operations at various points along a very extended line. Attacks demanded what were known as assault tanks, tanks following the original conception of helping the infantry forward but better than anything yet used. The KV series formed a sound foundation. Russian engineers declined to believe, as their British professional brethren did, that a turret cannot be enlarged to accommodate a gun bigger than that for which it was designed. They took a standard KV, lowered the top run of the tracks along with the rollers, sprockets and idlers, and extended the hull top sideways. This gave the extra width needed and a bigger turret-ring was inserted. On to this was mounted a gun beside which all others looked like toys. The 122- mm was a piece of medium artillery, near enough equivalent to the British 5′ 5″. No tank was able to outdistance it for the next thirty years, nor could any field-work survive even the briefest shelling. The Josef Stalin was ringmaster; no Tiger or Panther could stand in its presence. With the T 34 it made the best combination by far in the world of armour during the last year of the war. As a feat of mechanical engineering it was a masterpiece. Thus equipped, the Red Army began the last long drive to Berlin and Vienna. From a purely technical standpoint it would be interesting to know how the JS would have stood up to the rocket-firing Typhoon. The German Air Force in Russia no longer had power of that kind.

No invasion of Europe could, of course, be contemplated until air

superiority was complete. The first arrivals would go in by parachute and glider, arrivals that until the summer of 1944 had been
limited to men on foot carrying only light weapons. The Overlord
plan went beyond this. For the past four years the small Vickers
tank named Tetrarch had found no buyers but it was exactly what
the Airborne needed. It fitted fairly comfortably inside a specially
made glider, the Hamilcar, and had been up-gunned from a mere 11
mm to a 2-pdr Littlejohn cannon. This, insisted BSA who had made
it, was 'Britain's real answer to the Tiger'. The crews were not entirely persuaded. To punch holes in a captive on a range is one
thing; for a 7-tonner to encounter something eight times its size in a
country lane is quite another.

The infantry also were very different from the infantry of pre-
Dunkirk days. Then the basis of their training had been that laid
down in the famous Army Training Memorandum No 35 which
extolled the skills of that minority of the civil population normally
employed as poachers and cat-burglars and enjoined those of other
callings to acquire them. These arts were undoubtedly useful in
campaigns such as those in Italy and Burma but they were wasted in
France. In 1940 the emphasis in defence had been placed upon anti-
aircraft; when the first Brens had arrived they had come with complicated mountings resembling bicycle frames which were intended
for use both as tripods for turning the Bren into a poor substitute for
the Vickers and, when assembled differently, to raise one leg sky-
ward and make it into an anti-aircraft weapon. It was standard practice upon occupying a position first to erect these and to prepare to
receive Stukas. Tanks were hardly considered; nobody took the
Boys rifle seriously. The only action that could be taken when tanks
appeared was to make oneself as nearly invisible as could be con-
trived. As time went by infantry battalions were provided with the
weapons once claimed by the Artillery as their own, the 2-pdr and,
later, the 6-pdr gun. They were specialist weapons and only one platoon in the battalion operated them. For a long time the search went
on for something smaller that any rifleman could pick up and fire
with a reasonable chance of doing some damage.

This task had been entrusted to Millis Jefferis and his co-adjutors
at The Firs, Whitchurch. Jefferis, now a Brigadier, had presided
over the making and trials of several weapons of only modified success but the Prime Minister retained a touching faith in his ingenuity. The Sticky Bomb was of little value; in case anybody should
think of trying the same thing with its adhesion caused by a magnet

the Germans had taken to smearing the outsides of all their tanks with a paste called Zimmerit which would repel them. Next came the Blacker Bombard, named after an eccentric Irish Colonel who claimed to be both a TA officer and the only private arms manufacturer in England. His gun was unique in that it had no barrel. A bomb containing a 10-lb charge consisted of a shaped head containing the explosive, a tail tube with stabilizing fins and a spigot off which it was fired. Its best point was the explosive which 'poulticed' on to the target before it detonated and thus multiplied its power for destruction. On 28 July, 1940, Blacker demonstrated it at Chequers and the Prime Minister was vastly taken. Jefferis, then no more than Major, was given £5,000 and told to make better ones. The Ordnance Board put every possible difficulty in the way; it should not be blamed too much, for the next performance, at Shoeburyness nearly a year later, was 'a complete flop'. Macrae, Jefferis' assistant, says that he found on his desk one morning a Minute ordering Blacker's removal. After the war the Royal Commission on Awards to Inventors gave Blacker 'a very large sum indeed mainly on the strength of this Bombard invention'.

Jefferis persevered. One day, long afterwards, Macrae found him poking about in the workshop among the remains of Blacker's ironmongery and examining a contraption worked by a long rusty spring. With Blacker's permission Jefferis amused himself by taking it to pieces and reassembling it in a way that would permit the thing to fire a 2″ mortar bomb. It worked fairly well but the kick from the released spring was nearly disabling. Jefferis set himself to study the mechanics of it and worked out a formula for calculating the requirements of compression springs used in shoulder-guns. That done, he made with his own hands a specimen that worked very well indeed. By coincidence he had been working at the same time upon something called the Neumann effect on shaped or hollow charges. It appears that if an explosive charge is placed behind a metal cone with the concave part facing forwards and the device is stood off from the target for a prescribed distance the charge on detonation will give great penetration over a small area. Thus, against armour, it will not dissipate itself but will punch a hole.

The Jefferis Shoulder Gun had its first trial at Bisley where a QMSI from the Small Arms School was detailed to loose it off at a sheet of thick armour plate. The plate was duly holed but so was the firer. A slug of metal came back through the tube in the opposite direction and went straight through him. Not to be deterred, Jefferis picked up his weapon and fired several rounds without unto-ward consequences. Only a small piece of re-designing was needed to make it safe. Then, as the thing had obvious value, it was handed over to Lord Melchett, the Chairman of ICI, who had made all the bits and pieces, including both hollow-charge A/T rounds and ordi-nary anti-personnel ones, at his Company's Billingham factory. The Ordnance people, said Macrae indignantly, insisted that the name Jefferis Shoulder Gun be changed to Projector, Infantry, Anti-Tank. Thus came the PIAT. Mr Churchill shared Macrae's indig-nation. On 11 April, 1943, he minuted to the War Office that 'It seems a little hard to grudge having Jefferis' name attached to the shoulder gun, especially as everyone speaks of Mills grenades, Stokes guns, Hawkins mines, Kerrison predictors, Northover pro-jectors, etc.' It made no difference – PIAT it was, and as such the infantry of Montgomery's armies came to know, if not to love, it. The range was very short – barely 100 yards – and the kick was un-pleasant but the Neumann effect worked. Macrae quotes an anony-mous letter telling of how Canadians, crawling to within five or ten feet, burnt out twenty-nine Panther or Tiger tanks with it. Though this would not have been the common experience of infantrymen, the PIAT was a most useful addition to the armoury. Macrae, poss-ibly not an unprejudiced witness, says that it was by far the most effective anti-tank weapon produced for the infantryman, not excepting the American bazooka which came later. It certainly made the foot soldier far more able to take care of himself than anything that he had had before.

CHAPTER TWENTY

'The More You Have the Less You Lose'
GENERAL SIR WILLIAM SLIM

Among the names of the distinguished corps of war correspondents none stand higher than Christopher Buckley (killed in Korea not long afterwards) and Alan Moorehead. Both of them had seen it all and their opinions command respect. Buckley has already been quoted. Consider now Moorehead.

'By any standard it [Normandy] was extremely unsound country for tanks – especially our tanks. Our tanks were Shermans, Churchills and Cromwells. None of them was the equal of the German Mark Five [the Panther] or the Mark Six [the Tiger]: nor could all the ministerial statements in the House of Commons make them equal. It was, after all, solely a matter of plain figures, and the tank being a fairly out-of-date weapon it is not difficult to define.

'The German tanks had 88-millimetre guns. We had 75-millimetre guns. The Germans had much thicker armour than we had. Their tanks were effective at a thousand yards or more; ours at ranges around five hundred yards. We had a tank known as the Firefly which was a Sherman with a 17-pounder gun. We also had a new type of ammunition. But both the Firefly and the new ammunition scarcely existed in France during the vital battles of the bridgehead. In the end we used rocket-firing Typhoon aircraft with which to fight the German tanks and they were a great success. Whenever we sighted German tanks we called up the Typhoons. Our own tanks were unequal to the job because they were not good enough. There may be various ways of dodging this plain truth but anyone who wishes to do so will find himself arguing with the crews of more than three British armoured divisions which fought in France. A destroyer does not engage a cruiser on equal terms. One can only hope that sooner or later the scandal of British tank manufacture will come out, just as the shell scandal of the last war was ventilated. In fairness it must be admitted that neither Tigers nor Panthers could have exploited the break-through in the way the Shermans and the Cromwells did. I am simply asserting here that our tanks were inferior to the German models.' Nobody was in a better position to know.

His view was confirmed by a professional soldier: 'These tanks [Tigers and Panthers] were, of course, just what was required for this close fighting. Our Shermans and Cromwells were no match for them and our Churchills were only a little better. What we wanted in this type of warfare was the new design of really heavy infantry tanks which we had always asked for, but this was not available.' Thus wrote General Martel a year later. Nor was he much taken by Montgomery's tactics: 'The armoured divisions could not fight their way through any more than they had done at Alamein; in fact we saw a repetition of that mistake again.' It was not, he insisted, the work for which they had been created; their business was the pursuit, as the Americans had always insisted.

The Churchills in Normandy were, for the most part, of the last kind, Mks 7 and 8 with a 75 mm gun and a 95 mm howitzer respectively. Both weapons were British-made but all ammunition for the 75 came from America. The Instruction Book, issued by the Chief Inspector of Fighting Vehicles, lets a small cat out of the bag. The section on ammunition treats of high-explosive shells and both armour-piercing and semi-armour-piercing shot. This might have been expected; less so was the chemical shell painted grey with green bands. There were two varieties, described as holding either persistent or non-persistent gas. None seems to have been issued, but they were on hand should a desperate Hitler resort to such expedients on his own. None of these projectiles, with their short ranges, made the Churchill equal to its foes.

Nevertheless, it was the tanks that made invasion possible. Hobart's 79th Division did everything that had been expected of it and the Americans came to regret that, except for the DDs, they had decided against using 'Funnies'. In their sector even the ones they did employ were not always a success. The sea off Omaha beach on the day following a storm that had forced postponement of the invasion by twenty-four hours was more than they could cope with and only three managed to struggle ashore. The loss of their fire power was serious and it was only the courage and determination of US infantry soldiers that got them established in their beach-head. Casualties at Omaha were far heavier than elsewhere and the fighting much harder.

On those beaches allotted to the British and Canadians, which enjoyed better shelter, things went more smoothly. The Crabs whirled their chains and cleared mines very satisfactorily; a few Shermans descended slowly into quicksands but the Bobbins served their purpose. Best value of all were the DDs, launched at distances between two and four miles from the shore into choppy water through which they swam gamely until their tracks found something upon which to take hold. First on the scene were the Royal Engineers, making lanes through the German works with their stange but effective equipment until the way was clear for the assaulters. One AVRE, its sapper crew tired of waiting for supporters to arrive, turned itself into an infantry tank and set about the blockhouse that had once been Hamel sanitorium. Sherman DDs came up behind the Assault Squadrons, dropped their skirts and drove into the hinterland. By dusk the bridgehead was six miles deep and the first patrols were making their way into Bayeux. It is unsurprising that the plan did not always go like clockwork. Near Bernières the infantry arrived first and a mighty traffic jam built up. Further east, a pair of the DDs, still swimming hard, were rammed and sunk by a flotilla of LCTs which cut across their bows. But, one way or another, the business was done and D-day ended with a lodgement in force on a respectable-sized piece of coast. One mischance has to be recorded. The gliders duly appeared overhead and the eight Tetrarchs started up their engines before touching down. As the little tanks clattered out and began to deploy for battle they crossed a field littered with discarded parachutes whose lines wrapped themselves round the sprockets as nets do around fishermen's propellers. Their moment of glory was postponed but eight more arrived by sea and they gave valuable service during the hard battle fought by the Airborne. A few days later they were replaced by Cromwells.

Most spectacular were the Crocodiles. Two of these landed, four having been drowned, with the first flight manned by 141st RAC, still known to themselves as 7th Buffs. The badge of The Buffs is the fire-breathing dragon and the dragon still appeared in their

190

hats.* Their strangest adventure happened at dawn on the second morning. The Crocodile needs to clear its tubes as a matter of routine before going into battle. One of them directed itself towards a wood, apparently unoccupied, and eructated. A battery of German artillery, unknown to anybody, was lurking there. Those gunners who were not incinerated wasted no more time before surrendering. One cannot blame them. The breath of the Crocodile was a fearsome thing. Later on it was instrumental in compelling the garrisons of Le Havre and, under American command, of Brest to lay down their arms. So successful were the flame-throwers that the two more RAC regiments were hastily converted to them.

On D plus nine a news flash reached the Tank Board: 'The 95 mm Centaurs have been in action from the ships. No information yet available as to their performance ashore.' The Royal Marines had made their contribution; lobbing shells ashore from a ship's deck was all that the Centaurs were fit for. The Leathernecks deserved better.

If it was the specialized armour that made the landing possible, it was the air forces that enabled it to be sustained. Lying in wait behind Caen was the 21st Panzer Division which had the power to drive the Allies back into the sea. The knowledge that any forward move on its part would have brought down the full weight of an enormous air arm kept it immobile during the critical hours. Two others, the 12th SS Panzer and Panzer Lehr – theoretically a demonstration unit but in fact a very formidable one – made up Rommel's armoured corps; both of them were still on the wrong side, for him, of the Seine and were under orders to stay there until Hitler personally gave the word to move. In the middle of the morning of D plus one the 21st Panzer attacked with ninety tanks. By then the British 3rd Division, once Montgomery's pride, was ready for them. The anti-tank guns opened up at 2,000 yards and eleven Panzers were left burning. The remainder swung westwards to find a gap and some even reached the sea by Luc-sur-Mer. It was the sudden arrival of the Air Landing Brigade, with its Tetrarchs, that prevented them from making use of this. When the SS Panzers arrived near Caen, much battered all the way by the RAF, it was too late. First the Canadians and then the 3rd Division were already on the

* Those who remember him will not need to be told that this was due to the first CO, Lieut-Colonel Roscow Reid. When ordered to convert his battalion to armour he accepted the necessity but demanded that they fight, as The Buffs had done since 1572, under the dragon badge. Few General Officers dared oppose him.

move and the SS were thrown on to the defensive. Panzer Lehr, with most of its soft-skinned transport left burning by the roadside, did not turn up until the 8th. By then the tanks that had smelt salt water had been eliminated.

All the same the advance of Second Army did not display any great dash. The 7th Armoured Division had all its tanks ashore by 7 June but four days were to pass before it was turned loose. Away to the west the Americans seemed to be making better progress. Nevertheless the battle for the beaches had been won and the build-up continued.

Once the British armour had got on the move its general line of advance ran towards the south-east. This was a misfortune, since all the roads the French describe as *'carrossable'* trended south-westerly, leaving only sunken lanes which wander up and down and are frequently so deep and narrow that a tank, once in any of them, could not traverse its gun, let alone turn round. It was often impossible to see above the hedges and, once in a lane, there was no getting out of it. For the big German tanks it could not have been arranged better. Moorehead saw as much of it as any one man could. He tells of the armoured thrust towards Villers Bocage that Liddell Hart says 'had not gone according to plan': 'Then our tanks were engaged. They were dispersed hull-down behind the hedges but every time they moved the Germans sighted them and hit them. Eventually the whole squadron was cut off, and while the German infantry began pressing in on the flanks the rest of us drew back out of Villers Bocage. You could never be sure of where the fire was coming from. Every time a tank turned the corner of a road it ran the danger of being ambushed by an anti-tank gun. When the infantry went forward through the breast-high wheat to get at the enemy gun they found themselves enfiladed. At this stage the Germans were far ahead of us in using the country. Their infantry smothered themselves in leaves and branches. They crawled up to the forward positions on their bellies. They never showed themselves. Whole platoons of snipers would tie themselves into the leafy branches of the trees, and there they would wait silently for hours, even days, until they got the chance of a shot. The snipers were something new in our experience. They were deadly.' Apparently the army had forgotten Gort's Army Training Memorandum No 35 which had insisted upon the importance of what it called the sniper-stalker. He is one of the essentials of an army at war. The British infantry soon got the hang of it again, but many good men were picked off because another ancient skill had been allowed to fall into disuse.

It was at about this time that the need for some gadget to help tanks over the hedges and ditches of the bocage became strident. Eisenhower tells of how an American Sergeant named Culin worried it out. His answer was 'fastening to the front of the tank two sturdy blades of steel which, acting somewhat as scythes, cut through the bank of earth and hedges. This not only allowed the tank to penetrate the obstacle on an even keel and with its guns firing, but actually allowed it to carry forward for some distance a natural camouflage of amputated hedge.' The Germans provided the steel; there was plenty of it in the obstacles still cluttering up the beaches.

As neither tanks nor infantry could succeed in taking Villers Bocage the bombers were called in and they flattened it. The German troops had sense enough to take to the fields and came through unscathed. All the bombing achieved was to give more practice to the armoured bulldozers in clearing rubble.

It was on 13 June that the inadequacy of the Allied tanks were given a practical demonstration. A detachment of the vastly experienced 4th County of London Yeomanry drove through Villers Bocage from the west and pushed along the Caen road until they reached a hill called Point 213. A single Tiger crawled out from the woods, knocked out the leading half-track with its first shot and then gave its attention to the armour. Within a few minutes its great gun had set twenty-five British tanks ablaze, the Tiger contemptuously shrugging off the few shells that hit it. That took care of regimental HQ and the reconnaissance troop. It was a higher score than Haig's legendary German officer who, at Cambrai, had been supposed to knock out sixteen tanks single-handed with his gun. A complete squadron was ambushed by Tigers and Panzer IVs a little further on; every tank was destroyed from a range of 2,000 yards. The Germans took no hurt. It was no comfort to learn that the Tigers and their friends soon went the same way when they tried to attack the town and walked into the 17-pdrs. TOG would have been able to give them a better fight than this. And almost any of the Russians would have made cat's meat of them. Next day, on almost the same spot, the 1st RTR knocked out a couple more Panthers and slew many German infantrymen with their Besas. It was only the equipment that should be criticized, along with those responsible for it. General Bayerlein, commanding Panzer Lehr, did not feel the conscious superiority of the Germans that Moorehead ascribed to them. On 19 June he said, according to Liddell Hart: 'My chance to drive to the sea was lost. We had lost about a hundred tanks against the British. Half my striking force was gone.' Then came a month during which nothing of much importance happened to the armour of either side. An intended German counter-attack in strength was ruined by the RAF. On 9 June it bombed General Geyr von Schweppenberg's HQ so comprehensively that all his Staff were either killed or wounded. This is what Fuller had laid down as being tank business in his Plan 1919. Events had now overtaken him. More factory space and skilled labour was allocated in 1944 to Bomber Command than to the whole of the army. Sir Arthur Harris would have claimed that this was entirely as it should have been. Beyond question the bombers had put paid to any serious German comeback.

By mid-June the Allies had great numerical superiority in armour with some 1200 tanks ashore, not counting about 300 of the specialized machines. Rommel mustered about 500 – 152 Panthers and the rest Mk IVs, plus a company of forty-five Tigers. In the air he was even worse off, with about 400 machines to face the Allies' 13,000 of all kinds. To round it off he also had 2,300 guns against him. Apart from the air it was not quite as bad as it looked on paper, for the Allies were of necessity the attackers and masses of second-rate tanks could easily become masses of first-rate targets, which they did when the 11th Armoured Division made its debut. One encouraging thing for the RAC was that Churchills, the Matilda 1s of 1944, proved able to take a lot of punishment and when they burned they did it slowly. Panthers, as often as not, blew up. For this the Army had to thank Bomber Command. A report prepared just after the war observes that 'Panther plate was, for the first time, inconsistent and often cracked up badly'. It was assumed, probably rightly, that the havoc wrought by Harris' young men had compelled the use of factories that did not really understand the making of armour. The same thing as mentioned earlier had happened here. Nevertheless it did not appear in that light to the men on the ground. In the desert, as you may remember, it had been official philosophy that in order to take on a German tank three British ones were needed. During the bocage fighting it was worse. The general, and probably well founded, doctrine was that whenever a Tiger appeared four Churchills were needed to cope with it and three of these would be lost.

The countryside south of Caen is known to the guide books by the banal but not entirely inapt name of La Suisse Normande. It was not far from here that Montgomery had taken on the role of Arnold von Winkelried, the heroic Swiss who, as every schoolboy knows, gathered all the Austrian spears into his own breast in order that his comrades might fall upon their enemy undistracted. This did not mean setting up a line of guns and beckoning the three SS Panzer Divisions, two of them lately arrived after an eventful journey from Poland, to come and immolate themselves. His armoured regiments, though well aware of the inferiority of their tanks, set out time and again to hammer them. It was an expensive business and many fell prey to the waiting Tigers and prowling Panthers. The Press, especially in America, did not fully understand what the British General was about, and a great deal was written about his slowness. 'Why don't the British do some fighting?' was an elegant extract quoted by de Guingand. Tripe à la mode de Caen has long been famous.

These days, all through the battles for a break-out, were bad ones for the RAC; one may try to imagine how it felt to drive along a country lane, not once but often, knowing that any moment might bring a shell from some unseen gun which would end a Churchill's career along with those of some of the occupants. The Corps came out of it with great credit and, despite all handicaps, the British tanks left their mark on the Germans. How much more effectively they might have done so, and at how much less cost, given proper heavy tanks of their own can only be guessed at.

One may to some extent get inside Montgomery's mind by considering his choice of Corps Commanders. General Crocker had done course and distance before in 1940 with the impossibly placed 1st Armoured Division and under more or less continuous air attack. He had every claim to a place among the high commanders. General O'Connor, who had enlarged himself from an Italian prison camp, had been in at the beginning of the desert war and had also given his proofs. General Ritchie, who arrived in mid-July as GOC 12 Corps, had not been the most successful commander of the Eighth Army but merited another chance at a lower level. There were, however, two notable absentees. General Gatehouse at the age of 23 had commanded a Tank Battalion during the last battles of 1918; after treading water for 20 years he had commanded another in 1940. After that he had won the confidence of everybody but one in the desert. The one was General Montgomery who had never forgiven him for, as he asserted, being a mile behind his leading troops at Alamein. The fact that Gatehouse had been compelled to come back that distance in order to speak to his Chief on the telephone was neither here nor there. In Montgomery's eyes Gatehouse was finished; he took over from Pratt in Washington.

The other missing figure was General Lumsden. As a 12th Lancer he had done famously with the armoured cars both in France and Libya and had risen swiftly. Because he had not achieved the impossible at Alamein he too was what the cavalry called 'cast'. When, in private conversation, Montgomery told a junior officer that Lumsden was 'yellow' the hot answer came that he was speaking of one of the bravest men in the army. It made no difference. Lumsden came to his death in a manner uncommon among cavalrymen. He was sent on a liaison mission with the Americans in the Pacific and was killed on the bridge of the USS *New Mexico* by a Japanese kamikaze pilot.

The Americans were, by design, the beneficiaries of the spear-gathering at Caen. Montgomery, who did not make a vice of modesty, implied that this gave them something like a walkover. Nothing could have been further from the truth. The US troops, most of them gaining their experience as the British had had to do by trial and error, had a hard task ahead and they stood to it like men. They too were imperfectly equipped, with no Churchill but only the Sherman and some self-propelled guns used as tank-destroyers. Priests and Sextons had been around for a long time but both American and British soldiers had little benefit of clergy. There were not nearly enough of them.

There was, however, a new weapon of greater power in tank-smashing than any gun. When von Kluge attacked the US VIIth Corps with some 500 tanks in five Panzer Divisions he made its acquaintance for the first time. The Americans put up a staunch resistance but it was the air that won the battle for them. By the time the fighter-bombers had launched their last rockets more than ninety Panthers were out of action, not simply holed but ripped open and torn apart in a fashion not seen before. The German armour, less that part of it which was now scrap metal, abandoned the field. The rocket-firing Typhoons and Thunderbolts, better by far than any Stuka, were undoubtedly the sovereign anti-tank weapon but they were not a substitute for weapons the Allied armies should have had. It was seldom possible to call one up when suddenly confronted by a Tiger at the bend in a lane. The one weakness in the equipment of General Bradley's armies was in their anti-tank weapons. The US 76 mm gun was worthless.

As some sort of compensation the US commander of the armoured forces that would have to do the fighting was an exceptional man. General George Smith Patton, Jr., was born out of his time. Had he been an Englishman he would probably have followed the Hobart trail, being little regarded, and less liked, by his peers, but drawn to the Prime Minister as by a lodestone. Pattons was all the Wolfes, Clives and Ruperts that Mr Churchill loved. Being born where he was, the resemblance is more to that of George Custer, reincarnated but with a brain. He had, of course, an advantage that nobody would be churlish enough to grudge. American young manhood was almost inexhaustible; in Britain the supply was drying up and the time was not distant when entire divisions would fade away for lack of men. Every casualty counted and no commander dared risk running up what our grandfathers called a butcher's bill.

At the end of July the German army suffered a loss that even its enemies felt to be sad. The RAF shot up Rommel and he went home and killed himself. To describe him as the du Guesclin to Montgomery's Sir John Chandos would be putting things a little high but there was certainly no rejoicing over his death. Had the same happened to his successor, General von Kluge, nobody would have minded in the least. He was a practising Nazi; Rommel was not. Professional soldiers seldom hate each other, though an exception must be made for the Japanese.

At near enough the same time the British–Canadian army, with three Armoured Divisions – Guards, 7th and 11th – made a mighty effort to incorporate tanks with heavy bombers and thus blast a way through to the Falaise plain where tanks might operate according to their nature. The bombers were to give up bombing such recognizable objects as town and bridges; instead the 4-engined Lancasters – one of the things British engineers made extremely well – would lay 'strips', a path of bombs along each side of the tank run. This should obliterate all the guns, big and small alike. That done, the light bombers would go over the course again with anti-personnel bombs that left no craters. Finally the artillery would wall off both sides and add a creeping barrage along the front. Under such treatment nothing could live. The tanks would have little to do but keep on the move. Everything depended on timing.

It went wrong. As always seemed to happen, the German gunners surfaced unscathed as soon as the bombers had gone and opened fire on the approaching tanks at very short ranges. In a matter of hours they knocked out 200. Then the Tigers and Panthers came back, slaughtering everything they could find. The German Air Force made one of its now rare appearances and caught a number of replacement crews as they sheltered for the night by one of the three bridges across the Orne Canal. The great attack fizzled out. A few days later new ideas were tried. Pink smoke was put up as a cover, the bombers were told to bomb closer to our own troops and coloured lights were fired towards the German positions as a guide. The Germans promptly fired them back at British positions. It is hard to blame Bomber Command for demolishing an HQ and causing hundreds of Canadian casualties. Much the same happened to the Americans. At St Lo a US General was killed and ordinary soldiers viewed the approach of their own aircraft without enthusiasm. The heavy bombers were called off and sent to ply their proper trade far away. The Typhoons, rapidly becoming expert at picking off single Tigers and Panthers, did the job far better, so long as the weather was fine. Low cloud, however, made them unavailable.

24 July, 1944, was one of the most important dates in the war. General Bradley broke through at St Lo and unleashed Patton's Shermans on their ride, not through Georgia but across an obligingly flat French countryside. As at Waterloo the whole line began to move forward. On 7 August British soldiers at last stood on top of Mont Pinçon and looked towards the flames coming from Falaise. The Canadians fought their way into the town with their infantry riding on the tanks and von Kluge's men found themselves firmly inside the killing ground. The Falaise Gap was the decisive battle of the war in northwest Europe. From then on it would very largely be a cruiser war and the Cromwell would be able to show what it could do. The cost in matériel had been heavy indeed. Moorehead remarks that it was not uncommon to find a field with 100 wrecked Shermans in it. So long as the crews had escaped, as more often than not they did, it was no great matter, but it still seems an odd way for the world's greatest industrial nations to launch their young men into battle. Tanks had seemingly become as expendable as an empty cartridge case. Apologists could fairly point out that it had worked. One may still legitimately wonder whether a few regiments of British and American heavies might not have worked it more quickly and cheaply, and have spared Europe a dreadful winter war.

One man was unafflicted by the smallest doubt. General Martel, writing about the Russians crossing of the Vistula, told of how the

Stalin tanks broke through all resistance and cleared the way for the T34s to exploit their success: 'This was exactly the technique which we had adopted and developed and which had paid us so well until we had foolishly ceased developing and manufacturing improved models of heavier infantry tanks. If we had possessed these tanks we would have been equally successful in the early stages of our breakthrough operations on the Western Front.' No man was in a better position to express a firm opinion. His successor, General Brocas Burrows, had nothing like the same cordial relationship with Russian officers and was not shown how far they had developed armoured machines since Martel's departure. In 1943 the Germans had produced a massive piece of self-propelled artillery named variously the Ferdinand, after Dr Porsche who had designed it, or Elefant. It mounted a long-barrelled 88 and the experimental model contained a petrol-electric transmission not very different from the one Stern had tried out in TOG. Dr Porsche, amongst whose designs was the Volkswagen Beetle, held this to be the smoothest and most effective drive system for a heavy tracked vehicle but in practice it worked no better for him either. The production model was of a more conventional kind. Ferdinand was not one of the Doctor's successes. On its first appearance during the Kursk offensive it looked, with its 65 tons of solid metal, like one of the Maginot forts broken loose. Possibly the Germans had grown over-confident, for the manner in which Ferdinand was put into battle asked for trouble. The eighty-three machines used were no more reliable mechanically than the Crusader and, just as serious, they lacked any machine-guns for their own protection. Because they were so slow they became separated from the tanks and the Russian infantry swarmed over them. Very few Ferdinands survived and those that did were sent off to Italy. Russian engineers dissected them thoughtfully and came up with a model of their own. It was not entirely a novelty to them for a KV chassis bearing a 152 mm howitzer had been used against the Mannerheim Line in 1940 with only limited success. Since then they had gained much experience and early in 1944 they put it to good use. From factories beyond the Urals emerged Tyrannosaurus Rex himself, the great Josef Stalin 3. For many years to come this was the finest tank in the world, with a 122 mm gun the size of that carried by a Navy cruiser, beautifully sloped armour and a reliable V12 diesel engine. No other tank could stand against it, for JS3 was used as a Tiger shooter rather than as a piece of ordinary medium artillery. Some 2,000 of them were produced and they justified every kopeck put into them. From about the same time that the Allies were landing in Normandy the Russian steam-roller – no longer the imaginary one of 1914 but demonstrably real – began to roll forward.

The British Second Army would have rolled faster and further but for one thing. According to the Administrative History of 21 Army Group, when September came 1400 3-ton lorries were found useless by reason of faulty pistons. The replacement engines were the same.

CHAPTER TWENTY ONE
Tiger Tiger Burning Bright

The last German offensive, von Rundstedt's Christmas attack through the Ardennes, demonstrates the truth of the adage that there are horses for courses. For some time past the German High Command had been putting together all the forces it could muster for a last throw and they were formidable indeed. Three complete Panzer Armies, an air force powerful enough to gain at any rate local superiority and a force of parachute troops to beat up the rear areas were thrown in. Their target was an American army in no great strength and unorganized to resist such an onslaught. Leading it were many of the great King Tigers, travelling fortresses of a size not seen or heard of on a front that did not know of the Josef Stalin.

Everything about the King Tiger was spectacular and likely to strike dread into the heart of any infantryman. It turned the scale at 67 tons, was wrapped in armour 6 inches thick and carried a long-barrelled 88 capable of smashing any Allied tank long before it could come into range. In Normandy any British commander would willingly have exchanged a whole squadron of Shermans for one of these. Now, however, the cause was altered. The Americans refused to be panicked and fought back hard. The King Tigers penetrated their lines, impervious to anything that could be fired at them and saved by cloud from the Typhoons. Even so their advances of five or six miles a day were far behind Rommel's figures for 1940. Excellent American generalship kept them walled into a narrow corridor and the price for using such monsters had to be paid. They ran out of fuel, the skies began to clear and the Typhoons came down. Such King Tigers as remained made for home. It had been a great waste of a mighty weapon. This had been cruiser work and it is not impossible that some Tiger commanders might have been willing to exchange for Cromwells. They had lost some 400 tanks and about 100,000 trained men. It all pointed the lessons not only of the fairly recent past but of the early days of armoured warfare. The King Tigers had punched the hole: that done, it was the business of the lighter, faster and less thirsty members of the tank family to take over and perform the old light cavalry functions of tearing into a beaten enemy and cutting him up. We had no Tigers for the first part: the Germans had no Shermans or Cromwells for the second. As said before, there are horses for courses.

Now that the war in Europe was nearly over, the English factories handed over some tanks of excellent quality. Just as von Rundstedt's King Tigers were heaving over the skyline the 11th Armoured Division received its first Comets. They were Leyland products, based originally upon the Cromwell and its Rolls-Royce engine, but so worked over as to be a very different affair. It was slightly heavier than the Sherman, at about 33 tons, but better armoured and carrying a gun tailor-made for it by Vickers after the Cromwell fiasco. Though called a 77 mm it was for all practical purposes a 17-pdr and could take on a Panther with a sporting chance of killing it. No Comet crew would have thought for a moment of exchanging it for anything.

There were still wars going on outside France and Belgium. When Alexander set out north from Rome his armies had been much reduced and strangely diluted. Fortunately this did not apply to his air forces which still held complete mastery. A new armoured Division, the 6th South African, had now teamed up with the 6th (British) Armoured and was a welcome accretion of strength. The work went on in much the same fashion. In close country it fell upon the Churchills, those with the 95 mm howitzer being particularly useful in the infantry support role. The attacks on the Gothic Line and the disagreeable winter campaign were followed by Alexander's offensive of April 1945 and the triumphant advance to Venice and Milan. These were, for the most part, old-style battles with armour being secondary to the foot and guns. Martel makes the point once more: 'The lack was felt by both armies (Fifth and Eighth) of a powerful infantry tank for this type of fighting.' Italy had not been a tank man's dream.

There was yet another country that was nearer to nightmare. Burma is very beautiful but so designed by Providence that if men have to fight battles there they can only be of one kind. A single instance may serve to explain. General Slim badly needed to have a substantial body of troops in the Kaladan Valley as the left flank-guard of his Corps in the Arakan. Between his existing positions and that place stretch many miles of jungle and mountain which contain nothing that could by any generosity be called so much as a path. Most of it appears on the map in a pleasing shade of green marked: 'Dense mixed jungle mainly bamboo; unsurveyed'. He took his difficulty to the Army Group Commander, General Sir George Giffard. Giffard had served many years with the Royal West African Frontier Force and had lately been its Inspector General. A complete division of the RWAFF had lately arrived in India and was training in the Western Ghats. All, incidentally, were volunteers, for the force had no obligations outside Africa. Sir George knew that, of all men, these were the best suited for the task. They set off on foot, every man from General Woolner downwards carrying his kit on his back. They cut, climbed, waded, swam and slithered until they arrived, living entirely on air supply that never failed. Behind them they trailed, spider-fashion, a jeep track called West African Way. Only then was it possible for anything on wheels to reach their valley. It does not seem likely that those who had tried to foresee the shape of the war and had talked airily of great armoured forces sweeping over the battlefield had imagined anything like this.

Slim's last campaign began with the monsoon. To think of this as the rainy season, imagining the kind of steady downpour familiar to the English but bigger, is understandable but wrong. Better to imagine oneself standing underneath a lake from which the bottom is suddenly removed. Add jungle, mountains, leeches, rivers, swamps and unusual diseases and one may realize that no enemy is needed to make Burma 'not tank country'. The fact remained that, as a strong Japanese army stood between him and his goal, Slim had to make it one.

By the expenditure of much sweat and, probably, some tears his men achieved this. Half a million soldiers of many nationalities took their orders from Slim but, apart from its air support, the Fourteenth was an old-fashioned army. Slim cheerfully admitted it: 'We were an old-fashioned army and we insisted on its outward signs. In the Fourteenth Army we expected soldiers to salute officers – and officers to salute in return.'

Only two of his brigades were armoured, equipped with a miscellany of Grants and Shermans, plus a solitary Stuart left behind in

1942 and picked up on the way back still in running order. Half the armoured regiments were British and the Indian half contained such famous names from the past as Probyn's, the 7th Cavalry, the 19th and 24th Lancers, Indian Army. As the Japanese were not strong in tanks and the Irrawaddy Valley was the only area where armour could operate, the cruisers would do well enough. Heavy tanks would have been useful in overcoming bunkers but their weight would in all probability have bogged them down.

First there was sapper work to be done and the Indian Sappers and Miners showed that they were as good as any. The floating Bailey bridge that they pushed across the Chindwin on 10 December, 1943, was, at 1154 feet, the biggest of its kind in the world. It would still be a long time before the tanks, carried on transporters, could give of their best, for months of old-style foot and guns battles, incongruously thickened up by the air, had to be fought before the crust was broken and the green fields appeared. The transporters served purposes for which they had never been built, carting such things as motor-launches and railway locomotives over what might imaginatively be called roads made moderately firm by coverings of tarred hessian. Anti-tank guns were little needed. Rocket-firing Hurricanes did the job very adequately against the medium tanks of the only Japanese armoured regiment. Bombers took over the tasks of heavy artillery, which did not exist. The Fourteenth was the orphan among armies, denied almost everything it needed and on occasions being made to hand back even that which it had. Once the tanks were cast loose near Meiktila in February, 1945, there was no stopping them. The Japanese had no experience of mass attack of this kind and were incapable of doing much about it. Behind them, dog-dirty and loaded for bear, trudged Slim's army, heading back to Rangoon.

A month earlier, on 12 January, 1945, the greatest concentration of tanks ever seen or likely to be seen began to roll westwards into the heartlands of Germany. The Red Army, divided into seven Groups, now mustered an unimaginable 300 divisions and twenty-five Tank Armies. Headed by the Josef Stalins as dreadnoughts and with T34s as the cruiser squadrons, they rolled inexorably across the Central European Plain against a crumbling opposition. By the end of the next month they were closing in on Vienna. Six weeks later another Group entered the suburbs of Berlin.

In the West the only tank business remaining that greatly differed from other affairs was the crossing of the Rhine. It had been considered by Stern and his friends as long ago as 1915 when they had made a mock-up of a machine called The Big Wheel for that very purpose. Thirty years later the problem remained, but a better answer had come up. Hobart's DD tanks were not conspicuously successful since the mud was too much for them. The antidote came up in the shape of the Buffalo, an American machine born in the Florida Everglades and originally intended for use by the Marine Corps in the Pacific. It was not, in strictness, a tank at all but rather an armoured and amphibious infantry carrier propelled through the water by its own tracks serving as paddles. The crossing took about four minutes; a troop of Buffalos carried a company and during the evening of 23 March and the early hours of the following morning the two battalions equipped with them ferried the first flight of the 51st and 15th Divisions across. This night also saw the first and only public appearance of Fuller's Canal Defence Lights. A single squadron furnished what was called 'movement and direction light' to guard the upstream flank against possible mines or frogmen. It was not much to show for all the work that had gone into them.

In Italy the war went on in the same disagreeable way as before. Against opposition that was still formidable the Fifth Army crossed the Po on 25 April and three days later the Eighth marched into Venice. For lack of an infantry tank better than the Churchill armour had little to contribute.

The end came on 8 May with the German surrender. When news of this came over the 18 set at a certain brigade HQ in Burma the only comment was an ungrateful 'About time too'.

The war being over in Europe, the army received the best British tank of the war. In September, 1942, at about the time of the 'nothing over 40 tons' decision, the Tank Design Department had bullied the War Office into withdrawing the requirement that all tanks should be capable of travel by rail. With that out of the way the Department had been able to get down to designing something of a superior kind. It was not, however, given immediate leave to have a model made, the policy still being to allow work on nothing that could not be in service during 1944. After much nagging the go-ahead was given in July, 1943, and the AEC Company was entrusted with making the pilot model. It was to be a genuine battle tank, armoured thickly enough to keep out 88s, to be armed with a 17-pdr, and to have the armour properly sloped as the Germans and the Russians did. Speed on roads was unimportant provided that it did well across rough country. For engine it could have the Rolls-Royce

Meteor. The weight was estimated at 46 tons and the designers calculated that this would be too much for the Christie suspension. A modified system known as the Hortsmann was designed for it and the Merritt Brown gear-box would be fitted. The hull design was boat-shaped to lessen the effect of mines and a 20 mm Polsten gun was put in as its secondary armament. A separate engine, taken from the Morris Minor, worked the fans and charged the dynamo. The first six were delivered at the beginning of May and were rushed out to Germany, under the name of Centurion, in hope of some battle experience. They were just too late.

Centurion was a very fine tank indeed, evidence of British engineering skill equal to any Spitfire or Lancaster. This was the kind of machine Martel had had in mind when he told Stern that the cruiser and the infantry tank would tend to come together. In 1942 and onwards no evidence had existed that British factories were capable of turning out something of this quality and for that reason knowledgeable men demanded the two kinds, heavy and light. With Centurion the need was gone. There seems no justifiable reason why it could not have come into existence a couple of years earlier. It had long been evident that the days when a tank was railed to the edge of its battlefield and railed back again afterwards were over and would not come again. The trouble was that tanks had been nobody's business and nobody of sufficient stature was greatly interested in them.

Centurion came in May: the atomic bomb followed in August. Every country of substance has been making bigger and better tanks for the past 40 years. In 1945 Alan Moorehead called them an out-of-date weapon and both Mr Churchill and General Brooke were of opinion that their day was over.

Another expert, then recently deceased, clung to the opposite view until the bitter end. Adolf Hitler, still convinced that something might happen between the stirrup and the ground, continued with tank designs of a Wagnerian kind. Most remarkable was the Sturmtiger, a machine thought out to take over the work of fighting in built-up areas which had begun at Stalingrad. In this art there is one inflexible rule. Once inside a building the attacker must on no account show his face again in the street. To get from one house to another he nips across roofs or 'mouse-holes' through walls. The Sturmtiger would take over the business and be to the infantry as a pile-driver to a tack-hammer. Its 380 mm rocket gun had been designed for the Germany Navy as an anti-submarine weapon and was a monstrous affair firing a half-ton projectile with a maximum range of some three miles. In theory a few Sturmtigers could clear an entire town within minutes. In practice it was quite useless. Ten of the machines were built, by the Alkett Company in Berlin, but they were dinosaurs. Every one was picked off before it was able to fire a shot. The Führer's supple mind had not stopped there. He also had dreamt up a Ramm-Tiger, half heavy tank and half bulldozer, whose task was much the same as that of Sturmtiger but with the added duty of ramming enemy vehicles trireme-fashion and crushing them. None was ever made. Adolf Hitler went to meet his Maker still dreaming of Tigers, V-weapons, rocket-propelled fighters and super-submarines. He had come quite near enough to seeing them all.

It is to be hoped that we shall never learn which of them, Churchill or Hitler, was right. Newspapers regularly tell of inventions which, properly applied, will reduce the finest of tanks to a cupful of molten metal. It may be so. Equally, it may not.

A note on Sources

By far the greatest part of the material for this book can be found among the archives of the RAC Tank Museum at Bovington Camp. The bound Minutes of the Tank Board, the Reports of the Purchasing Mission in the United States and the Report on Armoured Fighting Vehicles in The Mediterranean Theatre hold a mass of information. No single book of this size could contain it all. In addition to these, the papers of Sir Albert Stern held at the Liddell Hart Centre, King's College, London, contain much that will not be found elsewhere. Inevitably there is a good deal of matter based upon personal experience and what is usually called 'private information', things that were told to me either at the time or later by my contemporaries. The published books upon which I have relied are set out in the short bibliography. There are, of course, many more but I see no object in setting out a long list.

The comments on the 2-pdr gun at Netheravon in 1938 and the mines at Hythe a year later come from personal knowledge. I was a student on both courses. Those on the Territorial labour divisions of 1940 are, again, first hand. The Official History is not entirely accurate in some details.

References to General Martel are drawn almost entirely from his two books *In The Wake of The Tank* and *Our Armoured Forces*. Mr J. K. Frankish and Mr H. A. Dean, both of Vauxhalls, have told me much about the beginnings of the Churchill tank. Major J. F. Mayo Perrott, late the 2nd (Cheshire) Field Squadron RE (TA) has added much to my knowledge of the minefields at Alamein. Mr Terry All-nutt, late of 141st RAC (The Buffs), is my informant about the Crocodiles.

I cannot imagine that any possible reader of this book would thank me for distracting him by the insertion of little numerals scattered throughout which would, after putting him to some trouble, identify every source for everything. They should, I hope, explain themselves.

Bibliography

As most of the information used in making this book came from records, both official and unofficial, together with much more given to me by people with first-hand experience I have relied only a little upon printed books. Each of those listed below has told me something I needed to know. There are omissions that may seem strange but it was surprising to find how many authorities are silent upon the subject of the merits or otherwise of various tanks. Lord Montgomery, for example, asserts more than once that a strong factor in building morale is confidence in one's weapons. Beyond that he does not go. Much the same can be said about the memoirs of many senior commanders.

The most useful books, set out in no particular order, are these:

Vickers: A History, J. D. Scott, Weidenfeld & Nicolson 1962.
British War Production, M. M. Postan, HMSO 1952
The Other Battle, D. M. Ward, Privately published 1946
Winston Churchill's Toyshop, S. Macrae, Roundwood 1971
The War Office, Hampden Gordon, Putnam 1934
Our Armoured Forces, Sir G. Le Q Martel, Faber 1945
The Ironside Diaries 1937–40, Constable 1962
Panzer Leader, Guderian, Michael Joseph 1952
The Tanks, B. H. Liddell Hart, Cassell 1959
The Struggle for Europe, Chester Wilmot, Collins 1952
Alamein, C. E. Lucas Philipps, Heinemann 1962
Prejudice and Judgment, P. J. Grigg, Cape 1943
With Prejudice, Tedder, Cassell 1966
Wars & Rumours of Wars, Sir J. Marshall-Cornwall, Leo Cooper 1984
Peace and War, Sir F. Morgan, Hodder 1961
Ack Ack, Sir F. Pile, Harrap 1949
The Business of Tanks, MacLeod Ross, Stockwell, 1976

A Full Life, Sir B. Horrocks, Collins 1960
Greek Tragedy 1941, Baillie Grohman, Blond 1961
Personal Experience 1939–46, Ld. Casey, Constable 1962
Auchinleck, Philip Warner, Buchan & Enright 1981
Looking for Trouble, Virginia Cowles, Hamish Hamilton 1941
The End in Africa, Alan Moorehead, Hamish Hamilton 1943
Eclipse, Alan Moorehead, Hamish Hamilton 1945
The Road to Rome, Christopher Buckley, Hodder 1945
The Plain Cook & The Great Showman, Gregory Blaxland, Kimber 1977
War As I Knew It, Gen. George S. Patton, W. H. Allen 1945
The Exploits of Brigadier Gerard, Sir A. Conan Doyle, Newnes 1896

The last-named book furnishes but one passage, at the beginning of its second chapter. It reads thus:- 'I am talking about what my ears have heard and my eyes have seen, so you must not try to confute me by quoting the opinions of some student or man of the pen who has written a book of history or memoirs. There is much which is unknown by such people, and much which will never be known by the world.' Amen to that.

Index